Taiwan's Buddhist Nuns

Taiwan's Buddhist Nuns

Elise Anne DeVido

Published by State University of New York Press, Albany

© 2010 State University of New York

All rights reserved

Printed in the United States of America

No part of this book may be used or reproduced in any manner whatsoever without written permission. No part of this book may be stored in a retrieval system or transmitted in any form or by any means including electronic, electrostatic, magnetic tape, mechanical, photocopying, recording, or otherwise without the prior permission in writing of the publisher.

For information, contact State University of New York Press, Albany, NY
www.sunypress.edu

Production by Kelli W. LeRoux
Marketing by Michael Campochiaro

Library of Congress Cataloging-in-Publication Data

DeVido, Elise Anne.
   Taiwan's Buddhist nuns / Elise Anne Devido.
      p. cm.
   Includes bibliographical references and index.
   ISBN 978-1-4384-3147-5 (hardcover : alk. paper)
   ISBN 978-1-4384-3148-2 (pbk. : alk. paper)
   1. Buddhist nuns—Taiwan. 2. Women in Buddhism—Taiwan. I. Title.

BQ6160.T28D48 2010
294.3'657—dc22
                                                        2009034300

10 9 8 7 6 5 4 3 2 1

For Robert, Diane, Judith, and Philip

Contents

List of Maps and Illustrations — ix

Preface — xi

Credits and Acknowledgments — xiii

Note on Romanizations and Names — xv

Introduction — 1

Chapter 1
The Infinite Worlds of Taiwan's Buddhist Nuns — 7

Chapter 2
An Audience with Master Zhengyan — 29

Chapter 3
"Project Hope": The Ciji Compassion-Relief Foundation's
Post-'9.21 Earthquake' School Reconstruction Plan in Taiwan — 49

Chapter 4
The Women of Ciji: Nuns, Laypeople, and the Bodhisattva Guanyin — 63

Chapter 5
Jueshu renhua—"Cultivating Buddhist Leaders, Awakening
Humanity's Essence through Education": The Nuns of
Luminary Buddhist Institute — 79

Chapter 6
"Buddhism for the Human Realm" and Women — 93

Conclusion
Buddhism, Women, and Civil Society in Taiwan — 111

Notes — 119

Glossary of Selected Chinese Characters — 159

Bibliography — 163

Index — 181

List of Maps and Illustrations

Map 1	Map of Taiwan and Nearby Countries	xvi
Map 2	Map of Taiwan	xvii
Figure 1.1	Statue of Guanyin	11
Figure 1.2	Master Hiuwan writing the Chinese character for "Buddha"	20
Figure 2.1	Master Zhengyan	30
Figure 2.2	Still Thoughts Abode, Hualian	32
Figure 2.3	Still Thoughts Hall, Hualian	35
Figure 2.4	Master Zhengyan helping the poor in Taiwan	44
Figure 3.1	Sheliao Primary School, Nantou County	53
Figure 4.1	Master Zhengyan and the first Commissioners in Taipei	64
Figure 5.1	Master Wu Yin and her disciples during the Vassa (Rains-Retreat) Ceremony at Buddha Hall, Luminary Temple	80
Figure 6.1	Master Chao Hwei at anti-nuclear rally	102
Figure 6.2	Master Chao Hwei	103
Figure 6.3	Nuns of the Hongshi Institute at rally to save the Lo Sheng Leprosarium	104

Preface

This book began as a research project at the Taipei Ricci Institute for Chinese Studies, and I offer my heartfelt thanks to the Ricci's Academic Director Benoît Vermander for his support and guidance, and also to the Institute of Missiology Missio, e.V. (Aachen, Germany) for providing generous funding. I am especially grateful to Nancy Ellegate, Allison B. Lee, and Rebecca Searl of the State University of New York Press for their patience and encouragement throughout the publishing process. Without Nicola Thackeray's computer expertise, the book could not have been finished. I also thank the two anonymous reviewers of my manuscript for their many insightful suggestions for improvement; I fear, however, that the book falls far short of the reviewers' high expectations.

It is impossible to adequately thank the following friends and scholars who kindly shared their time and expertise with me, and without whom I could not have completed this book. I am indebted to (in alphabetical order): Marcus Bingenheimer, Christie Yu-ling Chang, Chen Kuo-chuan, Wei-yi Cheng, the Ciji organization's nuns and lay-members, Ding Min, Greg Epp, Vincent Goossaert, Beata Grant, Karen Shu-ch'ing Huang, Jiang Canteng, Charles B. Jones, Norman A. Kutcher, André Laliberté, Yuzhen Li, Lin Mei-Rong, Jun'an Liu, Lu Hwei-syin, Mi Gao, my colleagues at the NTNU Department of History, David Schak, Shi Mingjia, Shi Zhengyan, Shi Zifan, Shi Zinai, Shi Huiyan, Shih Heng Ching, Shih Chao Hwei and the nuns of the Hongshi Institute, Shih Wu Yin and the nuns of the Luminary Institute, the Taipei Ricci Institute, Nicola Thackeray, Ting Jen-Chieh, Karma Lekshe Tsomo, Dominique Tyl, Benoît Vermander, Wang Fansen, Yo Hsiang Chou, and Yü Chün-fang.

I would like to especially thank Jammy and Ian Lee for their constant guidance and support and also my wonderful students Han-chieh Chen, Snowting Liu, I-Chiao Wang, and Peter Fan-i Yang for their invaluable assistance and unwavering humor and friendship over the years. I dedicate this book to my parents, sister, and son: "*Alpha et omega estis!*"

Any errors of fact or judgment in this book are my responsibility and I welcome suggestions for improvement. Undertaking this study has been a rare learning experience and an inspirational journey, ever since the beginning years ago, when I sought refuge in a small Buddhist temple on a cliff above the sea where the sound of the bell and the drum and the warmth of many red candles vanquished the raw winter dark.

Credits and Acknowledgments

Map of Taiwan, permission granted by Chen Kuo-chuan
Map of Taiwan and Nearby Countries, permission granted by Chen Kuo-chuan
Statue of Guanyin, by Elise A. DeVido
Master Hiuwan writing the character for "Buddha," permission granted by Shih Jenlang
Master Zhengyan, permission granted by the Ciji Foundation
Still Thoughts Abode, Hualian, by Elise A. DeVido
Still Thoughts Hall, Hualian, permission granted by Elizabeth Zielinska
Master Zhengyan helping the poor in Taiwan, permission granted by the Ciji Foundation
Sheliao Primary School, Nantou County, by Elise A. DeVido
Master Zhengyan and the first Commissioners in Taipei, permission granted by the Ciji Foundation
Master Wu Yin and her disciples during the Vassa (Rains-Retreat) Ceremony at Buddha Hall, Luminary Temple, permission granted by Shih Wu Yin
Master Chao Hwei at antinuclear rally, permission granted by Shih Chao Hwei
Master Chao Hwei, permission granted by Shih Chao Hwei
Nuns of the Hongshi Institute at rally to save the Lo Sheng Leprosarium, permission granted by Shih Chao Hwei
Earlier forms of Chapter 1 appeared in the *Taipei Ricci Bulletin* 3, 1999–2000: 79–89, and in Karma Lekshe Tsomo, ed. *Buddhist Women and Social Justice* NY: SUNY Press, 2004: 219–231.
An earlier form of Chapter 2 was published in DeVido and Vermander, eds., *Creeds, Rites, and Videotapes: Narrating Religious Experience in East Asia*. Taipei: Taipei Ricci Institute, 2004: 75–103.
An earlier form of Chapter 3 was published in Chinese, "Xiwang gongcheng: Fojiao Ciji jijinhui 9.21 zaiqu xuexiao chongjian gongzuo," [Project Hope: Ciji's Post-9.21 Earthquake School Reconstruction Plan] in Lin, Ting, and Chan, eds. 2004: 439–460.

An earlier form of Chapter 6 was published as "Mapping the Trajectories of Engaged Buddhism fromz China to Taiwan and Vietnam" in *Out of the Shadows: Socially Engaged Buddhist Women*, edited by Karma Lekshe Tsomo. New Delhi: Sri Satguru Publications, India Books Centre, 2006: 261–281.

Master Zhengyan (Figure 2.1), Master Zhengyan helping the Poor (Figure 2.4), and Master Zhengyan and First Commissioners (Figure 4.1), Copyright 2009, Buddhist Compassion Relief Tzu Chi Foundation of the Republic of China, a.k.a. Buddhist Compassion Relief Tzu Chi Foundation. All Rights Reserved.

Note on Romanizations and Names

As a rule, this book uses the *Hanyu pinyin* romanization system for Chinese terms and names, except for certain well-known names and places (such as Chiang Kai-shek and Taipei) with an alternative romanization provided when helpful, such as Jilong (Keelung), but retains the romanization styles preferred by Shih Chao Hwei, Chern Meei-Hwa, and Lu Hwei-Syin, for example. As for the prolific scholar Jiang Canteng, I have seen at least four different romanizations of his name, and I have taken the liberty to use the *Hanyu pinyin* version. *Pai sey!*

This book uses both Sanskrit and Pāli terms according to the source quoted.

The real names of informants in this book are used with their permission; in other cases, names are omitted upon their request.

A glossary of selected Chinese characters begins on page 159.

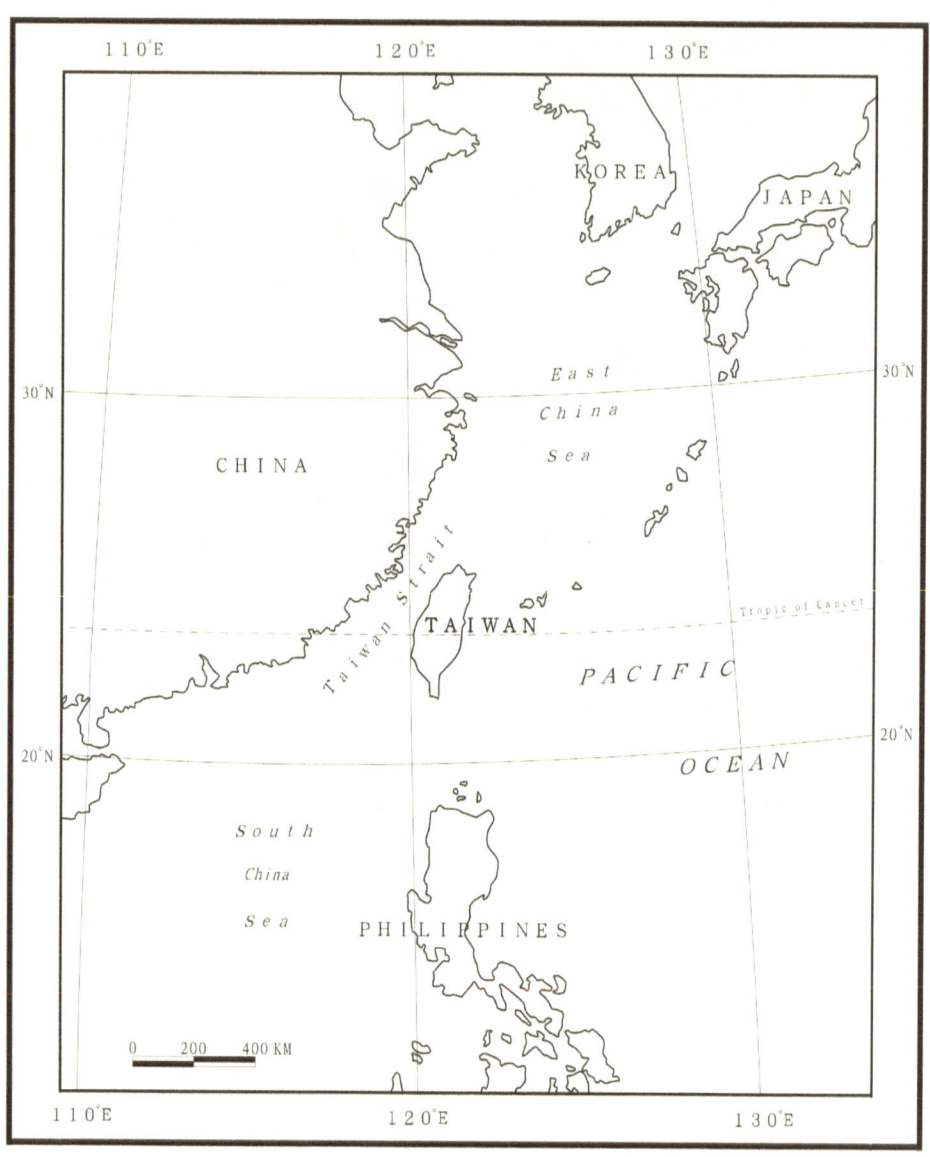

Map 1. Map of Taiwan and Nearby Countries (Chen Kuo-chuan)

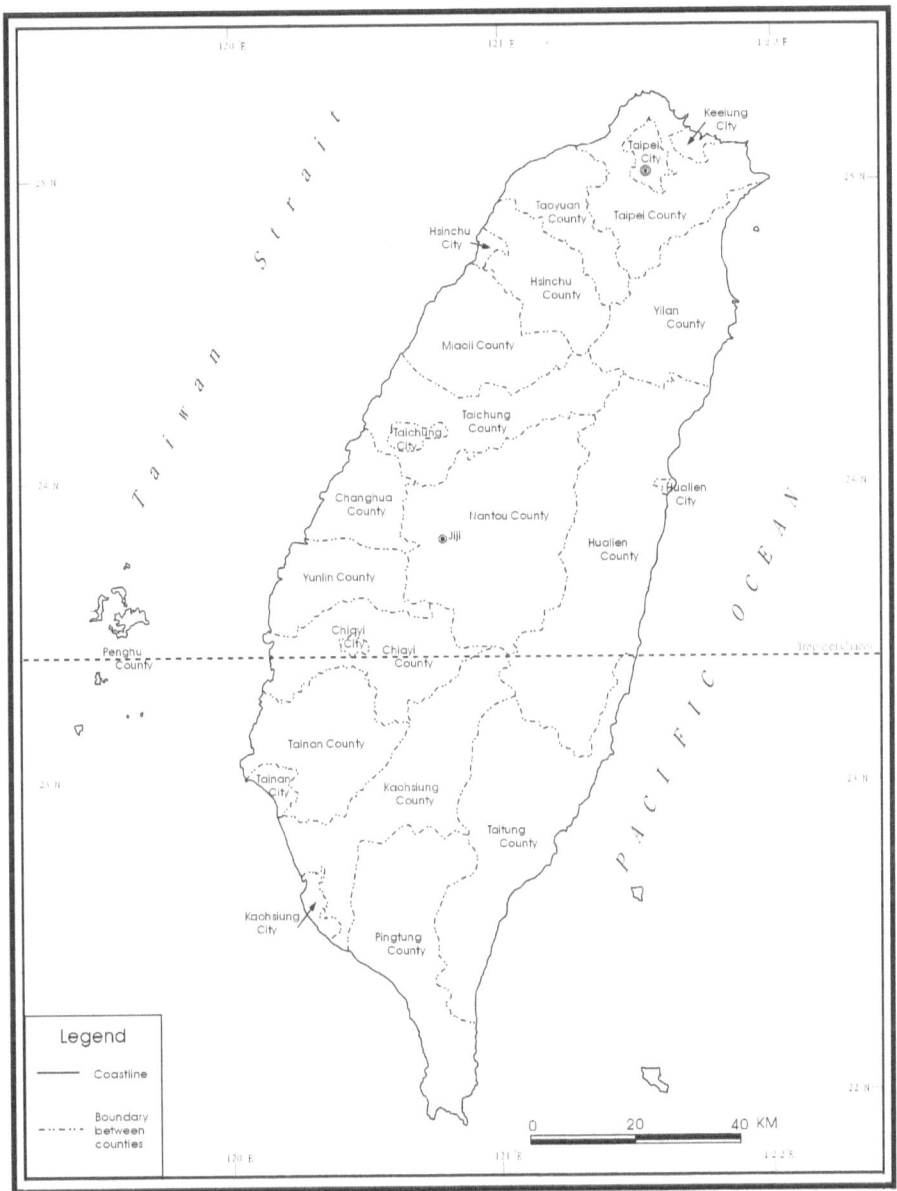

Map 2. Map of Taiwan (Chen Kuo-chuan)

Introduction

In 1995 I came to Taiwan expecting I would revise my doctoral dissertation on the pre-1949 Communist movement in China. However, my employment brought me in contact with Taiwan's religious landscape: first, as a study-abroad program director arranging field trips for foreign students in Taiwan, and then, as a research associate with the Taipei Ricci Institute for Chinese Studies. I learned that since the 1980s, Taiwan has experienced a religious revival, not only within the popular religious sphere, but also within institutionalized Buddhism. In particular, it intrigued me that Taiwan has the highest number of Buddhist nuns in the world and also a greater proportion relative to monks, a situation in monastic Buddhism unlike any other on earth.[1] Of the total number of nuns and monks ordained since 1953, nuns constitute about 75 percent of this cleric population, based on estimating annual ordination records from the years 1953-1987 and 1988-1998.[2] The total number of nuns ordained from 1953-1987 was 7,078, while the number of nuns ordained from 1988 to 1998 was 4,819.[3] Except for the year 1961, the number of female ordination candidates surpassed male candidates at Taiwan's triple altar ordination ceremonies from 1953-1987 by two or three times the number; after 1987, this trend continued. While there are no precise statistics available about monks and nuns in Taiwan, it is estimated that there are around 15,000 nuns active in Taiwan at present.[4]

Why do Buddhism and the life of a celibate religious monastic appeal to so many women in a society noted for its strong family bonds, as well as a shrewd pragmatism and an unabashed materialist outlook? This phenomenon is especially noteworthy because many people in Taiwan are not officially and regularly affiliated with a formal, organized religion, be it Buddhism, Daoism, Christianity, Islam, or syncretic sects and New Age religions. Rather, they may undertake certain rituals and celebrate on various holidays according to the Chinese almanac. Besides the rituals of ancestor worship, routine petitions to the gods and goddesses include praying for success in examinations, health, wealth, to beget sons, for protection against accidents and harm, and exorcism of malevolent spirits. At the very least, most Taiwanese will duly carry out traditional funeral and mourning rituals.[5]

Yet, though precise numbers are unclear, Taiwan has seen a dramatic upward trend over the past twenty-five years in numbers of Buddhist believers and Buddhist organizations in Taiwan.[6] The implications of the "Buddhist renaissance" in Taiwan, and in particular the contributions made by nuns, are profound. Not only will Taiwanese institutionalized Buddhism continue to transform and stimulate world Buddhism, but this Buddhist renaissance, through its notable contributions to charitable and philanthropic causes, secular and religious education, publishing, mass media, the arts, environmentalism, animal rights, opposition to nuclear power, and disaster relief, also plays a crucial role in the construction of a civil society in post-authoritarian Taiwan. Finally, the preponderance of women, both monastic and lay, in these developments is at once a product of accelerated socioeconomic change in Taiwan since the 1970s, and a force that is creating more diverse life opportunities and choices for women in Taiwan. How the phenomenon of Taiwan's Buddhist nuns is linked to feminism is a complex question. As I undertook research about Taiwan's Buddhist nuns, I realized that this topic is inseparable from larger issues regarding women, gender, and civil society in Taiwan, as well as the history of modern Chinese and global Buddhism.

Only in recent years have scholars begun to study Taiwan's Buddhist nuns as a discrete topic.[7] There are also works that discuss nuns in the context of temple histories; the *vinaya* (monastic rules for monks and nuns) studies; or biographies of nuns,[8] while other works mention nuns as peripheral to the general history of Buddhism in Taiwan.[9] Although Taiwan's nuns and laywomen are the subjects of numerous essays and several doctoral dissertations,[10] this is the first monograph in English devoted to the phenomenon of women in Taiwan's Buddhism.[11] Reflecting my training in modern Chinese history, this book is primarily a historical study, though I also draw upon scholarship in Buddhist studies, anthropology, and sociology. In addition to written sources, this study also utilizes information gleaned from interviews, field trips, and participation in Buddhist study camps, supplemented by my personal observations from living nearly half of my life in Taiwan.

This inquiry is not a comprehensive history of Buddhist women or Buddhist nuns in Taiwan, but, focusing on the post-1949 period and the recent decades of Buddhist revival in Taiwan, centers on three questions:

1. How have women shaped Taiwan's Buddhism?
2. How has Buddhism shaped the role and identity of Taiwanese women?
3. How are Buddhist women shaping the future of Taiwanese society?

When speaking of "Buddhist women in Taiwan," I include both nuns and laywomen. As the nun Yikong points out, laywomen supporters, many of whom have "taken refuge" and follow the five precepts, have contributed invaluably to the development of Taiwan's Buddhism, whether volunteering in countless ways with daily temple operations and activities, or as lay *dharma* teachers,[12] not to mention their monetary support of temples and masters. I regret, however, that this study does not offer personal or ethnographic portraits of laywomen and nuns as individuals or communities. "The fact [is] that nuns are the majority in Taiwan's *sangha* and their high quality and numerous achievements make Taiwan's Buddhism flourish. But behind this 'brightness,' it is very difficult to know what the nuns' lives at various *sangha* communities are really like and how the life experiences of each *sangha* are woven . . ." unless you live with a Buddhist community for an extended period and even then, nuns, like any person, may never reveal their real feelings and thoughts.[13]

Chapter Outline

Chapter 1 presents brief historical overviews of Buddhist women in China and Taiwan, explores the various reasons for the flourishing of the nuns' order in Taiwan, and illustrates the diversity among nuns in contemporary Taiwan. This chapter also points out some problems for further research in the historiography of Qing-era Buddhism in Taiwan and nuns in Qing-era China and Taiwan.

Chapter 2 focuses on Zhengyan, arguably the most famous nun in Taiwan. Over the past forty years Zhengyan has, together with her nuns and vast numbers of lay disciples, created what some sources claim is the largest non-governmental organization (NGO) in Taiwan, the Buddhist Compassion-Relief Foundation (Ciji), which has made important contributions in the fields of charity, medicine, education, and culture.[14] This chapter, based in part on the author's participant-observer experiences with the Ciji (Tzu Chi) organization, suggests a number of reasons why the Ciji organization has met with such astounding success.

Chapter 3 is the first study in English on "Project Hope": Ciji's project of rebuilding of fifty public schools destroyed or damaged in the earthquake of September 21, 1999. After describing the special characteristics of "Project Hope," this chapter explores the implications of Ciji's ultimate goal to create a "new Taiwan civilization," as well as the question of religious organizations' involvement in public schools.

Chapter 4 discusses the women of Ciji, including the nuns, various groupings of lay disciples, and the Bodhisattva Guanyin, who is the main inspiration for Zhengyan and her missions. This chapter will show how "the women of Ciji" have promoted the ideal of Buddhist compassion as the world-saving "Bodhisattva as mother," with great success. It also addresses the questions: How and to what extent does Ciji empower women and what does this reveal about Taiwanese women and Taiwanese society? And, Can Ciji's calls for a feminization of Taiwan's society through Ciji's interpretation of Buddhism be a long-term solution to Taiwan's discontents?

Important as the Ciji organization is, there are many other thriving groups of Buddhist women in Taiwan. Chapter 5 introduces the nuns of Luminary Buddhist Institute based in southern Taiwan, whose primary mission is training nuns as *dharma* masters and scholars, and offering classes in Buddhism to the public. This chapter gives the history of Luminary and explains the content and purpose of their education and cultural missions, as well as discusses Luminary's social welfare projects, one involving post-earthquake reconstruction, and another, classes to help "foreign brides" from Southeast Asia. A look at the Luminary Buddhist Institute will reveal these nuns' multilayered and at times contradictory outlook toward gender identity, gender roles, empowerment of women, and feminism, and proves an instructive comparison with the women of Ciji.

Chapter 6 explores the links between "Buddhism for the Human Realm" and women. The Buddhist renaissance in Taiwan has been greatly inspired by the philosophy of "Buddhism for the Human Realm," *Renjian fojiao*, developed by the twentieth century reformist monks, Taixu (1890–1947) and Yinshun (1906–2005).[15] After giving a historical overview of Buddhism for the Human Realm from its origin in China and its evolution in Taiwan, the chapter compares and contrasts Buddhism for the Human Realm with global variations of "Engaged Buddhism." The chapter also examines the questions: Is Buddhism for the Human Realm especially supportive of Buddhist women, nuns, and laywomen, and thus would help explain the predominance of women in Taiwanese Buddhism? And, does being a "socially-engaged" Buddhist necessarily entail working for women's rights and gender equality, including advocating for the nuns' order? Central to a discussion about the links among *renjian fojiao*, Buddhist social activism, and gender equality are the crucial contributions made by Chao Hwei and her Hongshi Institute, a special focus of this chapter.

The Conclusion attempts to answer the focalizing questions posed in the Introduction: How have women shaped Taiwan's Buddhism and how are Taiwan's Buddhist women participating in the global Buddhist women's movement? How has Buddhism shaped the role and identity of Taiwanese women? How have Taiwan's Buddhist women found spiritual, professional, and social liberation? How are Buddhist women shaping the future of Taiwanese society, especially, how and to what extent are Taiwan's Buddhist organizations contributing to civil society in Taiwan? Finally, in what ways are Taiwan's Buddhist nuns unique in the world?

I hope that this book, despite its shortcomings, will encourage future studies on women in Taiwan's Buddhism from all historical periods, including detailed studies of individual nuns and their monasteries, and further illuminate how Buddhist women in Taiwan are transmitting and invigorating for future generations the world's oldest and continuous *bhikkhunī sangha* tradition.

Chapter 1

The Infinite Worlds of Taiwan's Buddhist Nuns[1]

Oral and written sources often describe Taiwan as the *tiankong* (literally, heaven, or sky) for Buddhist nuns.[2] I translate this term as "infinite worlds" for two reasons. First, to indicate that Taiwan is a free and open space for Buddhist nuns' development, in stark contrast with China where the nuns are "utterly dependent on [the] patrilineal political hierarchy"[3] of the Communist party-state and its Buddhist Association.

Taiwan's developed economy and open civil society have directly facilitated the rapid development of Buddhism and the nuns' order in recent decades. Furthermore, since the end of martial law in 1987, there has been no central Buddhist or government authority in Taiwan, as in China or in other Buddhist countries, controlling ordinations and directing or coordinating the activities of Buddhist monasteries, temples, lay associations, and so forth. Li Yuzhen argues that even at the height of the Buddhist Association of the Republic of China (BAROC)'s influence in Taiwan from 1949 to 1987, though it alone administered the ordination system during that time and supposedly had direct access to the Nationalist party-state power structure and its resources, BAROC never completely functioned as a central ecclesiastic authority. Thus, she writes: "In order to understand the consequent vitality of Taiwanese nuns after the 1970s, it is important for us to remember this decentralized structure in Taiwanese Buddhism,"[4] in which temples and monasteries are independent, self-administered, and must find their own means of financial support.

Second, "infinite worlds" connotes the great variety among Buddhist nuns in Taiwan, to be illustrated later in this chapter. Significant differences exist within each monastic community (according to monastic generation, family and educational background, talents, and temperament), not to mention the differences among monasteries, due to the free and decentralized environment mentioned above. Also, in Taiwan there are monasteries composed only of nuns, or only of monks, as well as mixed-sangha communities.[5] The Taiwanese model of the mixed-sex sangha, where monks and nuns worship and work on the same premises, is not found in the orthodox Chinese Buddhist tradition, nor is a mixed-sex sangha found anywhere else in Asia. This unusual arrangement evolved out of special historical circumstances that will be related below.

Reconstructing Taiwan's Buddhist History: Problems and Prospects

Scholars in Taiwan have belatedly begun research on Qing-era Buddhist institutional history in Taiwan, having previously focused on twentieth-century developments, especially the post-1949 period and the recent decades of Buddhist revival in Taiwan. However, Buddhist institutions and practices have been an integral part of Taiwan history since the early Chinese settlement of the island. There is a record of Chinese immigration to Taiwan at least from the fourteenth century, and subsequent peaks in immigration occurred around the fall of the Ming dynasty in 1644 and also around 1661 with the arrival of anti-Qing military leader Zheng Cheng'gong. The Zheng family ruled Taiwan for twenty-two years from 1661, the year Zheng Cheng'gong expelled the Dutch colonists from Taiwan, until 1683, when Qing authorities occupied Taiwan and designated it as a prefecture of Fujian province. The Chinese immigrants brought with them their deities such as the Bodhisattva of compassion, Guanyin; the "goddess of the sea," Mazu; and the "Royal Lords," *wangye,* deities capable of preventing plagues and calamities. Qing sources note that during the "Zheng period," government and local gentry established three Buddhist temples in the Tainan area, and Qing records mention the presence of a few Buddhist monks sent from China.[6] The "Zheng period" was also known for its "six eminent Buddhist teachers," including one laywoman, a member of the ousted Ming royal family.[7]

In Fu-Ch'üan Hs'ing's estimation of the Qing historical records, the Qing era "... was a period of prosperity for Taiwanese Buddhism" due to political and economic support from the government authorities, literati, merchants, and the populace.[8] The Taiwan County Gazetteer of 1720 notes the existence of six Buddhist temples in Tainan and Tainan County, including one Guangci An, possibly a nunnery.[9] Thereafter, Buddhist temples were also built in Taipei, Jilong (Keelung), and Xinzhu (Hsinchu), such as Dizang An (1757). Government officials and literati founded some temples, and merchants founded others; donations by non-elite lay believers were crucial, as always.[10]

Chinese and Taiwanese Buddhist circles maintained constant interaction from the Zheng period on (1661–1683).[11] Temples such as Kaiyuan Temple (1689) in Tainan and Longshan Temple in Taipei (1740), for example, were "branch" temples named for their "root" temples in China. Kaiyuan Temple, supported and funded by officials and literati, was the largest Buddhist temple in Taiwan during the Qing dynasty and was one of Tainan's "five great monasteries of the Qing," including Zhuxi Temple, Mituo Temple, Fahua Temple, and Longhu Yan.[12] Chinese temples sent monks to Taiwan to serve as abbots, and potential ordinands in Taiwan traveled to Fujian (especially, Gushan's Yongquan Temple) or to Xiamen to become formally ordained and returned to Taiwan to the temple where they had been tonsured, or were assigned to other temples in Taiwan.[13]

An in-depth history of Qing-era Buddhist personnel and institutions in Taiwan is beyond the scope of this book. At the least, however, we should note the discrepancy between the overall positive impression of Qing-era Buddhism in Taiwan offered by Hs'ing (1983) and Shi Huiyan (1996, 1999) with other statements about the "weak condition" of Buddhism in the "wild frontier" of Taiwan: "Chinese and Japanese scholars are unanimous in their negative assessment of the state of Buddhism in Taiwan in the period between . . . Zheng Cheng'gong and the cessation of Taiwan to Japan in 1895."[14] Based on sources published in the 1970s, Jones writes that "monks in Taiwan . . . were few in number and for the most part not of high quality; . . . (t)he monastic establishment contained a few virtuous monks and not a few charlatans. . . ."[15]

This derogatory attitude toward Taiwan's pre-twentieth-century Buddhist personnel and institutions is a recurrent strain found in Japanese colonial-era sources (which dismiss Taiwan's monastics and laypeople as "ignorant" and "superstitious"), Nationalist government documents, and some contemporary works. A book of 1995 edited by a monk in Taiwan bluntly claimed that from the seventeenth century to 1895, "formally-ordained monastics were few; Buddhism in Taiwan was a mostly strange and bizarre kind."[16]

However, the more nuanced works of Hs'ing (1983), Kan (1999), and Shi Huiyan (1996, 1999), based on a wide range of sources from various periods in the Qing, portray the continuous growth and development of Buddhist institutions in Taiwan as spreading out from Tainan and important urban areas. Additionally, Vincent Goossaert argues that it is not tenable to argue that Taiwan's Buddhism was "weak" because it lacked a monastic ordination center.[17] In China, large wealthy monasteries, especially those that traditionally held ordination ceremonies, were found only in a few provinces. Furthermore, as of 1900, " 'Buddhism' [in terms of practice] was totally integrated with 'Chinese popular religion' " so that to call the extant syncretic practices heterodox, bizarre, or superstitious is to employ the critical rhetoric of Buddhist modernizers.[18] Thus, we should note that the above-mentioned critical assessments reflect the biases of Japanese colonial and Nationalist "modernizing" authorities intent on transforming and co-opting Buddhist institutions and practices in Taiwan, in tandem with the agenda of Chinese Buddhist reformers, who sought to separate "Buddhism," centered on the learning and propagation of selected Buddhist *sūtras*, from "superstitious devotional practices."[19] At any rate, to reach substantive conclusions about the state of

Taiwan's monastics and Buddhist institutions of the Qing period will require more evidence and more research regarding the numbers and background of monastics, the relations between temples and ruling elites, and varying local cultic and liturgical needs and practices.

Buddhist Women in Taiwan During the Qing Period

Thanks to the efforts undertaken by a few scholars in Taiwan in recent years, we can sketch out a broad outline of Buddhist women's diverse practices in Qing-era Taiwan (17th c.–1895). During this period, women in Taiwan were excluded from the Confucian public sphere, nor could they train or serve as Daoist priests, though they could become spirit mediums, some involved with spirit-writing connected with "phoenix halls."[20] Numerous women participated in the popular religious sects called the *zhaijiao*, "vegetarian religions," whose followers kept a partial or total vegetarian diet, and were devoted to worship of Guanyin, or to the Eternal Mother, *wusheng laomu*.[21] Taiwan's *zhaijiao* sects had both male and female members, but the Japanese colonial government noted "the presence of a large number of female *zhaijiao* members,"[22] as was also the case in rural Guangdong at the turn of the century.[23] One could practice *zhaijiao* without "leaving home," however, entering a *zhaijiao* order might offer young women a temporary or permanent alternative to an arranged marriage, or widows a refuge from oppressive families.

In Taiwan, evidence for *zhaijiao* practice dates back to at least the seventeenth century, and the sects' relationship to institutional Buddhism is complex. Scholars like Topley and Jiang focus on the sectarian nature of the *zhaijiao* distinct from Buddhism, with their own "... independent texts, patriarchal lineage, initiation rituals, ecclesiastical hierarchy, and institutions."[24] In Li Yuzhen's analysis, *zhaijiao* and the varieties of female practitioners in Taiwan are more usefully studied together with institutional Buddhism and she suggests the following typology (excluding here the priests and nuns belonging to Japanese sects in Taiwan):[25]

> The female non-celibate followers of *zhaijiao* who lived at home but worshipped at Vegetarian Halls.
>
> The female celibate members of *zhaijiao* living in family *zhaitang* or at community *caitang*. Many *zhaitang* were built by pious families; several famous and wealthy lineages in Taiwan including the Banqiao Lim family; the Xinzhu Zheng family; and the Wufeng Lim family and other families built *zhaitang* for their unmarried daughters to live and practice in, and sometimes administer. Some

all-female *zhaitang* were headed by a female[26] but many *zhaitang* were led by a male priest, *caigong*, with his wife referred to as *caipo*. Depending on the type of *zhaitang*, property and leadership positions were often inheritable, whether within families or transmitted from master to disciple.

Non-ordained vegetarian women, *caigu* or *zhaigu*, residing at private Buddhist Halls, *fotang*, or at Mountain Buddhist Nunneries associated with the temples on the Guanyin pilgrimage routes in Taiwan. Along with Mount Putuo off the Zhejiang coast, Taiwan has for centuries been a major pilgrimage center for Guanyin devotees (Figure 1.1). One famous site for Guanyin worship is Longshan Temple founded in Taipei, 1740, but in addition to the many urban temples dedicated to Guanyin, pilgrims traveled outside cities to Guanyin temples called *yansi*, located at the border between local settled communities and the mountain "wilderness."[27]

Finally, we come to the category of Buddhist nuns affiliated with Chinese Buddhist institutions such as *fosi*, *chansi*, and *chanyuan*.

Figure 1.1. Statue of Guanyin (Elise A. DeVido)

The Enigma of Nuns in Qing Taiwan

The few scholars who have studied this issue have great faith in the supposed efficacy of Qing religious laws, as well as the accuracy of Japanese colonial officials' findings. First, there is the mantra that "Qing law of 1764 forbade women under forty years old to enter Buddhist nunneries."[28] But these scholars, like Jiang Canteng for example, do not elaborate upon where and how such a law was effective, given the huge geographical expanse of the Qing empire.

However, in undertaking his path-breaking project to map Chinese "religious" and "clerical" geography in late Imperial times, Vincent Goossaert has found much material on Qing-era female registered and unregistered clergy (Buddhist and Daoist), and doubts that either Qing laws or Confucian anti-clerical literature met with great success in preventing women from joining religious orders. He has found that in some regions of China there were large numbers of nunneries; furthermore, many female clerics were employed as managers in local temples.[29] Therefore, it may be premature to infer, as Jiang Canteng and Charles B. Jones do, that Qing laws successfully barred women from becoming nuns in Taiwan.[30]

Second, scholars place much weight on a report on religion in Taiwan published in March 1919 by the Japanese colonial government that claimed there were no ordained nuns in Taiwan, "only *zhaigu*."[31] However, this is an official report on the state of religion in Taiwan from the Japanese perspective, and furthermore it is not a comprehensive history of Buddhist practices and female religious in Taiwan. What appeared to be true to the Japanese colonial government as of March 1919 should not be presumed as the situation obtaining fifty, one hundred, or two hundred years previously in Taiwan.

The enigma of nuns in Qing-era Taiwan deserves a separate and full study, and regrettably can only be hinted at here, in two examples. One is taken from a local gazetteer first published in 1720 by Tainan official Chen Wenda:

> Monks and nuns (*sengni*) are of the populace (*min*) but they are heterodox. Yet they have not been abolished in all the past dynasties because they take care of widows, widowers, orphans, people without means of support, and comfort them in their sorrow when facing sickness and death. In Taiwan, many monks are handsome young men; they chew betel nut and watch dramas in open-air theaters. The old nuns (*laoni*) raise teenage boys and girls to be their disciples. This greatly offends the harmony of heaven and earth and is deleterious to the people's customs.[32]

The local official in Tainan who wrote this passage in the early eighteenth century is ambivalent about *sengni*: though praising them for their compassion and social welfare contributions throughout history, he still characterizes them as "heterodox." He casually mentions the precept-breaking behavior of the "handsome young monks," but directly criticizes "old nuns" for violating Confucian norms regarding segregation of the sexes.

Another brief allusion to nuns dates from 1811. In that year, local officials in Tainan seized a temple dedicated to the Daoist immortal Lu Dongbin and renamed it the Yinxin Academy *(Yinxin shuyuan)*. The officials' excuse for seizing this property was that the nuns *(biqiuni)* residing there had "violated temple regulations *(qing'gui)*." No further explanation is given, except that one of the accounts, the "Education Record" section, calls this temple a "White Lotus Vegetarian Hall," suggesting sectarian and thus prohibited religious activity. It cannot be ascertained from these two accounts exactly what type of Buddhist practices the nuns were engaging in, "White Lotus" or otherwise, and the sectarian accusation seems a pretext for official confiscation of temple property.[33] But it is worth noting that the term used here is not *zhaigu*, but *biqiuni*, though their ordination status cannot be confirmed.

During the Qing period, monks from Taiwan regularly travelled to Fujian to be ordained; perhaps they brought their sisters or mothers to be ordained as well.[34] Another possibility is that "... Chinese monasteries running ordination altars allowed women to mail in an ordination fee and gain an ordination certificate without attending the ordination in person," called *jijie*, mail-in ordination,[35] but it is yet unclear how many Taiwanese women religious did this.[36]

Records once held by Qing-era Buddhist temples in Taiwan are lost or incomplete, partly because the Japanese colonial authorities "... destroyed many temple and meeting-hall records and historical documents..." during their rule.[37] Further research in this area would necessitate the combing of the historical records, if they still exist, from ordination centers in Fujian, Xiamen, etc., to find possible mention of nuns from Taiwan. But even without a determination of how many nuns in Taiwan before 1919[38] received formal ordination, it would still be valuable to know more about the lives and practices of the *ni* and *biqiuni* of the eighteenth and nineteenth centuries so fleetingly mentioned in the sources above.

Buddhist Women during the Japanese Colonial Period, 1895–1945

The Japanese colonial authorities propagated State Shintō and facilitated the development of "eight schools and twelve sects of Japanese Buddhism" in Taiwan, with Sōtō and Rinzai Zen and the True Pure Land sects predominating.[39] Japanese Buddhist sects, especially Sōtō Zen, eventually seized control over most of the *zhaijiao* sects.[40] However, monks such as Jueli, Shanhui, Benyuan, and

Yongding endeavored to sustain and develop Chinese Buddhism in Taiwan, even as they cooperated with Japanese colonial and Buddhist authorities.[41] Continuing Taiwan's long tradition of Buddhist exchanges with China, Shanhui for example invited Buddhist monks from China to teach in Taiwan, such as the head of the Buddhist Association of the ROC, Yuanying, and famed Buddhist reformer Taixu; and monks from Taiwan studied at Taixu's Min'nan Buddhist Institute. Taiwan's monks also organized the first ordinations held on the island: Kaiyuan Temple held the first ordination ceremony in Taiwan for monks in 1917 (at which Taixu officiated) and for nuns in 1919; ordinations continued at different temples until 1942.[42] Not surprisingly, given Taiwan's large number of female Buddhist practitioners, in the ordinations of 1924, 1934, and 1940, female ordinands outnumbered male by a large margin.[43]

Jueli in particular is noted for his efforts to educate and train Buddhist women by holding public classes and founding the Fayun Women's Research Institute and four nunneries.[44] The three largest nunneries in the Japanese period were Longhu An in Dagang, founded by the monk Yongding in 1908; Pilu Chan Temple in Houli, founded by Jueli in 1928; and Yuantong Chan Temple, founded by Jueli's disciple, the nun Miaoqing, in 1927 in Taipei County. A number of nuns from these temples become important personnel in post-war Buddhist circles in Taiwan.[45]

Furthermore, the monk Jueli accompanied his nun disciple Miaoqing (1901-1956) to Yongquan Temple in Fujian to receive full ordination (year unknown), and Miaoqing thereafter lectured on the *dharma* to women at Fayun Temple and Longshan Temple, both headed by Jueli.[46] Another of Jueli's nun disciples Miaoxiu (1875-1952) was also ordained at Yongquan Temple, year unknown,[47] and Shanhui's disciple Deqin (1888-1961) went there to study Buddhism in 1935.[48] However Jueli, for one, had to endure criticism by conservatives for his support of nuns and Buddhist women.[49]

As for Taiwanese women's options within Japanese Buddhism, some women were ordained as Rinzai nuns. The Japanese authorities in Taiwan provided some opportunities for women's Buddhist education and occupational training,[50] but the Japanese set quotas favorable to Taiwanese men seeking Buddhist education; and only men could be ordained as priests, with full ritual, administrative, and financial powers.[51] A number of Taiwanese women from wealthy families studied in Japan and some became important bridges between the pre- and post-1949 Buddhist traditions in Taiwan.[52]

The Flourishing of the Nuns' Order after 1949

After the defeat of the Nationalist government in China in 1949, Buddhist monks, mainly from Jiangsu and Zhejiang, sought refuge in Taiwan.[53] Though among these were some monks well-known in China, they were not necessarily welcomed and assisted in Taiwan. Most did not speak Taiwanese and many were turned away from Taiwanese temples onto the streets to fend for themselves. Due to the chaotic and dangerous conditions of the transition from Japanese to Chinese rule and the subsequent anti-Communist campaigns, these monks often proselytized in secret, necessarily moving from temple to temple. Unless they enjoyed direct Nationalist government political protection, they risked harassment and arrest.

Monks from China such as Baisheng (1904–1989), Cihang (1893–1954), Yinshun (1906–2005), and Xingyun (b. 1927) fundamentally depended upon Taiwan's native Buddhist women for day-to-day survival. Nuns active from 1945 to the 1980s were great pioneers, such as Yuanrong, Tianyi, Ciguan, Cihui, Daxin, Xiuguan, Xiuhui, Ruxue, Miaoqing, and others. These nuns were the bridge between the Japanese period of Buddhism and the re-establishment of Chinese institutional Buddhism, working with monks from China, building temples and Buddhist institutes, translating monks' *dharma* talks into Taiwanese, teaching the *dharma*, transmitting the formal precepts, and cultivating new generations of nuns. However, they deferred to the monk-centered system and did not, or could not, gain public credit for their hard work.[54]

Thus, the drastic sociopolitical changes after 1949 had different repercussions for male and female Buddhists. The incoming Buddhist authorities were determined to "cleanse" Taiwanese Buddhism of its "heterodox" characteristics such as married male priests, non-tonsured nuns, and non-vegetarian practices, and to establish in Taiwan what they recognized as Orthodox Chinese Buddhism. In the process, BAROC and their allies clashed with the Japanese married priests and Taiwanese monks, with their own lineages and local networks, with struggles, some to the death, over leadership and property.[55] But to many *zhaigu* and nuns ordained during the Japanese era, accepting the authority of BAROC and becoming tonsured and fully-ordained by this organization represented a promotion in status, and could lead to positions in temple administration and ordination platforms,[56] though the "price" was to acquiesce to the authority of male monks from China.[57]

There are a number of reasons why the nuns' order flourished in Taiwan after 1949. Monk leaders in Taiwan faced what they believed was a "crisis," even signalling "*mofa*," the end of the *dharma*:[58] Women outnumbered men in Taiwanese Buddhism, as evidenced by numbers of *zhaigu* and in numbers of candidates at ordination altars. Monks arriving from China were surprised by the large numbers of *zhaigu* entering Buddhist institutes for study; the large numbers of *zhaigu* becoming nuns; and the long-standing Taiwanese custom of male and female Buddhist practitioners living and/or worshipping together at the same temple; and some suggested that the BAROC restrict these developments.[59] According to the Chinese monk Dongchu in 1950, ". . . There are more than two thousand Buddhist monks, nuns, and *zhaijiao* women in Taiwan; (the number of monks is less than one-tenth of the nuns). Less than ten percent of them ever directly received the real [sic] Buddhist education."[60]

Turning to "skillful means," some monks realized the necessity of developing the nuns' order, and over time, came to emphasize the Buddhist teachings on equality and have invested time and resources in Buddhist women's education and training, while, relatively speaking, in comparison with the situation in other Buddhist countries, they have muted other teachings regarding female pollution, female deficiencies, and female karmic burdens found in Buddhist literature.[61]

"Instead of complaining about the decrease of monks, Ven. Baisheng encouraged Chinese monks to ordain and educate Taiwanese nuns in order to maintain the Buddhist heritage in this period of transmission and wait for an increase of monks in the future."[62] For example, Baisheng (a leading monk who served as BAROC president several times) sponsored nuns to attend summer study retreats and together with nuns, Baisheng founded the Chinese Buddhist Tripiṭaka Institute, while Yinshun established the Fuyan Buddhist Institute for Women, Cihang founded the Maitreya Inner Hall, and Xingyun founded the Shoushan Buddhist Institute.[63]

Asserting that "Buddhist women should lead Buddhist women,"[64] Baisheng realized the need for more female instructors and masters at ordination platforms to attend to the many female candidates at ordination.[65] As so many women sought ordination, Baisheng encouraged training of both nun ritual masters to teach the correct body postures for monastics, and nun ordination masters to ask the proper questions of female ordinands.

Baisheng may not have foreseen what the ultimate result of his promotion of nuns as ritual and ordination masters together with his strict propagation of the *vinaya* would be: nuns working for the re-establishment of the dual ordination system. Li Yuzhen argues that the phenomenon of dual ordination, which "had been absent from the Chinese Buddhist tradition for centuries," is another reason for the strength of the nuns' order in Taiwan in recent decades,[66] but took several decades of struggle to establish. The learned and experienced nun Yuanrong (1905–1969) held an ordination for nuns at the Mt. East Chan nunnery in 1957 that was boycotted by nearly all monks. But Baisheng encouraged the Hong Kong nun Foying to produce an *Annotation of the Bhikkhunī Vinaya* in 1961, which Baisheng used to train nuns, and Foying herself became a popular lecturer at Taiwan's nunneries.[67] At the urging of nuns, Baisheng held the first dual ordination at Linji Temple, Taipei, in 1970 without much incident; but Yuanrong's disciple nun Tianyi (1924–1980) met with great censure and controversy when she took charge of a *bhikkhunī* ordination at the Longhu Nunnery in 1976.[68] Except for Baisheng, the other male ordination masters quit, but junior monks filled their places on the ordination platform; Xingyun and his nun disciple Yikong participated as well. Many nunneries sent their novices to be ordained, and after many obstacles, the 1976 ordination was successfully carried out and marked a breakthrough for dual ordination in Taiwan. Since the 1980s, Taiwan Buddhists have regularly held dual ordinations in Taiwan and abroad.

In addition to empowering nuns through their training as ritual and ordination masters, gaining invaluable administration and leadership experience, "(t)he process of dual ordination entails the transmission of the lineage from senior *bhikkhunīs* to novices, confirming a sense of shared identity and commitment among women from generation to generation."[69]

Yet another aspect conducive to development of the nuns' order in Taiwan was the leading monk Yinshun's emphasis on the doctrines in Buddhism that advocated gender equality:

> Buddhism has made no distinction between men and women in faith, correct practice, wisdom ... Women and men, both and alike, can practice the Way and reach liberation ... Women are wise and strong, and at the same time not inferior.[70]

Significantly, in March 1965 leading masters Yinshun and Shengyan agreed that Taiwan's Buddhists need not "overly stress" the Eight Special Rules that historically kept nuns in an inferior and subservient position to monks, and instead, Taiwan's Buddhists should stress Buddhist teachings on "equality."[71]

However, not all Buddhists in the post-war era were so pragmatic and open-minded as to encourage the nuns' order, and the Buddhist leadership still worried about how to recruit new monks. In the mid-1960s, Japanese scholar Fujiyoshi Jikai, upon visiting Taiwanese temples, wondered if an overly lax or flawed ordination process was the reason for the "strange" phenomenon of more nuns than monks in Taiwan. In response, a writer using the pen name "Chun Lei" wrote a scathing article entitled "Taiwan's Buddhism That's Lost Its Brightness." Without considering at all women's religious belief or any other positive motivation on the part of women, without taking into account any other special characteristics of Taiwan's religious history, the author points the blame at two reasons: First, the prevalence of "adopted daughters" (*yangnu*) in Taiwan, and second, the unrestrained and flawed ordination process, which basically functions as "a nun-manufacturing place"; a meal-ticket trade exchange; a market. He refuses to explain more about Taiwan's *yangnu* (or precisely how *yangnu* and flawed ordination processes are related) saying that *yangnu* is "too big a topic," but if we read between the lines, he implies that many adopted daughters, once grown up, are unable to find a job or marry so become nuns as a means of survival.[72]

The author claims that at Taiwan's ordination ceremonies anyone is accepted, without asking motivation, personal background, or education level. "Such a 'manufacturing-place,' *zhizao suo*, produces monastics who only seek donations and build temples, become abbots/abbesses, accept disciples, and chat about myths; these monastics are abnormal outgrowths, excrescences, completely useless to the world.... The fact that nuns are numerous does not mean Buddhism is thriving; proof of progress in Buddhism is high-quality monks."[73]

"Chun Lei" obviously holds ugly biases against women and Buddhist women. While the larger issue of whether Taiwan's ordinations in the 1950s–60s were lax or irregular cannot be explored here, it suffices to say that respected monks such as Ven. Shengyan and others also were concerned about the ordination processes and insufficient education resources and facilities to train monks and nuns.[74] But to single out Buddhist women for censure is unfair and inaccurate. Many ordination candidates were indeed *zhaijiao* women, but demobilized soldiers came as well. Some ordination candidates, both male and female, were in fact illiterate or minimally educated, some were very old and looking for food and shelter, others not sound in body or mind,[75] but we are not told precise statistics or details. Furthermore, being illiterate did not hinder the monk Ven. Guangqin (1892–1986) from becoming a famous Pure Land/Chan master in Taiwan, who taught several generations of monastic and lay disciples.[76] Chinese Buddhist history was filled with examples of illustrious male and female Buddhists who may have been poorly educated or "illiterate," yet still had knowledge of Buddhist scriptures through oral transmission, not to mention possessing great insight and wisdom.

Still, the post-war Buddhist leadership in Taiwan continually strove to attract young men to become monks in a society offering men many choices for successful secular career: a society in which sons were, as ever, expected to provide their parents with grandsons and life-long economic support. Furthermore, in Taiwan, unlike the general situation in Thailand or many Tibetan Buddhist communities, other religious "economies of merit" competed with the Buddhist one in garnering male resources and talents.[77] Probably the most successful conduit to recruit young monastics was through the Buddhist campus movement, the *dazhuan xuefo yundong*. Following the practice of Catholic and Protestant proselytizing methods among Taiwan's young people, from the late 1950s Buddhist monastics and women and men of Buddhist lay organizations such as the Lotus Societies began to establish study groups and scholarships in vocational schools, high schools, and universities, and issued popular publications and tapes of instructional lectures, Buddhist sūtras, prayers, and songs, etc.[78]

The layman Zhou Xuande (1899–1988) was a major leader in the Buddhist campus movement, starting in 1958. Zhou, like many Buddhist revivalists of the early twentieth century, was concerned that Chinese students should not lose their own Confucian-Buddhist moral culture in the face of the forces of Westernization and Christianity. Zhou lamented that "[i]n Taiwan's Buddhist environment, women outnumber men, the old outnumber the young, there is no distinction between the gods and Buddha, the Buddhist environment is superstitious and passive/pessimistic, all this needs active rectification."[79]

Thus, the purpose of junior colleges and university campus study groups, with their lectures, camps, and scholarships, *was to attract male students in particular*, and many young men did decide to become ordained, yet still, in the long run, more women were recruited through the *dazhuan* Buddhist study groups, because increasing numbers of young women received secondary and higher education after 1968, when the government instituted a compulsory, universal, nine-year education system. Thus, the overall high level of co-education in Taiwan is another factor advantageous to the growth of the nuns' order, compared with other nations with a Buddhist heritage. As Shi Jianye comments, "after 1945 . . . [Taiwan's] nuns' growth occurred simultaneously with the [socio-economic] development of Taiwan . . . and rise in women's status."[80]

The Diversity of Nuns in Contemporary Taiwan

Taiwan is renowned for its highly educated nuns, outstanding in fields such as education, social service, and the arts.[81] A pioneer in several fields is Ven. Hiuwan (b. 1913 in Guangzhou, d. 2004, Taipei County), an artist of the Ling'nan school and a poet who became the first ordained female disciple of Tanxu, the 44th Patriarch of the Tiantai School in China (Figure 1.2, next page). She was also the first nun to teach at and become head of a graduate institute in Taiwan, the Chinese Cultural University in Taiwan; and her Lotus Buddhist Ashram has trained nuns for decades. At age seventy-six she decided to establish Huafan University (financed in part by selling her own paintings), the first Buddhist university in Taiwan to be recognized by the Ministry of Education.

Another pioneer is Ven. Heng Ching (b. 1943 in Taiwan) who became a nun in 1976 at Wanfocheng in San Francisco. She obtained her PhD at the University of Wisconsin, the first Buddhist nun to earn a doctorate from an American university, and became a full professor in the philosophy department at National Taiwan University (NTU). While at NTU she established the Center for Buddhist Studies, which is equipped with an academic library and extensive electronic databases. Heng Ching founded this Center with funds all donated by monastic and lay supporters: "Not a dime came from NTU."[82]

Foguangshan has produced many outstanding nuns who have been crucial to its development both in Taiwan and abroad.[83] One of Foguangshan's

Figure 1.2. Master Hiuwan writing the Chinese character for "Buddha" (Shih Jenlang)

protégés (and prodigies) is Ven. Yifa. Born in 1960, she became a nun in 1979, received a law degree from National Taiwan University, and her doctorate from Yale University. She teaches at Boston University and is closely involved with Foguangshan's University of the West; her areas of expertise include history of Chinese Buddhism, *vinaya* studies, women's equality in Buddhism, and interfaith dialogue.

Another nun with perseverance and creative vision is Liaoyi (b. *circa* 1960) of the Lingjiu Mountain monastery, founded by the Chan monk Xindao. Liaoyi is the main force behind the planning and operation of the Museum of World Religions (2001) in Taipei County; this museum is the first of its kind in the world.

Subsequent chapters in this book will focus on Zhengyan (b. 1937 in Taiwan) and Chao Hwei (b. 1957 in Myanmar). Zhengyan leads the large, international Ciji Buddhist Compassion Relief Foundation. Although over the past decades Zhengyan has cultivated a small core of nun disciples, the Ciji Foundation focuses on the philanthropic activities undertaken by its numerous lay-followers. Chao Hwei is an indefatigable academic and social activist; she is among the few self-proclaimed Buddhist feminists in Taiwan.

Yet Jiang Canteng reminds us of the varieties of Taiwanese nuns and temples besides the above-mentioned "star nuns" and nuns from international, high profile and resource-rich temples.[84] Women may choose to join one of numerous smaller monasteries situated in or outside major cities. These monasteries may concentrate on performing Buddhist funeral rituals and holding periodic public ceremonies to "alleviate disasters and pray for blessings," or offer services such as columbaria pagodas (to store the ashes and bones of the deceased). One of the many examples of such a small-scale temple is the Benyuan Temple in Kaohsiung city.[85] This group of six nuns, who chose to join this temple rather others in their area, is devoted to the Dizang (Earth-Treasury) Bodhisattva who made a vow not to rest until all suffering souls in hell are freed. They focus on Tiantai Chan practice and offer classes on meditation, sign language, and English to the local community.

Li Yuzhen mentions two other nuns, both with advanced education, devoted to Dizang. One nun, Dijiao, famed for her talents as a spiritual medium able to communicate with ghosts, has founded a nunnery and five meditation halls in Taiwan and six branches abroad. Another nun, Jingding, among her many achievements has founded several nunneries and *dharma* halls, helped Ven. Hiuwan build Huafan University, and developed a walking meditation practice.[86]

Monastics leading an ascetic and eremitic life centered on meditation are rare in contemporary Taiwan, but the nun Fuhui of Miaoli was one such example. Fuhui became famous for her miraculous healing and exorcistic powers; and her small temple is still a popular site, even after her death in 1985, for pilgrims seeking cures through the Great Compassion water blessed by Fuhui.[87]

Other types of nuns include:

> *Independent nun:* As mentioned above, National Taiwan University professor of philosophy *emerita* Ven. Heng Ching is an independent nun not affiliated with any temple and has devoted her life to teaching and scholarship. Another independent nun is Ven. Rongzhen. Born *circa* 1957 into a poor fisherman's family, she was unable to attain much education until she became a nun at Ven. Chao Hwei's Hongshi Institute in Taoyuan. Battling ill health, she lives by herself in a small Buddhist shrine in a Pingdong (Pingtung) County village, holding Buddhist classes and ministering to her neighbors who face serious problems with unemployment and alcoholism.[88]
>
> *Nun with charitable lay foundation but no nun disciples:* Lianchan (b. *circa* 1960 in Tainan) founded the Wuyan Association for the Protection of the Blind to teach the sight-impaired life-skills and Buddhism. Lianchan is a practitioner of Chinese and Tibetan Buddhism, is a calligrapher, and is editing a series entitled *Biographies of Taiwanese Nuns.*[89]

Nun living at a temple, but working elsewhere: Shanhui became a Buddhist nun in 1971 at Biyun Temple in Tainan County and in 1985 moved to Qianguang Temple in Jiayi (Chiayi) County. From the start she taught courses in Buddhism to local laypeople and in 1990 began to teach classes of 300 to 500 men in the Tainan Penitentiary. She also has taught classes of up to 2,000 at the Central Military Prison and the Jiayi Penitentiary. She has developed her own teaching materials and has acted as a mediator during times of prison unrest. Besides her prison classes, she holds night courses in Buddhism for laypeople. She devotes the entirety of each week to teaching and is exempt from temple administration and ritual duties. Her nun disciples carry out the tasks of chanting Buddhist sūtras at ceremonies such as funerals and groundbreaking rituals. Except for laypeople who help with classroom organizational matters, Shanhui works by herself. She has been awarded many achievement and service awards by local and central government officials.[90]

As the foregoing examples indicate, many Buddhist temples in Taiwan do not expressly refer to the term *renjian fojiao* nor claim links with or inspiration from Masters Taixu and Yinshun, but nonetheless utilize modern methods of organization and proselytization to "create a pure land on earth." One such example is Henan Temple, founded in 1967 by the monk Ven. Chuanqing, a disciple of the Chan-Pure Land Master Guangqin. Located in a scenic spot overlooking the sea near Hualian (Hualien), Henan Temple has twenty-one nuns, ranging in age from around twenty to sixty, many of whom are college educated and had prior work experience. The nuns carry out the standard Buddhist daily and year-round ceremonies as well as hold meditation sessions, but their special mission, begun by their master Chuanqing, focuses on propagating the *dharma* through the arts, literature, music, and multimedia presentations. More extensive research into the differences among Taiwanese Buddhist temples is necessary to assess the extent to which the body of doctrines and practices in modern Chinese Buddhism associated with the term *renjian fojiao* has or will become the mainstream in the Taiwan Buddhist world. With few exceptions, Buddhist nuns of all sects and lineages in Taiwan fully employ modern technologies and methods of organization, proselyztization, and education, and do not shun but seek engagement with society and "this world."

Why Become a Nun?

In different times and places, women have become Buddhist nuns for various psychological and socioeconomic reasons, and scholars who seek to reconstruct the history of Buddhist nuns must be aware of the tendency toward idealization in religious biographies, as well as be skeptical of the stereotypes and slander found in anti-clerical literature.[91] With this caveat in mind, some main points known about the history of the Chinese *bhikkhunī sangha* can be summarized as follows. While the earliest reference to Buddhism in China dates from 65 AD,[92] the first monastery for monks is said to have appeared in the second century, and the earliest known nunnery was founded in the fourth century. These early nuns had received ordination from monks only.[93] In the fifth century, delegations of nuns from Sri Lanka enabled the lineage of full *bhikkhunī* ordination to be established in China, and thereafter, nuns' communities grew apace, with some nunneries supporting hundreds of resident nuns.[94]

Biographies of monks throughout Chinese history abound, following the example of Huijiao's *Gaoseng zhuan, Lives of Eminent Monks*, published in 530 AD. For nuns, however, the sole equivalent account in the pre-modern period is the *Biqiuni zhuan, Lives of the Nuns*, (517), written by the monk Baochang, who describes the lives of sixty-five eminent nuns from the fourth to sixth centuries, of varying ages and marital statuses but from mostly elite and learned family backgrounds. Among these nuns were ascetics, contemplatives, teachers, and administrators, as well as examples of nuns undertaking self-immolation as an offering to the Buddha and to all sentient beings.[95]

In response to the Confucian critique that to "leave home," *chujia*, violated the strictures of filial piety and thus subverted the social order, Buddhists answered that, on the contrary, becoming a monastic is "the ultimate act of filial piety," for by undertaking prayers, rituals, and good works, one could help one's parents attain a better rebirth or even freedom from cycle of rebirth.[96] *Lives of the Nuns* recounts, for example, that An Lingshou wanted to become a nun but "... her parents opposed this decision and criticized her as selfish and unfilial." Lingshou responded by saying: "I am setting myself to cultivate the Way exactly because I want to free all living beings from suffering. How much more, then, do I want to deliver my parents from human form!"[97]

In recent decades, the pioneering research by Li, Levering, Hsieh, and Grant has documented for the Tang, Song, Ming, and early Qing periods many examples of female *dharma* masters and abbesses with lay and monastic disciples; some of these nuns had powerful connections to imperial and literati circles. These scholars have illuminated a long tradition of Chinese nuns renowned for their teaching, institution-building, literary accomplishments, ascetic practices, and charity works.[98]

In 1939, the monk Zhenhua (1908–1947, an artist and scholar from Zhenjiang, Jiangsu) published a sequel to Baochang's *Lives of the Nuns* that includes the biographies of 248 nuns from the Tang-Song, Ming, Qing, and Republican periods.[99] It is particularly important to note that Zhenhua found records pertaining to eighty-six nuns from various periods and regions during the Qing dynasty, records which help fill the glaring gap regarding the lives and practices of nuns during this period.[100] These nuns were devout practitioners of Chan and/or Chan/Pure Land traditions, and a number of them spent years in sealed confinement (*biguan*).[101] Zhenhua describes nuns whose outstanding Buddhist practice attracted nun and lay disciples; some were memorialized by Confucian elites and some left *yulu* (discourse records), many were skilled poets as well.[102]

Contrary to Confucian moralists' generalization of nunneries as "refuges of last resort" and nuns as social outcasts, these nuns' socioeconomic and educational backgrounds varied: Like nuns in previous dynasties, some hailed from Imperial families; some were raised in Buddhist families and were sent to nunneries as children; some joined nunneries as young women with their parents' blessing (sometimes sisters and/or cousins joined together); some became nuns to avoid arranged marriages; and some were widows.

The twenty-seven Republican biographies of nuns included in Zhenhua's book relate details about the nuns' family backgrounds, the nuns' place of ordination and their interactions with monks, local officials and laypeople, and their pilgrimages throughout China, Tibet, and abroad.[103] Again, Zhenhua portrays the nuns as active agents engaged in study, teaching and writing, building nunneries, institutes, and lay associations, and organizing charity missions; and as exemplary practitioners, whether chanting, meditating, or undertaking ascetic practices. Zhenhua's work awaits a full and detailed analysis that will, in particular, shed light on the lives and works of Buddhist nuns during the Qing and Republican periods.[104]

In Taiwan, despite its long tradition of Buddhist and *zhaijiao* women and the contributions of the post-war pioneering generation, nuns were, until the 1980s, often stereotyped as illiterate, poor, and as social outcasts.[105] But Li Yuzhen's study points out that some nuns came from wealthy families and/or famous Buddhist families. Furthermore, Li inquired into the cases of women aged 20 to 30 years becoming nuns before the 1980s and found that contrary to popular stereotype of these women as being unfilial, selfish, and "fleeing marriage," the young women had in fact sacrificed education and marriage opportunities to take factory or other jobs to support their families, widowed mothers, and younger siblings, especially younger brothers, and only after many years of carrying out arduous familial duties did they become nuns.[106]

Many nuns grew up in families who worshipped Guanyin, the Bodhisattva of compassion or the Eternal Mother, *Wusheng laomu*, a millenarian deity. Some had grandmothers or other older female relatives who were nuns, or mothers who, when young, were thwarted from being nuns.[107] Death or sickness of a parent or relative also influenced some young people toward Buddhism and the monastic path.[108] For many nuns, the point of entry into the orthodox Buddhist world was participation in Buddhist study groups in vocational schools, high schools, and universities.[109] Young women engaged in the study of arts and sciences, business, computer science, or vocational training hope to pursue more intensive study of Buddhism as a means of self-cultivation, toward the goal of enlightenment. Many nuns told me that learning about Buddhist doctrines and practices was opening a door to an entirely new world of spiritual development that had been completely absent from the Taiwan education system.

As these young women move from the secure and highly-protected harbor of the Taiwanese family and educational system into the world, they often grapple with questions involving identity, family, and relationships. Ven. Jianduan became a nun at age twenty-four not due, as many people in Taiwan assumed of Buddhist nuns, to an unhappy family life, setbacks in a romantic relationship, or unsuccessful studies. She recounts that her childhood was very happy, and she grew up with parents who treated their daughters and son equally; she never knew about "gender discrimination" until she reached college. But even as a child she realized that all human relationships eventually must end, and each of us must face the fact of being alone and relying on oneself. During her first year of college, Jianduan learned about the life of the Buddha and realized that the *dharma* taught the way to live life and find happiness in and by oneself. Besides caring about one's family, is there a way to be concerned with other things? So in college she assiduously studied Buddhism and upon reading Buddhist teachings on life's impermanence, was deeply moved, pondering, What do I want? What do I really want to accomplish in this life? How can I make my dreams become reality?[110]

At this juncture, young women, as Jianduan did, may consider entering monastic life, but must pass through the intensive, multi-step process of observation, examination, and evaluation necessary to reach the novitiate stage.[111] Some young women drawn to the possibility of the monastic life already possess skills in the areas of counseling, medicine, and children's education. Others are teachers who feel that they have reached a limit in the significance and effectiveness of their pedagogy, and find in Buddhism unmatched spiritual and philosophical inspiration. Still others consider careers in academia, publishing, communications, the arts, social work, adult or community education, or active social service, all of which are possible by joining one or another monastic community, each defined by an emphasis on its own particular missions. Another feature that may attract a woman to monastic life is that monasteries often sponsor the graduate studies for their nuns in Taiwan or abroad. For some women, this may represent their only chance to obtain advanced degrees.

Of course, it is not necessary to become a nun to develop one's individual career or spiritual path; one can remain a lay practitioner of Buddhism. Therefore, the purpose of the pre-novitiate and novitiate screening process is to identify those who are willing and able to uphold the precepts for a lifetime and are suited to living and working in a very disciplined, communal setting. Equally important is to identify those who are dedicated to furthering the interests and missions of that particular monastery. Finally, no matter what form their secular mission may take, the central responsibility of every monastic is to propagate the *dharma*.[112] Without sincere motivation and unusual strength of character, it would be very difficult to uphold the precepts and remain one's entire life in the sangha.[113]

The Question of Feminism

Having created such a strong and flourishing *bhikkhunī* order, we might assume that Buddhist women in Taiwan have identified or allied with the feminist movement, defined as working to gain equal opportunities for women, as well as to improve their legal status and quality of life.[114] Also, initiated by feminist Buddhists in the late 1980s, a global movement has developed to attain greater gender equality in Buddhist institutions and to work for the welfare and rights of Buddhist women worldwide.[115] Do Taiwan's nuns identify with, and are their views congruent with, those of the Taiwanese or international feminist movements? One might first draw this conclusion after observing the many self-reliant, self-administered communities of highly talented and hard-working Taiwanese Buddhist women. Yet when asked, the nuns cited their own hard work and essentialist notions of gender rather than credit the struggles of the feminist movement to explain the nuns' "success."[116] The nun Shanhui told me that women possess a mother's compassionate and warm heart and thus are suited for the life of the Bodhisattva's path.[117] Yikong believes that "(men) . . . are individualistic and want to establish their careers. Even if they become *bhikkhus,* they are reluctant to be bound by monastic rules. Women are gentle and yielding, and feel comfortable living in groups, so they are more likely to settle into long-term monastic life."[118] Jingxin claimed that women suffer more, and can better endure hardships and hard work than men, so are better suited for the monastic life.[119] Heng Ching asserted that women by nature are inclined to excel in the fields of culture, [secular] higher education and scholarship, Buddhist education, and adult/community education. Even the feminist Chao Hwei maintains that nuns have succeeded in Taiwan in propagating Buddhism due to their "gentle feminine nature, which makes people feel like they have been bathed by spring winds."[120] The so-called feminine virtues of compassion, nurturance, and conciliation are argued, in a perfect example of "skillful means," to correspond precisely with Buddhist virtues, thus women's strength lies in their difference.[121]

In fact, the flourishing of the nuns' order in Taiwan developed parallel to, not in coordination with, feminist movements in Taiwan or abroad. Nuns see themselves as working for the good of Taiwanese society as a whole, not especially for women's rights. Nuns say that they built the nuns' order through hard work and sacrifice, without the aid of feminist theory or praxis.[122] Many women interviewed for this book believe that women's progress in Taiwan over recent decades is the "natural result" of Taiwan's overall "progressive development," rather than acknowledge the feminist movement's contributions. Similarly, one theme that Li Yuzhen stresses in her dissertation is that the priority of Taiwan's nuns' struggle over the years has been to legitimize their monastic identity without openly challenging patriarchal society.

Conclusion

It would take a separate book or two to satisfactorily treat all the topics addressed in this chapter. Much research is still necessary to excavate the histories of three topics in particular: Buddhism in Qing Taiwan, nuns in Qing and Republican China, and nuns and other Buddhist women in pre-1949 Taiwan. This chapter devoted many pages to a historical review in order to show how the nuns' order in contemporary Taiwan is revitalizing the long tradition of Chinese nuns teaching, writing, and meditating, building institutions, and undertaking ascetic practices and charitable works. However, we must also point out a number of modern developments that are special to Taiwan's Buddhism: unprecedented support by monks for the education and career promotion of nuns (beginning in the Japanese colonial period); nuns' empowerment through the dual ordination system; leading monks' stress on the doctrines of equality in Buddhism; a lax attitude toward observance of the "Eight Special Rules"; a weak (and after 1987, decentralized) Buddhist authority structure; a high degree of religious freedom; the "Buddhist campus movement" to recruit young monks and nuns; and Taiwan's Buddhists' valorization of "feminine" and "maternal" traits.

These aforementioned features, in tandem with a developed economy, helped create a Buddhist environment in which a variety of nuns could prosper, including the nun Zhengyan and her Buddhist Ciji Compassion-Relief Foundation. We now turn to a discussion of Zhengyan, because she is the only nun heading one of the major Buddhist organizations in contemporary Taiwan (the Foguangshan, Fagushan, and Zhongtai Chan organizations are led by monks born in China), and because Zhengyan's teachings and practice embody what it means to be Buddhist and female for thousands of women in Taiwan.

Chapter 2

An Audience with Master Zhengyan[1]

Shi Zhengyan has been compared with Mother Teresa and Albert Schweitzer, and her followers consider her to be the Bodhisattva Guanyin incarnate, a loving, patient, and kind mother, and a benevolent and wise teacher (Figure 2.1). Since 1966, Shi Zhengyan has led the Ciji Compassion-Relief Foundation *(Fojiao ciji gongde hui)*, Ciji for short, an international NGO with a board of lay trustees claimed by some sources to be the largest civil organization in Taiwan.[2] Worldwide membership numbers over five million members, with branches all over Taiwan and in over twenty countries.[3] Ciji is primarily a lay organization whose missions include charity and disaster relief, medical care and research (including hospitals and the first bone marrow bank in Taiwan), an education system (from kindergarten to graduate school and a medical school), culture (TV stations, videos, magazines, books, cafés), and environmental protection.[4]

How did Zhengyan, "an unknown girl, a weak woman, a common nun," as phrased in the Ciji promotional literature, gain such a fervent lay following and come to build this stupendous philanthropic and medical organization? Of all the major Buddhist organizations in Taiwan, Ciji is unique in that its Master is both native Taiwanese and a nun. The story of Zhengyan and Ciji is an indispensable part of the answer to the question, "how have women shaped Taiwan's Buddhism?"[5]

In order to gain firsthand information, I made several visits to the Ciji headquarters in Hualian and also participated in a three-day camp for the Ciji Teachers' Association held there. The Teachers' Association is one of the various subgroups within Ciji, including the youth group and the entrepreneurs' group, that hold periodic camps and "retreats" at the Ciji headquarters. The Ciji's Teachers' Association was founded in 1992 and has developed its own pedagogy, with a series of textbooks, a TV program, a journal, camps, and workshops.

The purpose of the Ciji Teachers' Association *Still Thoughts* camp was to enable teachers from colleges and universities to learn more about Ciji and

Figure 2.1. Master Zhengyan (Ciji Foundation)

Zhengyan's core text, *Still Thoughts (Jingsi yu)* and incorporate it into their teaching "in order to cultivate young people and thus build a healthier, more peaceful and stable society." Zhengyan derived the title *Still Thoughts* from a passage in the *Wuliangyi jing (Sūtra on Immeasurable Meanings)*, a favorite *sūtra* of Zhengyan's on the Bodhisattva path of practicing compassion and the cultivation of *bodhicitta* in ourselves and for the benefit of all sentient beings. She explains this passage as follows:

> 'Still Thoughts,' as the term suggests, is to maintain a peaceful mind in any situation and to walk into the mundane world with a tranquil mind. Born into this world, we cannot detach ourselves from all the worldly affairs. However, affairs do not go as expected in this world. Therefore, we should deal with the constantly changing world by sticking to our principles while keeping a tranquil mind.[6]

Still Thoughts' popularity lies in how it presents central Buddhist and Confucian teachings in simple language. Ciji has promoted Buddhist teachings skillfully blended with familiar Confucian values like filial piety, social harmony, fulfillment of one's social roles, respect for authority, and the belief that individual moral rectification leads to rectification of the family, society, and nation.[7] *Still Thoughts* also offers practical and pithy advice on how to face and overcome challenges in love and friendship, marriage and the family, the workplace, and various problems of modern life. Though other Buddhist masters in Taiwan like Hiuwan and Xingyun have also promoted a Buddhist and Confucian "ethical-religious synthesis" for laypeople, *Still Thoughts* has become a best-selling book in the commercial market, and the "*Still Thoughts* Pedagogy" materials have been used in the public schools since 1992.[8]

Notes from "Still Thoughts Camp," April 1–3, 2000

The registration fee for the camp was NT $2500 (about US $80) and included lodging and meals. Ciji provided us with the unisex uniform for members of the Ciji Teachers' Association: White trousers, blue polo shirt, and a sturdy navy-blue book bag embossed with the Teachers' Association logo of three *bodhi* leaves nestled within lotus leaves shaped like two hands with palms upward. Also included was a reusable mess kit in a blue drawstring bag, a tote bag for shoes, and a Ciji belt and blue hair-ribbon, and a gray pajama outfit. According to the information sheet:

> We're sure that this will be a sweet and fulfilling spiritual journey for you...
> The daily schedule... is probably quite different than what you're used to, so please bear up, and joyfully try it out. We're sure that the care of the nuns and other full-time people at Ciji, as well as the intimacy, affection, and enthusiasm of all the Sisters and Brothers will bring you joy like being bathed by spring winds.
> At the 'Still Thoughts Abode,' your days marked by the sounds of the evening drums and morning bells, you can learn what a 'disciplined life' is.[9] (Figure 2.2, next page)

The Teachers' Association divides its membership into four major geographical areas with a leader for each; upon arrival at the Taipei Station, participants from northern Taiwan were divided further into small groups each led by a "Mama" or "Baba," an experienced Ciji commissioner. The next three days were spent under the watchful eye and firm thumb of our respective "mother"

Figure 2.2. Still Thought Abode, Hualian (Elise A. DeVido)

or "father," who made sure the participants adhered to the camp's schedule of events and maintained the proper protocol and group spirit of Ciji.

From the start, Ciji members stressed to newcomers the importance of a group identity as "Ciji people," first, regarding appearance: One's shirt is fully buttoned to the collar, hair brushed and tied back with a blue ribbon, shoe-laces tied evenly, book-bag fully zipped and hanging straight from right shoulder.[10] "The *Shangren* expects us to be neat and tidy."[11] The retreat also taught participants about basic "Buddhist etiquette" while walking, sitting, and eating, but Ciji goes further, with its own "code" regarding articulation of words and emotions.[12]

During the train trip to Hualian the group passed the time with self-introductions, and participated in group songs, clapping games, and sign-language practice. The schedule planned for the next three days was full and wide-ranging, and despite the early rising time, there was no time allotted for afternoon rest, unusual for Taiwan group activities. However, this was fully in keeping with Zhengyan's calls for self-discipline and self-abnegation, part of the Bodhisattva vow. "The meaning of rest should merely mean another way of doing work."[13]

Still Thoughts Camp for Teaching Professionals: Schedule of Events

Saturday, April 1	Sunday, April 2	Monday, April 3
Bodhisattva clouds congregate from all directions...	5:30–6 am Morning bell	3:50–4:20 am Arise to the sound of the wooden clapper
	6:00–6:40 Breakfast	4:20–5:40 Walk in the garden at dawn; attend morning worship service
	6:40 Assemble in Corridor	5:50–6:45 Breakfast and clean-up
	7:00–10:00 Tour of the Ciji school system from kindergarten through college;	6:45–8:20 Morning meeting for Ciji Volunteers
	Tour of hospital and medical school complex	8:20–8:50 Tour of the Still Thoughts Abode, the "Heart of Ciji" and the earliest extant architecture of the Ciji complex
		9:00–10:15 A lecture on how to help students handle male-female inter-relations, given by a school counselor
	10:20–11:50 Lecture by a nun on the etiquette and attitudes proper for Ciji members	10:30–11:40 "The Content and Praxis of Ven. Zhengyan's *Still Thoughts*," given by a senior Ciji member
	12 Noon–1:00 pm Lunch at Still Thoughts Abode	11:50–1:30 pm Lunch and rest
	1:00–1:30 Return to Lecture halls	1:30–2:00 Group rehearsal for the Closing Ceremony
	1:30–2:10 Historical Overview of Ciji Organization, given by a nun	2:00–4:00 Closing Ceremony
3:00–4:30 "Construction of Hope": Lecture by prominent Taiwanese engineer on the Ciji mission to redesign and rebuild fifty schools destroyed in the earthquake of Sept. 21, 1999	2:20–3:30 "Great Love Has No National Borders:" Lecture on Ciji's international relief work by its layman director	

continued on next page

Still Thoughts Camp for Teaching Professionals: Schedule of Events (con't.)

Saturday, April 1	Sunday, April 2	Monday, April 3
4:50–6:30 Tour of the "Still Thoughts Wisdom and Love Exhibition," a gallery of photos and text illustrating the scope of Ciji's four major missions in Taiwan and abroad: Charity; Medical Care and Research; Education; Culture. Also information about Ciji's Blood Marrow Bank, international disaster relief work, environmental protection work, community volunteer services, and post-earthquake relief and reconstruction	3:40–5:40 Audience with Master Zhengyan	4:00– Joyfully return home...
6:30–7:50 Dinner and bath	6:00–7:00 Dinner	
7:50–9:10 "Cultural Impression": Lecture on the potential of mass media and the Internet in the 21st century and how this can benefit Ciji's missions	7:00–20:50 Small group discussion	
9:10–10:00 Small-group discussions	9:00–9:30 *Still Thoughts* time	
10:30 Lights out	9:30 Lights out	

Upon arrival at the elegant *Still Thoughts* Hall in Hualian (Figure 2.3), teachers from all over Taiwan met together: some long-time Ciji members, some neophytes, sixty-three in all. New arrivals ran the gauntlet between two rows of student and adult Ciji volunteers who enthusiastically sang and

Figure 2.3. Still Thoughts Hall, Hualian (Elizabeth Zielinska)

clapped their hands. It is important to note that throughout the three days an audio-visual crew was present to document the entire proceedings including lectures, small group meetings, tours of grounds and facilities, meals, even in the hallway outside our dorm rooms as we settled in. Continuous "Omitofo" chants, set to "easy-listening" style orchestration, played in the background in public areas, and all meeting rooms and other public spaces were equipped with TV screens of various sizes not only to present videos and CDs but also to simultaneously broadcast the camp proceedings. Thus, the "Ciji experience" exists in three levels of narration:

Each person's individual experience, obliged to be verbally shared with others

The live, on-going recording by the audio-visual crew

Each person's viewing of the live recording on the TV screens

The above three experiences were then compressed into one, in the form of the official videotape that was shown in its entirety at the closing ceremony. Such audio-visual overload, this intensive recording and broadcasting of events, is not unusual for group activities in Taiwan (including its large Buddhist organizations), but from my comparative experience, Ciji is the most anxious to record every detail of their activities. This can be explained partly for practical reasons, to record materials to be used later for proselytizing, but it also reveals the Ciji organization's self-conscious intention to "make history."[14]

As the camp schedule relates, events included the opening and closing ceremonies, lectures, tours of grounds and facilities, small group discussion, meals, and an audience with Master Zhengyan. The ceaseless group activity was challenging, due to the constant obligation to joyfully respond, to communicate one's emotional states, to physically and actively participate (smiling, singing, clapping, expressions of thanks, and calling the name of Amitābha). Participants masked their fatigue with varying degrees of success.[15] Furthermore, during the camp the only chance for individual privacy could be found in the bathroom; every other moment, sitting, standing, walking, eating, and sleeping, was spent as a part of one's "small team." For Ciji, solidarity is all. As one commissioner commented during a discussion session, "All is achieved through the group, through group effort, even wisdom." However, this commissioner did not clarify that while teachers and spiritual groups are important guides to wisdom, the cultivation of wisdom demands much individual effort: pursuit of oral and written knowledge; personal reflection; and meditation.[16]

Despite the exhausting pace, the camp's program was highly informative, and the audience with Master Zhengyan seemed to revive all participants. Experienced lay-members shepherded us into the Guanyin Hall. Seated on floor cushions, the teachers awaited the entrance of the *Shangren* and her entourage of nuns and senior lay cadres. While waiting, the audience sang Ciji songs and practiced sign language.[17] At the front of the room was Master Zhengyan's chair and writing table, on which her attendants had placed a floral arrangement, a microphone, and the Master's notebook and mechanical pencil.

Then came the call "All rise for the entrance of the *Shangren*," and all stood at attention as she, bathed in spotlights, glided silently in her gray robes through the center of the room to her desk, sat down, and nodded for us to be seated. Her assistants then helped adjust the microphone and audio-visual lines, all the while attempting to maintain a half-kneeling position in respect to the seated *Shangren*. The tension of expectation was palpable and no one dared to breathe. Zhengyan's every move was concentrated, spare, exquisite, and determined. Then she spoke to us about the importance of education and educators in society and the need for us to incorporate Buddhist teachings and the Ciji spirit into our work. She spoke primarily in Mandarin but used the Southern Min dialect when expressing humor and other strong feelings or to emphasize certain points, in the habit of those whose "mother tongue" is the Southern Min dialect. Her tone was like a teacher or parent affectionately and patiently exhorting a younger child. For example, she asked quasi-rhetorical questions to which we all responded "Right!" or "Wrong!" Her light, high voice has a polyvalent timbre, like alternating sunlight and shadows as clouds pass overhead.[18]

Based on my impression of this single occasion, I would not characterize her, as do her followers, as primarily conveying great expression of mother's-love. I saw her sincerely pleasant but reserved, a person with an incisive mind tempered by a wry and light humor. Here is the authority of a matriarch, or better, a patriarch, like a traditional high official wielding the power of the pen and the word, her utterances evoking the force of both ethics and law.[19]

After Zhengyan finished her lecture, audience members went to the front of the room, stood to the left of Zhengyan, and asked questions, raised issues of common interest, or shared personal testimony of their faith in Zhengyan and in the Ciji organization.[20] Both she and another nun beside her took copious notes.

In tears, with broken voices, women and men gave testimonials, similar to both Christian and Sōka Gakkai testimonials:[21]

(A woman): Through Ciji I discovered not only the true meaning of life and love but I also discovered myself as well.

(A woman): Every time I come back to the Still Thoughts Abode, I can't stop crying with happiness, because I feel like I've really returned home, this is my spiritual home. I'm crying from the moment I get here to the time I get back to Taipei!

(A man): I always thought that I was a good enough person. I worked hard and did my best to help people out. But you know, I never had the time to take care of my own parents! Then when I read the passage in *Still Thoughts* that says: "Life is short . . . there are two things that cannot wait: Fulfilling filial piety and doing good deeds . . ." how deeply I regretted my bad attitude, and felt so guilty! . . . Now I know just how wise the *Shangren* is!

(A man): I know they say "Men can't cry" but here at Ciji, I do, because we are all a big family.[22]

The teachers met with Master Zhengyan again at the camp's closing ceremony. Kneeling on the floor cushions, each participant held a red votive candle, handmade by the nuns, in a small glass candleholder shaped like a lotus flower. Row by row, hands piously clasped as if preparing to receive communion, we stood up and proceeded to the front where Zhengyan bestowed on each teacher a certificate of achievement. In addition, each small team had its group portrait taken with the *Shangren*. The teachers also received a laminated photo of Zhengyan giving a lecture; a pale-green, glow-in-the-dark prayer bead bracelet with one bead embossed with a sepia photo of the young Zhengyan, her best-known portrait; and bookmarks with quotations from *Still Thoughts*. Thus ended the camp, and all participants went their separate ways, "looking forward to meeting again, according to affinity," *yuanfen*.

In sum, this Still Thoughts camp did not explore the topics of equanimity and insight/wisdom of the *Sūtra on Immeasurable Meanings*. Nor did this retreat encourage free discussion about teaching Zhengyan's *Still Thoughts*, critical debates on Buddhism, or on any topic. The main purpose of this, as other Ciji retreats, is to initiate the participant, through choreographed manipulations of the emotions and strict discipline of the body, into Zhengyan's interpretation of Buddhism, the Ciji organization's activities, and Ciji's group identity.[23] It is claimed that at Ciji, like a circle, "all people are equal, there is no hierarchy of who's above, below, ahead, behind, high, low,"[24] and Ciji's lay and monastic members indeed represent many different places, education and family, and class backgrounds, etc. Or in another metaphor, the different subgroups of Ciji are like one wave after the other, relying on each other to maintain a surge force.[25] Yet, C. Julia Huang devotes three chapters of her dissertation to discussion of the hierarchical structure and consciousness of the Ciji organization, where access to various retreats at the Ciji headquarters is graded from "general-entry" to "exclusive," according to one's depth of commitment and experience as a Ciji volunteer.[26] Claims and beliefs in egalitarianism at Ciji notwithstanding, the group is in fact a clear pyramid-shaped hierarchy with Master Zhengyan at the top.[27]

Charisma

On the train returning to Taipei, the group tone was subdued: most simply went limp and collapsed into their seats with fatigue, retreated back into their selves, the self that had been clamped down for several days. Few people in the world possess the willpower and charisma of Zhengyan, which has enabled her, though described as "small, frail, weakened by bouts of serious illness and from ceaseless over-work," to lead the Ciji organization to carry out its tremendous philanthropic accomplishments. One image from the camp experience illustrates this well: At the start of the candle-lighting ceremony, the young laywoman in charge was unable to operate the large butane lighter to light the first candle, causing a slight awkward delay. Zhengyan herself stepped forward, seized the lighter and ignited the candle in one fell swoop. That one graceful yet forceful action declared that "the candle shall be lit . . . NOW." And the flame passed from person to person down the rows until the Guanyin Hall was aglow with golden silence.

C. Julia Huang writes, ". . . Zhengyan is not only the spiritual figure but also the ultimate decision-maker of the Ciji umbrella organization. The power of her charismatic authority is exercised at every level of Ciji. . . ."[28] Religious leaders by definition should possess strong will and clear vision, and radiate charisma to attract and keep disciples and lay-followers. As one Ciji member wondered: How is it that the *Shangren*, by uttering just one sentence, can motivate so many people?[29] We approach the answer if we can articulate the particular charisma of Zhengyan. Mircea Eliade's entry describes charisma as "a gift of grace, a spiritual gift with special endowments," as well as being blessed with ". . . power of leadership or authority" but this description begs the question. Max Weber is more helpful as he notes that charisma is manifested through an interactive process between leader and followers; it is a successful social relationship based on shared values. Marc Bloch describes the charisma of *les rois thaumaturges*, kings with "the royal touch" as "the collective ideas [of the people] and the individual ambitions [of these kings] blended into a kind of psychological complex [that] led the kings of France and England to claim this wonder-working power, and their subjects to recognize it." However, neither Weber nor Bloch elaborates upon how such an individual leads a growing institution over an extended period of time.

The charisma of Zhengyan lies in a powerful and fortuitous amalgamation, her will to achieve her particular vision of Buddhism that happened to mesh with the sociocultural background of her followers and the saga of the Taiwan Miracle. It is first necessary, however, to know something of Zhengyan's early years, her family background, and the circumstances that led her to become a Buddhist nun.

Narratives of Zhengyan's Early Life

Many of Zhengyan's contemporaries had similar childhood experiences with illness and death and grew up in far poorer households, yet the choices Zhengyan made in response to her experiences were extraordinary. The many works in English and Chinese about Zhengyan paint a similar portrait of her early years; my purpose here is not to repeat well-known details but to examine her early life to find the source of the spirit and will working through her, still unfolding through the ever-growing Ciji enterprise.

Wang Jinyun was born in Qingshui, Taichung County in 1937. Her paternal uncle and his wife adopted her when she was an infant and moved to Fengyuan; her coming "brought luck" to the childless couple as they subsequently had sons of their own.³⁰ Wang Jinyun grew up familiar with the countryside around the town of Fengyuan, although her adoptive parents were not farmers but owned various properties and managed movie theaters in the region. Allusions to the life and landscape of rural Taiwan predominate in Zhengyan's speeches and writings.

The official accounts say nothing about Jinyun's daily life such as schooling or relations with her extended family and friends. She first "became aware of the Bodhisattva Guanyin's compassion" during American air raids of Japanese-occupied Taiwan: She noticed people in the bomb shelter around her praying to Guanyin "to throw the bombs into the sea."³¹

As is often the case with hagiographies, early signs of unusual spiritual gifts are claimed. "Ever since she was young, Jinyun liked to engage in deep contemplation, asking questions such as where does life come from, and where do people go when they die? In between life and death, what do people live for?"³² Several biographies of Zhengyan mention the epiphanic power of three health crises involving her brother, mother, and father, and Zhengyan's exemplary action as filial daughter and compassionate sister. At around age ten, Jinyun looked after her brother while he lay in the hospital for eight months with a serious illness and she "admired the spirit of the doctors and nurses in saving the patients."³³ When she was fifteen (some accounts say twelve) years old:

> ... her mother had stomach ulcers and needed an operation. At that time operations were very risky. Out of filial piety for her mother, Jinyun ... vowed to dispel calamities for her mother and prayed to the Bodhisattva Guanyin ... 'I, Jinyun, am willing to shorten my own life by twelve years.' Perhaps the heavens and the earth were actually moved by her filial piety, for her mother's disease gradually and miraculously disappeared. Jinyun, full of gratitude, became a vegetarian."³⁴

After finishing middle school (few girls of her generation attended high school) Wang Jinyun as eldest child and daughter was obliged to help her family at home and with the movie theater business. Li Yuzhen adds that because Jinyun's stepmother was weakened by successive childbirths, Jinyun took on many of her mothers' duties for the family.³⁵ When Jinyun was twenty, her father suffered a stroke and died the next day. This sudden death of her father, who had always been strong and healthy, was "a major blow to [her].... She began to search for a place to take refuge, seeking the origin and boundaries of life, looking for the answers to the riddle of impermanence."³⁶ Acting in the capacity of both father and mother of the family, she first put family matters into order as best she could for her mother and four younger brothers and then began a several-years' journey into the wilderness of central and eastern Taiwan.[37] During this journey, she experienced a number of epiphanies that all (except a period of solitary meditation) involved pivotal encounters with women (her first Buddhist teacher and other nuns, devout laywomen, an ill aboriginal woman, and three Catholic nuns) and men (her second Buddhist teacher, layman Xu Zongming; and her teacher Yinshun, the distinguished Buddhist scholar and propagator of Buddhism for the Human Realm).

The Journey: A Series of Epiphanies

The journey into the wilderness, whether of Jesus, the early Church Fathers and Holy Men, Chinese eremites, or Mao on his Long March, invests the traveler with the spiritual capital and legitimacy upon which he or she will draw in the future. The traveler not only survives the trials but emerges victorious, diminished in body but fuller in energies to accomplish the projects to come. Over several years of spiritual cultivation Jinyun decided to become a nun; visualized her interpretation of Buddhism's essence; and formed in her mind the vehicle to realize her Bodhisattva vows: the founding of Ciji organization in 1966.

After the death of her father, Jinyun sought out Ven. Xiudao, head of the nearby Ciyun Temple for solace and spiritual guidance. Jinyun had grown up in the Taiwanese religious landscape, familiar with the popular worship of Guanyin, the Eternal Mother, and Mazu, but had not studied Buddhist scriptures: These were not yet published for distribution at large in Taiwan. Ven. Xiudao, one of a small number of Taiwanese nuns who had studied Zen Buddhism in Japan, became Jinyun's first teacher.[38] According to Chen Huijian's biography of Zhengyan, Ven. Xiudao and Jinyun had the following exchange that influenced her decision to become a nun:

> Jinyun asked, what kind of woman is happy?
>
> Xiudao answered: A woman who can carry a food basket.
>
> Jinyun thought: but I do that everyday, why aren't I happy?
> She then thought: what if a woman could be like a man and
> do great things for the world?

Here is one account of the moment when Jinyun decided to become a nun:

> When she was twenty-four years old, at the crossroads of summer and autumn, she passed by the paddy field of [Ciyun] monastery

and saw two Buddhist nuns harvesting rice. Acquainted with them, Jinyun joined them in their work. The rice plants moved, floating in the wind like a verse spoken for her. As she was cutting the rice plant, she gained an understanding, instantly attaining an awakening. At that moment, she felt really happy, as if all the secrets of the heavens were revealed in her heart. The sun was beginning to set, and their harvesting work came to an end. It was time to say good-bye. Suddenly, the young nun asked her: "Do you want to come with us?" Jinyun was not surprised by this sudden question, because she had already made up her mind. "Yes, now. Let's go now." Another nun, a little older than Jinyun, took her hand, and with her eyes shining brightly, asked: "Are you free from obstructions?" She nodded her head. "Free from obstructions." At the train station, the nuns asked: "Shall we go north? Or south?" [Jinyun] answered, "The direction of the first train that comes is the direction that we go. All in harmony with conditions."[39]

Master Xiudao and Wang Jinyun traveled to temples in Taichung and Kaohsiung, then settled for a time in a small village called Luye, near Taidong.[40] They led an ascetic life in a small temple dedicated to the Eternal Mother and survived by gathering wild vegetables and fruits and gleanings such as peanuts and yams. At one point Jinyun helped out a neighbor named Mrs. Zhou Jinru by drawing water for her at dawn and dusk. Mrs. Zhou asked her in to dinner and was impressed by the unusual resolve of this young woman. As winter approached, Mrs. Zhou was concerned about Jinyun's health and sewed for her a light blue dress and a warm quilt. But before she had the chance to give them to Jinyun, she discovered that Jinyun and Ven. Xiudao had left the area to go to other temples in Lanshan, Zhiben, and Hualian. Mrs. Zhou was worried, for the terrain in these areas was dangerous. She faced the mountains and prayed to the Eternal Mother to protect these young religious devotees.[41]

Jinyun was a stranger to Hualian but received help from a devout Buddhist couple, Mr. and Mrs. Xu Zongming whom she met at Dongjing Temple. Mr. Xu was well-versed in Buddhist scriptures and Jinyun asked him to be her second teacher. Jinyun took the tonsure herself but still needed to receive the official nun's precepts. She traveled all the way to Linji Temple in Taipei but was rejected because she had broken with precedent and lacked an official tonsure master. However, after a chance encounter with the esteemed monk Yinshun, she became his disciple, and Zhengyan, the name he bestowed upon her, could officially receive the precepts.

At age twenty-six Zhengyan returned to Hualian and continued her spiritual cultivation mainly based at Puming Temple. She quickly gained nun disciples and lay-followers through her public lectures on the *Earth Treasury* and *Lotus Sūtras*. She declined several offers to become the head of temples elsewhere; rather, she and her followers remained in Hualian and supported themselves through farming and handicrafts, neither seeking alms nor accepting offerings.[42]

The Candle *Samādhi*

After she was ordained, Zhengyan lived alone for about six months as an ascetic, intensely studying the *Lotus Sūtra*. One night while studying by candlelight Zhengyan had her great focalizing vision as she contemplated the flame. This vision epitomizes her cosmology and has animated all her actions and decisions since that moment:

> A candle cannot burn without a wick. Even if there were a wick, it must be burned to be meaningful. The lighted candle produces tears of wax, but it is better than not being burned at all. When a wax tear rolls down the candle, it is immediately stopped by a layer of thin membrane, just as in the heavens and earth there is a kind of consoling power, which is like skin. To prove this kind of power, she burned her right shoulder with incense as an offering to the Buddhas. In the instant that the skin was burned, there was immediately a coolness that covered the wound, which is really a soothing skin. In the Southern Min dialect, when children are hurt, the mother would say: Come, Mother will console you ... The suffering of birth and death is actually like a falling candle tear. It is like being hurt, but suddenly there is also consolation.[43]

In Buddhism and in the Chinese holistic conception of body and heart, suffering comprises both the physical and mental. To Zhengyan, Buddhist compassion, universal and unconditional, is akin to the "consoling power contained in the heavens and earth." Perhaps at that time, Zhengyan envisioned that, though life is precarious as a fragile membrane, compassion can heal the suffering and make the broken whole, individual energy passing forward like a chain reaction, or like the transmission of a candle flame to one's neighbor.[44]

Two other encounters in 1966 confirmed Zhengyan's intuition that her vocation lay in medicine and charity work. On a visit to a Fenglin clinic she was shocked to see a pool of blood on the floor and was told that an aboriginal woman had hemorrhaged from a miscarriage. Although four men had carried her across the mountains for eight hours to reach the clinic, she was refused medical care because her family could not afford the fees. The utter disregard for human life shown by the callous clinic personnel made Zhengyan dizzy with pain; she vowed to work to improve the state of health care in eastern Taiwan.[45] Upon her return to Hualian, three Catholic nuns called upon Zhengyan. In the course of their conversation, the nuns queried: Though the central tenet of Buddhism is compassion, how have Buddhists contributed to society, such as building schools and hospitals? At that time, Zhengyan could not answer them.

Heretofore, Zhengyan had thought that she and her disciples would follow a traditional Buddhist life of contemplation, shunning fame and fortune, *taoming, taoli*. But she reasoned that vast potential energies of Buddhist compassion could best be realized with strong organization and funding, for without it, compassion remains but an abstraction, and thus she founded the Ciji Compassion-Relief Foundation in 1966.[46] (Figure 2.4)

Figure 2.4. Master Zhengyan helping the poor in Taiwan (Ciji Foundation)

Ciji as Contrapuntal Narratives

Part of comprehending the charisma of Zhengyan emanates from her multifaceted self: at once a woman with a personal background similar to that of many Taiwanese, and at once a woman of unique and seemingly supernatural will and talents. Of all the large-scale Buddhist organizations in Taiwan, Zhengyan is the only leader who is a woman and a Taiwanese; furthermore, her fluency in the Southern Min dialect attracted many grassroots supporters.[47]

Putting together visual and aural evidence from official Ciji literature, from camp lectures and in-depth tours of grounds, facilities, schools, and medical complex, "the Ciji experience" communicates a number of simultaneous narratives, at once in tension, at once in harmony, the polyvalent sum of which creates a powerful web that reaches back and forth across times and spaces to draw supporters in, now at this point, now at that point.

The Past Is Always with Us

The past was bitter and poor, any Taiwanese over forty can relate to this either directly or indirectly. And although there are many kinds of poor and suffering ways of life in both urban and rural areas, the classic archetype in Taiwan is the agricultural laborer, in particular the rice farmer, working exhaustively to survive, relieved only by familial mutual aid. Although Zhengyan in fact was raised in a middle-class business family, she and her earliest followers grew up familiar with this milieu, and most importantly, the founding and early growth of the Ciji organization was undertaken in a self-reliant manner.

The story of the early years of Ciji is repeatedly told in the official literature; in old sepia and black and white photo exhibits at the Hualian headquarters; in the display of artifacts at the Still Thoughts Abode from the past such as kitchen utensils, agricultural tools, and implements involved in the nuns' handicrafts labor. Yet this is not only a museum of historical representations, it is still a working space for nuns who still produce health foods to sustain the nuns' livelihood.[48]

This narrative communicates the message that no degree of post-1980s *parvenu* material wealth and success can erase one's past, and furthermore, as one prevails over poverty and suffering, one gains great virtue and strength. The visitor also senses nostalgia for the merits of "traditional agrarian society," the Good Earth, the "Pure Land" abundant with "sincere and rich human feelings," where supposedly all knew and helped each other. The Ciji organization expressly tries to re-create this "big family" and "local community" *Gemutlichkeit* both at the Hualian headquarters and also in Ciji's community service volunteer groups. Upon completion of camps such as the one described above, one is directed to join the "big Ciji family" by working with the local chapter and encouraged to return to Hualian often, to your "spiritual home,"[49] for respite and rejuvenation from what Ciji members see as a chaotic, polluted, cold, urban world.

The Pure Land Is Now

Simultaneously, through the Ciji literature and Web site, from the exhibition entitled "The Still Thoughts Wisdom and Great Love Gallery," and throughout the imposing and modern facilities of the entire Hualian complex runs the pulse of modernity and the Chinese reformist "Buddhism for this world." Ciji critiques the alienation, selfishness, and excessive materialism of modernity, but does not reject its instruments in order to realize the exhortations of Zhengyan's master Yinshun, "At all times do everything for Buddhism, everything for sentient beings" and to focus on "Here ... now ... this person," and build a Pure Land on earth.

The "Taiwan Miracle," One Step at a Time

The popular phrase *yibu, yijiaoyin* (one step, one footprint) is often used to describe how the Taiwanese people built Taiwan into a developed nation, through self-reliance, frugality, and self-sacrifice (without mention of government policies); and Ciji borrows this trope to characterize its own rise and development. Ciji reflects Zhengyan who reflects Taiwan and its people, at once weak and strong, marginalized yet obliged to adapt to the challenges of globalization. Additionally, the "Taiwan Miracle" provided Ciji with material and human resources to realize Zhengyan's Bodhisattva's vows; yet to achieve this "miracle" Taiwan has undergone rapid economic, social, and political change, and faces an uncertain political and economic future. Out of this "desert," Taiwanese from a variety of social groups have come to Ciji and submit to the group's rules and regimen in their search for a parent, a teacher, an authoritative text and leader, and for answers to difficult existential questions, for consolation and love.[50] At the same time, Ciji members, like many laypeople in Chinese history before them, believe that doing good works accrues merit for oneself, one's family, and one's community, and doing so satisfies both Buddhist and Confucian expectations of what a good person should be.[51]

But Ciji radically differs from other Buddhist laygroups in the global scale of its missions and its particular global consciousness. A working sketch by the artist Tang Hui shows the Buddha, with the face of Zhengyan, standing behind the Earth, gazing down, as if healing the globe with her touch.[52] The Ciji members' Bodhisattva vows were greatly tested on September 21, 1999, when a major earthquake occurred in Central Taiwan. In "Project Hope," to which we now turn, Zhengyan took on the responsibility of not only providing relief, but also rebuilding fifty public schools, due to, as Zhengyan put it, the anguish that she felt as she viewed not only the pain and suffering of the earthquake victims, but also the ravaged, "wounded" landscape itself.[53]

Chapter 3

"Project Hope"

The Ciji Compassion-Relief Foundation's Post-'9.21 Earthquake' School Reconstruction Plan in Taiwan[1]

Excellent works are available on the nature and structure of the Ciji organization, about Zhengyan's charisma, about Ciji's achievements in charity, relief, and provision of medical care, and about emotions and gender in the Ciji organization.[2] This chapter studies Ciji's "Project Hope" (1999–2002), a plan to rebuild fifty schools destroyed by the earthquake of September 21 1999, in order to explore certain questions raised by Project Hope's ultimate goal of creating a "New Taiwan Civilization."[3]

The "9.21" earthquake measured 7.3 on the Richter scale, with 2,444 dead, 8,700 wounded, and 100,000 homeless. Many buildings were damaged or destroyed, including 1,759 schools in the central region of Taiwan: The epicentre was located in the town of Jiji.[4] The Ministry of Education and Ministry of the Interior, pushed and guided by private groups such as the Humanistic Education Foundation, the Organization of Urban Re's, the New Homeland Foundation, and Taiwan University's Graduate Institute of Building and Planning, launched the "New School Campus Movement," to rebuild 293 schools in Miaoli County, Taichung County and City; Nantou County; Tainan County and City, Yunlin County, Zhanghua County; Jiayi County and City, Taipei County, and Taoyuan County.[5] The government commissioned the private sector to rebuild 108 of these schools, of which fifty were completed by the Ciji Foundation, in Taichung, Nantou, and Jiayi Counties.[6]

Ciji's project, called "Project Hope," *Xiwang gongcheng*, began in November 1999 and involved over twenty architects, some of whom are natives of the stricken areas. Even though many of these and other professionals and volunteers donated their services, materials, and time to this project, overall costs still amounted to over US $312 million.[7] As of September 2002, all Project Hope schools were completed and open for classes.[8]

This chapter examines the distinguishing characteristics of Project Hope and its ultimate aim of creating a "new Taiwan civilization": a Buddhist-Confucian-Green synthesis, where men are civilized, women are gentle, and children are quiescent; a Taiwan "refined and cultured," purged of "superstition" and "bad habits," yet also firmly rooted in local soil.

But will all parties involved in Project Hope schools, most of whom are not Ciji members, continue to promote and develop Ciji's ideals? How and to what extent will the Ciji organization directly influence local public education and does this violate the issue of "principle of neutrality on school campuses" as expressed in national law? Moreover, are concerns raised in Taiwan about the increasing involvement of religious organizations in public schools, or does pragmatism (alleged lack of public funds, shortage of social welfare professionals, the free social benefits gained) take precedence in the above-mentioned questions? In fact, for the past fifty years in Taiwan, the government has gladly entrusted welfare and charity responsibilities to the private sector's religious and non-religious groups.[9] However, this instance of delegating such a large public works task, and rebuilding public schools, at that, to the private sector is unprecedented in Taiwan.[10]

Finally this chapter also seeks to clarify Project Hope's use of the term "humanism," a key term in Project Hope expressed in the term *yi ren wei ben*, "to consider humans as the core or foundation." According to the Buddhist modernizer Taixu, *yi ren wei ben* is a term with roots in ancient Greece, but is especially associated with post-Enlightenment modernity in the West.[11] Although Ciji uses the phrase *yi ren wei ben*, Ciji's humanism is not derived from Western philosophical sources, nor from the humanistic psychology of Abraham Maslow, as is the case of Taiwan's Humanistic Education Foundation (*Renben jiaoyu jijinhui*).[12] Ciji's use of *yi ren wei ben* is derived from Taixu's *renjian fojiao*, "Buddhism for this world," or "Buddhism for the human realm," for Taixu strove to emphasize and express, in modern forms, Buddhism's inherent tendency to consider humans as the foundation, while at the same time aiming to liberate all sentient beings.[13] In addition, Project Hope places a particularly strong emphasis on Confucian humanism. In the Confucian social order, the individual cannot live outside a web of social relations, and acts according to one's position and standing in family and society; the gentleman cultivates himself in order to serve as a moral example and lead others.[14] Ciji is a Buddhist organization that skillfully promulgates benevolence, compassion, filial piety, propriety, harmony, and the molding power of education as "traditional ethical values," familiar and acceptable to many people in Taiwan, whether they are Buddhist or not; and this is one reason for Ciji's success.

In sum, "Project Hope" comprises progressive goals such as family community engagement in schools and education, developing environmental awareness, and community building, while at the same time, in contrast with the Humanistic Education Foundation promotes Confucian humanism, encourages strict standards of behavior for men, women, and children, and traditional ideas about education. Before we can consider these issues further, we must examine the larger context in which "Project Hope" arose.

"Project Hope" as Part of the "New School Campus Movement"

First, a few words about the Ministry of Education's school reconstruction plan, called the "The New School Campus Movement," which was informed by recent trends promoted by the government, schools, and NGOs in Taiwan and abroad, such as education reform, community revitalization, strengthening local identity, etc.[15]

Besides Ciji, other groups such as Taiwan's media corporations; Taiwan Electric Company; Formosa Plastics; Xinguang Insurance Corporation; Evergreen Shipping Corporation; the Red Cross; the International Lions Association; and Foguangshan, also "adopted" schools to pay and arrange for schools' reconstruction. According to the Ministry of Education, out of the total 293 schools that were rebuilt, the private sector took responsibility for 108 schools; local governments, 122 schools;[16] the Ministry of the Interior, 41 schools; and the Ministry of Education's contracted company, the Yaxin Construction Company, 22 schools. Japan's public and private sectors also helped with the initial disaster relief and also with schools' re-designing and rebuilding.[17]

It should be noted that the Ministry of Education, the architects, and Ciji shared similar ideas about prioritizing safety, durability, and sustainable development; that schools should act as community centers for life-long learning; that education is an interactive process among schools, the parents' associations, and the community; and also shared the hope that rebuilding schools could stimulate the larger project of community renaissance.[18] The ideal was for schools and communities to create local exhibition halls, museums, music centers, and memorial sites—for schools to function also as cultural, social, and athletic centers for the local community. In addition, the new schools' designs endeavored to preserve the original trees, plants, and landscaping, and if possible, integrate the extant architecture, like a gate or wall. The New School Campus Movement did not merely aim to rebuild school buildings, but to re-envision and transform the content and process of education from traditional textbook- and teacher-centered education to a locale-centered comprehensive education, created and carried out in concert by the schools, families, local community, and the local education department.

How and to what extent the new schools will carry out these reform policies and ideas varies greatly, and depends on the teachers, administrators, and parents.[19] As several Project Hope school administrators phrased it: *shang you zhengce, xia you duice*; i.e., the locale will deal in their own way with government policies issued from above.

The Special Characteristics of Project Hope

Project Hope's schools comprise a major part of the New School Campus Movement, but are also a platform to promote Ciji's own Mission of Education. Although Ciji became famous through its achievements in charity and relief work, in recent years Ciji has also invested much energy and many resources in education, based on Zhengyan's Confucian conviction that a sound education is the foundation for families' well-being and for a harmonious society. Besides medical and nursing schools, Ciji has constructed an entire education system from kindergarten through graduate school at their Hualian headquarters, as well as developed teaching plans and materials based on Zhengyan's work, *Still Thoughts*. Ciji's Project Hope design claims to have its own distinctive "vocabulary," *yuhui*, and "spirit," *jingshen*, its own education ideals, and its own plans for long-term social reconstruction, distinct from, and at times, at odds with, the program of the Humanistic Education foundation and other advocates for education reform in Taiwan.

"Ciji Vocabulary," "Ciji Spirit"

The Still Thoughts Abode and Still Thoughts Hall at the Ciji headquarters were the models for the Project Hope Schools[20] (see Figures 2.3 and 2.4), although there is still is a degree of variation among the schools.[21] Zhengyan required the architects and engineers of Project Hope to "build to last a millennium...." All structures were built with steel-reinforced concrete, yet each school was designed to be aesthetically pleasing, according to the taste of Zhengyan: "It's not only to build a sturdy structure that will last 1,000 years but also create an artistic work that surges from the earth."[22] Zhengyan stipulated the color of the schools, including the roof, to be light gray[23] to provide students with a quiet and calm learning environment. Also, the outside walls were plastered with high-grade, finely-washed pebbles; this entailed extra time, negotiation, and expense, according to one study.[24]

Like Ciji's Still Thoughts Abode and Still Thoughts Hall in Hualian, many of the schools feature a traditional Chinese vertically-flared roof, a shape that to the Ciji group symbolizes *ren* (person), to connote Ciji's promulgation of Buddhism in the human realm and Confucian humanism (Figure 3.1). Ceilings are high, corridors and stairways are wide, and the broad balco-

Figure 3.1. Sheliao Primary School, Nantou County (Elise A. DeVido)

nies offer vistas looking out to both the landscaped campus and the distant scenery. The floors are designed to be non-slip and the school facilities are handicapped-accessible. The design is intended to give people a spacious and open feeling.[25] In He Youfeng's opinion, "... as for the notion of space, [this design] ... leans towards Buddhist traditions, that is, dignified, austere, neat, the spatial structure has a strong sense of proportion and is well-grounded. This form makes people feel peaceful and stable."[26]

But this could just as well be a description of a Confucian temple. Project Hope, as does Ciji in general, purports to promote Confucian moral ideals: Cultivate oneself and also create a refined campus; cultivate morals, quality, good taste ... take the right path ... stress self-cultivation and education as key to stable and healthy family and society.[27] Zhengyan believes "education must have its roots in childhood: one must make up one's mind to become a gentleman. The gentleman's heart is broad, he has compassion, he understands gratitude, and he follows the rules. To become a gentleman one must diligently study, respect your teachers, and be filial to your parents."[28] These are traditional Chinese educational values, echoed by a former principal at Yanping Primary School who wrote that he expects that the new school's design will create a study atmosphere that will make teachers and students "refined and elegant" and will make good citizens who are polite, maintain order, are neat and clean, studious, and love others.[29]

But to Luo Rong, schools designed like Ciji's Still Thoughts Hall, with its "Still Thoughts" message, may become "imprisoning," and may clamp down students' personality development. She adds that the schools' all-gray color scheme, intended to convey a calm, dignified, and quiet air, lacks the vitality and liveliness associated with developing children.[30] Her point becomes clear when one views the other schools of the New School Campus Movement, built with wood, brick, stone, and tiles, and using an array of lively colors and textures, some incorporating Southern Min, Hakka, or aboriginal styles, reflecting the local history, economy, and ecology traditions of their locales. Xitou's Neihu Primary School, for example, was designed like a Japanese traditional inn in the woods; not a few schools look like private homes, vacation villas, or summer camps. Many of the new schools have spurred tourism in their areas.

But the Ciji organization proceeds in its own orbit, with its own missions to accomplish. Unlike most religious or charitable organizations, Ciji has its own professional construction department and an architectural committee, with specific ideological goals that they are determined to attain.[31] One of the architects involved in Project Hope felt pressured to keep to Ciji's fast work-pace and strict timetable, and still meet their requirements about space allocations, school safety, and "educational ideals." He had to alter his original plans to fit Ciji's "vocabulary" and "spirit," which is, in a word, exemplified by Ciji's Still Thoughts Abode; but he diplomatically claimed he did not mind changing his design, since "Ciji's ideas are very meaningful."[32]

Another architect who rebuilt Project Hope schools felt he did have less freedom to design, choose materials, and so forth than he usually enjoys, for several reasons. He felt, first, that there was a consensus in the Ciji organization that Zhengyan's ideal is the Still Thoughts Abode style and that Ciji members wished to please her; and, second, that all parties involved were under great pressure to complete the schools for the 2002 academic year. For this architect, meeting the deadline took priority over his design freedom, since he could basically accept Ciji's aesthetics and philosophy. However, he added that, in his personal opinion, Buddhists should not adhere so closely to one "form" or "vocabulary" or "group identity"; this seems to contradict Buddhist teachings on non-self, non-duality, and non-attachment or equanimity.[33]

Luo Rong queried: "What does Ciji mean by putting up gray, grand, and imposing 'Still Thoughts Halls' all over Central Taiwan, and encouraging the teaching of *Still Thoughts* in the schools?"[34] She did not venture answers, but as this chapter argues throughout, Project Hope is one way through which Zhengyan and Ciji hope to realize their vision of a new Taiwan civilization.

Ciji's "Green" Philosophy

A "green" philosophy, one that stresses conservation and a sustainable type of development, is another basic principle of Project Hope, so the school communities strive to conserve water and other resources, sort and recycle waste, and recycle rainwater for use in restrooms. The buildings were designed to exploit natural light and good air circulation to avoid extra lighting and air conditioning, and tried to eliminate or minimize sources of noise pollution.[35]

Also, much attention was paid to the landscaping and protection of the natural topography and ecology of each school's campus; the plans tried to protect rare species and old trees on the campus, and as much as possible promote outdoor education and build multipurpose outdoor amphitheaters and stages.[36]

Since the 1980s, spurred by Taiwan's environmental movement, Ciji has promoted environmental awareness, recycling, and conservation to a greater extent than the other major Buddhist groups in Taiwan. Some statements of Zhengyan recall an "Earth-as-Gaia" philosophy articulated in the works of James Lovelock ([1995], 2000), Fritjof Capra (1997), and Anna Primavesi (2000), who hold that the earth is a living and breathing organism.[37] For the new millennium, Zhengyan believes the Buddha's mission is to save our Mother Earth and each of us must wash the earth clean and purify human hearts.[38]

As a Buddhist and a believer in Chinese correlative cosmology, in her view many natural disasters are in fact man-made, not only due to human abuse of the environment but also from humanity's "accumulated negative karma" and general human moral depravity which upsets cosmological harmony. She believes in the Buddhist notion of the apocalyptic potential for human renewal: Major disasters will awaken a few humans to repent, who can rebuild civilization. Moreover, Zhengyan believes that there is a direct connection between the turn of the new century and the great number of disasters occurring around the world; she claims that the world is now in the Buddhist period of "decline," akin to the Biblical apocalypse.[39] At the same time, she exhorts that we can and must do all to protect and restore the global environment: Humans must learn to peacefully coexist with nature to slow the current pace toward world destruction.[40]

One of the stated goals of Project Hope was to help restore "the local people's way of life" while carrying out long-term conservation efforts. However, Zhengyan does not name or criticize the specific causes of massive erosion in Taiwan such as non-sustainable construction and development projects, or over-cultivation of betel nut trees and other cash crops in mountain areas, which is often the "local people's way of life."[41] Absent from Zhengyan's sermons overall is any specific critique of the structural causes of environmental degradation such as government support of boundless industrial development or flagrant disregard of pollution and construction regulations. On the contrary, Zhengyan believes social and global change will occur most meaningfully by cultivating individual morality, self-restraint, and the powers of empathy. Drawing from the *Book of Rites* and the *Analects*, Zhengyan (and Ciji) promotes the "*keji fuli* movement": Overcome one's desires and revive courtesy, not only to reduce one's needs and consumption habits but to shape harmonious ties of mutual respect among people.[42]

"Refined and Cultured," Purged of "Superstition and Bad Habits..."

Furthermore, Ciji urged all involved in Project Hope to be "rational," forget about *fengshui* and choosing auspicious days, etc.[43] Here Zhengyan expressed the stance of *renjian fojiao* as it developed around the time of the New Culture Movement in early twentieth-century China: "Superstition is the way of ghosts and spirits and is not the way of true Buddhism... Buddhism is not only a religious faith but even more is concerned with the improvement of life and the promotion of science."[44]

And the Ciji organization wants to purge the Taiwanese of their "bad habits" ("waste" of materials and resources; littered working conditions; betel-nut chewing, spitting, smoking, drinking, coarse or "aggressive" language). Purging "superstitions" and "bad habits" echoes the exhortations of various "New Culture Movements" in modern Chinese history such as the May Fourth activists' call to "purge the accumulated poisons in traditional Chinese culture," or Chiang Kai-shek's "New Life Movement," or Mao Zedong's slogan "separate the gold from the dross in Chinese culture."

Ciji's series of books on the Project Hope Schools included testimonies of success in "reforming" and "refining" the (primarily male) construction workers, how "they too can learn manners and civilization"... learn sign language and songs... be gentle and compassionate... "hands that are strong as steel can also be gentle." Some workers claim that due to the ameliorative influence of *Still Thoughts*, they ended their habits of smoking, drinking, betel-nut chewing, swearing, and explosive tempers. During my visit to school sites with the Ciji Teachers' Association, we met one such "converted" worker who designed his own "holy cards" decorated with a photo of Zhengyan out of gratitude to her. It is not known how numerous or permanent these conversions were. But Zhengyan ceaselessly promotes a certain definition of "culture" among her Ciji members as well as among the construction workers: "clean, quiet, no drinking, smoking, or chewing betel-nut."[45]

Of course intoxicants, anger, and harmful speech contravene Buddhist principles, but here also is a clash of class cultures, as Ciji attempted to "civilize the coarse and hard sun-darkened workers," recalling the historical example of nineteenth-century middle-class Christian reformers who hoped "to uplift" workers and immigrants in Britain and America. Though social reformers may have felt compassion for these people, they were also determined to eradicate such behavior such as "loudly and rudely eating, drinking and making love" in public areas. The reformers thus betrayed their psychological and social anxiety, to clearly place themselves in a higher class, and especially in the American case, to demarcate themselves from a "lower class" some had only too recently "escaped."[46] Robert Weller has also compared Ciji members with nineteenth-century Christian social reformers and found that both hailed primarily from urban new middle classes, and both faced societies undergoing rapid and unsettling economic and political change. Confronted with such change, both groups expressed their fears as the danger of losing "traditional community and family values" (as if there ever existed one clear set).[47]

Again like their nineteenth-century predecessors, Ciji volunteers involved with the Project Hope school reconstruction project acted as benevolent authority figures. Both male and female members made frequent, even daily, visits to each work site, and provided material and moral support to the workers (rest stations, periodic snacks, group spirit activities) but also demanded on-site adherence to safety and high quality construction, while at the same time they expected orderliness, recycling of refuse, a high degree of efficiency, and adherence to work schedules. Zhengyan, her vice executive director Lin Biyu, Ciji's architectural committee, and various Ciji volunteer groups consistently monitored the progress at all sites to ensure that the spirit and letter of the original designs were carried out.[48]

Besides Class Bias, Ciji Promotes Traditional Feminine Ideals

Ciji hopes not only to civilize males but also to temper females: to refine and soften the so-called Taiwan Superwoman, *Taiwan nuqiangren*. This term often refers to a career woman who may or may not take on each and every duty expected of a "wife-and-mother," including valet to husband, tutor and "homework coach" for the children, family nurse, family cook and maid, family secretary, family accountant, and caretaker of elders on both sides of the family. To undertake so many roles, Taiwanese women must be strong and able to express their opinions. But *nuqiangren* is usually used pejoratively to criticize an "over-opinionated," "aggressive," "strong," and by deduction, "unfeminine" woman.[49]

While visiting Project Hope's Fengdong Middle School, our teachers' group was entertained with a hand-puppet skit centered around this topic: "... She was a Superwoman who struck fear and trembling into people's hearts, but now, because she's experienced the Enlightened Love of Ciji, she's been transformed into a soft and gentle bird, a little bird who relies on others ... thus her relations with family and friends are more harmonious and happier than before...." Visitors to the school handled the puppets while the male puppeteer, a Ciji volunteer, delivered lively voice narration, acting four different roles. This skit evinced laughter from the audience, but laughter can convey uneasiness or skepticism as well as signify revelation and affirmation.

Toward a New Taiwan Civilization?

Project Hope's missions to promote community engagement in schools and education, as well as active concern for the environment, promise great benefits to Taiwanese society. Teachers, students, and parents actively participated in various ways during the planning and construction of Project Hope schools; and Ciji volunteers provided material and moral support (rest stations, snacks, group activities) to the workers, did the post-construction landscaping at some schools, organized fund-raising events such as charity auctions and flea markets, and organized cultural and recreational activities in the schools and for the local communities. According to Yao Taishan's study of Project Hope, Ciji's activities during the construction process reduced the gap between Ciji, the schools, and parents, and "the infectious power" and "cohesive power" of the Ciji volunteers inspired and mobilized teachers, administrators, and parents to stand up and take a more active role in their local schools.[50]

But Project Hope raises important questions about Ciji's aim of long-term sociocultural reform. Although promoting recycling and environmental protection is commendable, Ciji's "New Taiwan Civilization" aims to replace Taiwan culture's pluralistic, colorful, and boisterous characteristics, as well as democratic dissent and debate, with a quiet and obedient collective conformity.[51]

Furthermore, to what extent does the Ciji organization continue its involvement in public schools and do teachers and administrators teach *Still Thoughts* in their classrooms? During "family activities" on the weekend, Ciji members teach the "Lesson on Giving Thanks," a central tenet of Ciji culture, and explore this as a theme to be practiced at home, at school, and in the community. Furthermore, Fugui Primary School, along with other Project Hope schools, sets aside time for students to read *Still Thoughts* to cultivate a grateful heart.[52] A number of schools have posted quotations from Zhengyan's *Still Thoughts* in classrooms—along the corridors and in the bathroom—and students copied them into their notebooks. To teachers and administrators, the *Still Thoughts* curriculum teaches "ethical values" and "wisdom for daily life." Parents and teachers view this as a wholesome character-building activity, not religious proselytizing, even though, over the course of Project Hope, teachers, administrators, and parents did become Ciji members.[53]

A former principal of Jiji Middle School, in gratitude to Ciji, had the school's Counseling Room decorated with a picture of the Buddha and a smaller photo of Zhengyan, and some teachers involved in student counseling at the Middle School are Ciji members. Is this religious proselytizing, or simply psychological and moral guidance? A teacher at Jiji Primary School told me Ciji promotes concern about humanity and inspires students to "do good," and these are ideals welcomed by Taiwan's society. Or to cite another example, Yanping Primary School has a large concrete multifunctional structure shaped like the Buddha's Hand for children to clamber upon and slide down; it also functions as a stage. A former principal wrote that the "Buddha's Hand" not only makes students very happy but also can cultivate an enlightened mind in the teachers and great compassion in the students' hearts, to become a school that can sow the seeds of great compassion. The Buddha Hand ". . . is a welcoming hand, a hand of great compassion, a comforting and accepting hand."[54]

In yet another example, the Foguangshan Buddhist group funded the rebuilding of Zhongke Primary School; the building uses red bricks and wood, and the design is supposed to represent a Hakka style of architecture. Interestingly, next to a wooden shrine (donated by local merchants) dedicated to Confucius, there is a statue of Guanyin put up by the school in gratitude to Foguangshan and also to remind students to count their blessings and be grateful.[55]

The question is, do these cases violate the principle of "neutrality" stipulated in Article Six of the "Basic Education Law of the Republic of China" which prohibits proselytizing by religious or political groups on public school campuses?[56] In fact, Ciji has promoted *Still Thoughts* programs in Taiwan's public schools since 1992, before the promulgation of Article Six in 1999.[57] Academic studies on teaching *Still Thoughts* in Taiwan's public schools do not discuss the legal issues involved but, instead, affirm these programs' pedagogical efficacy, approach to teaching moral values, etc.[58]

So far, there is little, if any, open debate in Taiwan about promoting *Still Thoughts* in the public schools. Perhaps the following factors render legalistic reservations pedantic and irrelevant:

- The Taiwan government's alleged shortage of reconstruction funds

- The indisputable fact of positive benefits gained by all

- The current trend in Taiwan to implement curricula like "Life Studies" (courses exploring bioethics and counseling) and "Comprehensive Education" (education of mind, body, heart), which Christian and Buddhist groups have helped develop.[59]

- The current trend in education policy toward a 'school-based curriculum' that favors the initiative and authority of the locale (each school administration and faculty together with their parents' associations) after decades of centrally-dictated education.

Evidently, citizens in Taiwan take a pragmatic approach in this case that the excellent ends justify the means. One can hardly reject "love," [especially when it is presented in the form of parental love] positive and energetic volunteers, and wholesome ideas, all free goods and offered in good faith.[60]

But in the long run, will the teachers and parents necessarily welcome so much participation from outside groups, and to what degree would principals allow teachers or Ciji volunteers to teach *Still Thoughts* and Ciji to use public schools as a recruiting ground? The Ciji volunteers were most active in the new schools during the first year or so after the schools' completion, and thereafter have come periodically for storytelling and skits, to help during lunch, and to participate in the graduation ceremony. In general, if the principal, teachers, and/or parents are Ciji members, then the school has more Ciji-related teaching and activities.[61]

Rare questioning voices are Huang and Chen (2002), who argue that teaching *Still Thoughts* in public schools may violate the principle of neutrality and suggest that the relationship between religions and the schools should be clarified further, through regulations enforcing Article Six. Another writer, alluding to Ciji, is grateful to "the enterprise" for its generous contributions of funds and its supreme efforts in rebuilding the schools, but claims "the enterprise forced" the architects to change their design to fit "the enterprise's culture," and forbade the use of too much color in the design, despite the requests of the students, teachers, and local community.[62] Also, she continues, "the enterprise" distributed Buddhist books in the schools and wanted the students to study Buddhism at school. Adults should encourage students to do good deeds but, "good deeds should be done anonymously"; the writer hopes that the reconstructed schools don't become the totem of enterprise-culture.[63] Finally, C. Julia Huang declares that "[t]he significance of *Still Thoughts* pedagogy lies in its transforming the public school system into a field of Buddhist education among the people by turning the public school teachers from agents of the state into agents of Dharma socialization."[64]

But according to my limited inquiry, teachers, administrators, and parents see the teaching of *Still Thoughts* not as "Dharma socialization" but as acceptable neo-traditionalist values and actively promote these in the Project Hope schools, in part due to the ambivalence of teachers, administrators, and parents regarding recent education reforms and de-Sinicization policies undertaken by the government. As one school principal commented, *Still Thoughts* provides a set of standards and a moral compass that he feels Taiwan sorely lacks.

Open criticism of Ciji in any aspect is rare in Taiwan, other than that "Ciji absorbs too many donations and resources."[65] Still, why do so many people support Ciji? Chapter 2 suggested a number of reasons, but the next chapter will probe why Ciji's interpretation of Buddhism, with particular reference to its set of gender ideals, attracts so many women and men.

Chapter 4

The Women of Ciji

Nuns, Laypeople, and the Bodhisattva Guanyin

As we saw in Chapter 2, Zhengyan emanates an androgynous multifaceted personality: Buddhist master, visionary, mother, patriarch, commander-in-chief. In her youth she struggled with her mother and her family, rejected the roles of wife and mother, wandered in the wilderness of eastern Taiwan, and became a Buddhist nun. In all these acts, Zhengyan was a rebel, yet she became famous as a champion of traditional Confucian ideals of the primacy of the patriarchal family, filial piety, and "women-as-mothers" through her particular interpretation of Buddhism.

From the 1960s to 1990, the Ciji organization grew primarily due to the efforts of Zhengyan, her nuns, Ciji's volunteer female devotees, and a select group of female commissioners, major donors of time, skills, and money (Figure 4.1, next page). Men have always participated as volunteers, then as members of the Compassion Faith Corps founded in 1990, and as commissioners. In addition to its volunteer forces, Ciji also employs female and male professionals in the fields of medicine, medical technology, computers, education, media, publishing, engineering, and architecture. In 2004 the Ciji organization upgraded the male faith corps to the same organizational level as the (mostly female) commissioners.[1] Although male participation is important and growing in Ciji[2] this chapter argues that Ciji's reinterpretation and propagation of so-called "feminine values" was and continues to be integral to its mission and worldview. There are numerous women's groups, Buddhist groups, NGOs, and social welfare groups, but Ciji is the largest and most famous of these in Taiwan.

Lu Hwei-syin (1998; 2000a,b); Huang and Weller (1998); Robert Weller (1999); and Yang and Zhang (2004a) argue that one reason for Ciji's phenomenal success is that Ciji empowers women, as Ciji membership develops women's identities and potentials. "Empowerment" is a term prevalent in current academic and popular discourse, but what does it actually mean for women, particularly Buddhist women, in Taiwan?[3] How and to what extent

Figure 4.1. Master Zhengyan and the first Commissioners in Taipei (Ciji Foundation)

does Ciji empower women, and what does this reveal about Taiwanese women and Taiwanese society?

In order to explore these questions, this chapter discusses the following categories of "The Women of Ciji." The first section introduces Zhengyan's nuns and her expectations of them to become *da zhangfu*, "great men," and notes how different this expectation is from the Woman-Mother-Bodhisattva ideal she demands of lay supporters. The second section makes the point that while Ciji as a lay organization shares certain aspects with traditional lay-groups in Chinese and Taiwanese history, Ciji's members comprise volunteer and professional women and men of diverse backgrounds, and the content and scope of Ciji missions is unparalleled in Chinese Buddhist history.

The third section highlights another important "woman" of Ciji, the Guanyin Bodhisattva. (See Figure 1.1.) Ciji has successfully exploited the symbolism of the popular cult of Guanyin/Miaoshan to a greater extent than other Buddhist masters in Taiwan and Ciji's valorization of "feminine" and "maternal" virtues makes a striking comparison to the circumscribed and/or negative view of the same values in Tibetan and Theravādin traditions. How does Ciji's interpretation of a modern Guanyin both empower and delimit women?

The chapter concludes that Ciji does not challenge or subvert traditional ideas about women's nature and roles, but has extended women's so-called nurturing and healing roles from home to society, and in the process has convinced many Taiwanese to empathize with and assist people beyond their immediate social circles of family and friends. This is a profound example of social transformation for Taiwan, as was the case historically in China: "It is widely held that an important legacy of Buddhism in Chinese society was that it fostered a 'universalistic ethics' vis-à-vis Confucian familism and led to a great increase in charitable activities."[4]

Such a social transformation, this large-scale mobilization of citizens to undertake compassionate acts to relieve suffering, is an achievement seemingly beyond reproach, but in doing so, the Ciji organization has taken for granted and reproduced essentialist notions of gender,[5] though at the same time, other women and men in Taiwan are working assiduously to promote gender equality in education, law, political representation, and career opportunity. For how much longer can Ciji draw from the well of gender essentialism of Taiwan society? Is Ciji's vision of Bodhisattva-as-mother reactionary or revolutionary? To attempt to answer these questions, it is necessary to first discuss the women closest to Zhengyan, her nun disciples.

The Nuns of the Still Thoughts Abode

A noteworthy Buddhist nun or monk usually attracts and cultivates a group of like-minded monastic disciples and establishes a distinctive temple community and legacy. However, not much is known about Zhengyan's nuns: Ciji official publications and academic studies of Ciji barely mention them.[6] There are about 140 nuns affiliated with the Still Thoughts Abode, the heart of Ciji's Hualian headquarters. The nuns, ranging in age from twenty-one to over seventy (average age 45 to 50), are the core support group, *houdun*, and the force of stability for the entire Ciji organization.

> With lay members far outnumbering the nuns, it is mostly lay people (volunteers and paid professionals) carrying out the Ciji missions of charity, medicine, education, and culture. Though nuns also participate in these missions, their main role is to follow the spirit and letter and traditional ethics, protect the roots [of Ciji] and play the role of transmitters of traditional concepts; in the end it is the Master, through her deeds, who is leading everyone.[7]

Ciji sources often compare Ciji to a tree, in this way: Ciji is a tree that has grown tall and broad due to the dedication and willpower of Master Zhengyan; Ciji's roots are the nuns and permanent residents of the Still Thoughts Abode, while its branches and leaves are Ciji's lay-members: all are tightly bound together as one.[8]

Zhengyan began her enterprise in 1966 with a close-knit group of nuns.[9] They evidently dedicated themselves to Zhengyan heart and soul, and together they lived through several arduous years farming and making handicrafts by day and studying at night by candlelight. At times they had nothing to eat but soy sauce and rice; at night, mice ran around the room as "the sisters" attempted to sleep huddled together on two tatami mats, sharing two quilts. Zhengyan built "sororal ties" with her first disciples and the first generation of thirty lay disciples, as Robert Weller aptly phrased it,[10] but more than sisters, these women became comrades bonded through shared experiences of triumph over suffering and hardship.

According to Charles B. Jones' interpretation, "... the Still Thoughts Abode is very small and does not serve as the main symbol of the organization; that role is reserved to the white marble hospital buildings."[11] On the contrary, I argue that the primary role of Ciji's nuns, both in practice and symbolically, is protector of the roots of Ciji Buddhist spirit and mission and I agree with C. Julia Huang that the Still Thoughts Abode is the heart and home of the Ciji organization.[12]

Life at the Still Thoughts Abode

The founding and early growth of the Ciji organization was undertaken strictly in a self-reliant manner, expressly not relying on lay offerings, by keeping a frugal lifestyle, growing their own food, and also making and selling a variety of hand-made or self-cultivated items over the years such as sweaters, gloves, diapers, circuit breakers, chrysanthemums, pottery, plastic flowers, bean powder, and candles.

New nuns at the Still Thoughts Abode follow the life and work style originally fashioned by Zhengyan and her first five or six nuns. This is a lifestyle of self-reliance based on a passage from Tang dynasty Chan master Baizhang: "A day of no work means a day without eating."[13] Following a daily schedule similar to other Chinese monasteries, the sound of the wooden clapper wakens the nuns at 3:50 a.m., then bell and drums summon all to morning service. Next is preparing breakfast for all residents and guests. Daily indoor and outdoor chores follow, including tending the garden and making their own organic fertilizer. Other nuns attend to guests, manage the bookstore, lead tours of Still Thoughts Abode, answer the phone, take messages, and field inquiries about Buddhism, Zhengyan, and the Ciji enterprise.

As for production work, the nuns produce bean and barley powder (sold as health foods). As they have since the beginning, the nuns rely upon this work to cover their daily expenses: All donations to the Ciji organization go to Ciji's missions, not to Zhengyan or her nun disciples.[14] All monasteries do early morning chores not only out of necessity but as part of their Buddhist practice, and many grow fruits and vegetables; but to Ciji this tradition of self-reliant production is inherently virtuous, it carries central moral authority, it is a symbolic capital fund, which Zhengyan and her nuns draw from and constantly refer back to in their daily routines at the Still Thoughts Abode.[15]

In an article describing the resident nuns of Ciji, most of the photos highlight the nuns engaged in physical labor as gardeners of the Ciji spirit.[16] This is in contrast with other all-nun groups such as the Luminary Temple in Jiayi whose Master, Wu Yin, has focused on training nuns, and has developed a complete pedagogical system toward this end (see Chapter 5). Likewise, Ven. Hiuwan's Lotus Buddhist Ashram trains nuns and is affiliated with Huafan University, the first university founded by a monastic to be recognized by the Ministry of Education. Foguangshan monastery has trained nuns at their Buddhist Institute since 1967 and has run a separate institute for monks since 1985. Ciji has a school system open to the public comprising each level of schooling, from kindergarten to graduate school, but no Buddhist institute to train the nuns.

In the early days of Ciji, Zhengyan led her disciples in Buddhist studies, in keeping with the Chan Buddhist ideal *chaogeng, yedu* [farm in the morning, study at night], but in recent years, all Tuesday and Wednesday evenings are set aside for study, hearing guest lecturers, and informing the nuns on the progress of Ciji's missions as well as news and developments in Taiwan and around the world. One nun who has been with Zhengyan for over a decade said that she and her Master have not said much to each other, rather, that her Master teaches the *dharma* primarily not through lectures but from the example of her actions.

A potential novitiate first would have to fully identify with the missions and orientation of Ciji. In the case of Ven. Deni, she had already heard two other famous Buddhist masters in Taiwan lecture on the *dharma*, but still didn't understand the essence of Buddhism until she came into contact with Ciji. While serving as a Ciji volunteer in Taichung, she was greatly inspired by the dedication and selflessness, strong will, and down-to-earth attitude of the housewife volunteers, who faced all kinds of difficulties to carry out the Bodhisattva vow.[17]

Some nuns, like Ven. Deni, had been Ciji volunteers, some had been in the Youth Corps, and some have mothers and fathers who are active Ciji volunteers. Zhengyan prefers that candidates have some work experience before deciding to become a novitiate at Ciji. Novitiates spend a varying number of years participating in all aspects of life and work at the Still Thoughts Abode; Zhengyan decides who is suitable to be tonsured. This group must pass through another two-year observation period before Zhengyan finally decides who can be fully ordained. Candidates at Ciji, as is standard in Buddhism, must obtain parental approval before becoming ordained, and Zhengyan prefers that parents attend the ordination ceremony.[18]

According to their talents and experiences, some Ciji nuns work with the Ciji's missions of charity, medical care, education, and culture, and utilize their skills in computers, photography, music, writing, publishing, and administration. Others organize and carry out the numerous camps for children, teachers, volunteers, and others. The nuns closest to her, her disciples for the longest number of years, serve as assistants and secretaries.

To "Leave Home" Is to Become a Great Man: *Chujia nai da zhangfu shi*

Zhengyan requires both lay followers and nuns to be self-sacrificing, ever-striving, conscientious, and perfectionist, but in comparison with her expectations of her lay followers, Zhengyan does not request her nuns to be "good mothers." Nuns belong to a different category, that of a monastic, whose inner attitude and outer behavior should be, according to the Buddhist *si weiyi* [the four postures]: "Moving like the wind, standing like a pine-tree, sitting like a bell, lying down like a bow."

Furthermore, following long-standing Chan tradition, they have become *da zhangfu*, a great man: "From this time on you must totally transform yourself, from having the heart/mind of the common man to the heart/mind of a Buddha, of a Bodhisattva... You must have willpower, courage, be able to bear suffering and carry great burdens, at all times and forever work to realize the spirit of Buddhism within the human realm.[19] This includes "offering up of their life, to sacrifice one's bodily comforts and rest, to carry out their vow: let all sentient beings be free of suffering and be happy, and that there be no disasters in the world. To press on despite pain and fatigue, tempering and refining one's heart and will; to sacrifice to the utmost, to stand and work together as one, to endure what others cannot endure."[20]

As Miriam Levering explains,

> The term da zhangfu has a long history in Chinese classics and other literature, beginning with the Mencius. From the first its root meaning seems to have been "a great and powerful man." Confucian moralists seem to have attempted to transform its meaning from physical strength and power of will alone to moral greatness, but they also specifically underlined the term's meaning of "manliness" as opposed to "womanliness."[21]

In Linji Chan Buddhist texts, the term took on an additional meaning of one who can reach enlightenment directly, unburdened by arguments and words and intellectual distractions.[22] Such great heroes are Bodhisattvas who act spontaneously out of compassion. However, and crucially, it is the *da zhangfu's* manly qualities of courage, strength of will, and determination, that Chan Buddhists believe crucial to attain enlightenment.[23] Levering, Hsieh, and Grant have shown that in Chan Buddhist texts from the Song onward, male Buddhist writers "saw" and praised outstanding and enlightened female laywomen and nuns as *da zhangfu*, a development in Buddhist discourse that transmitted mixed messages to women then and now. On the one hand, such texts, in contrast to misogynist passages in other Buddhist literature, argued that women were capable of study and enlightenment equal to men, and related many cases of esteemed nuns teaching laypeople, named in *dharma* lineages, and managing their own monastic affairs. Yet Levering concludes that Chan Buddhism's "... rhetoric of equality cannot stand up against the rhetoric of masculine heroism, when the latter is supported by gender distinctions so 'real' to the culture and remain unambiguous."[24]

Androcentric or not, the *da zhangfu* ideal greatly appealed to Zhengyan, through which she could realize her youthful aspiration: "What if a woman could be like a man and do great things for the world?"[25] Ciji nuns Defu and Deni stated that to become a monastic is to accept a great mission: to "do your part in the family of the Buddha," *chengdan rulai jiaye*.[26] According to Ven. Defu, becoming a *da zhangfu* is not actually becoming male, nor is it a neutralizing of nuns' femaleness, but it is manifesting "male" characteristics such as bravery, as opposed to "female" characteristics such as softness. To become a monastic, she says, is to bear any burden, and donate one's heart and all bodily powers to society. To Ven. Deni, the *da zhangfu* is a gentleman, with a good moral character; his word is his honor and he is broad-minded, as opposed to "female" tendencies toward jealousy, narrow-heartedness, gossiping, obsessing, and fantasizing.[27]

Dwelling on the obvious gender-neutral and/or androcentric features shared by monks and nuns regarding clothing, the tonsure, deportment, and so on can lead to the hasty conclusion that Taiwan's nuns have "suppressed their femininity" and/or have "transcended gender."[28] But further research is needed to ascertain to what degree Ciji's nuns (or other nuns in Taiwan) identify with the masculine *da zhangfu* role relative to other aspects of their identity such as "Taiwanese female" or "professional religious."[29] Contradictory identities are not necessarily problematic: Wenjie Qin shows convincingly for nuns in China that they can "... make strategic use of their gender ambiguity;" which "... contains a liberating and empowering potential," as they make use of their feminine, masculine, and "neutral" characteristics according to necessity and circumstance.[30]

In sum, the nuns of the Still Thoughts Abode are important symbolically for the Ciji myth and are invaluable to Zhengyan, personally, to the daily operation of the Still Thoughts Abode, and in the many activities of the Ciji Foundation in Taiwan and overseas. However, in terms of membership and the focus of its missions, Ciji is primarily a lay organization. The next section therefore will discuss Ciji's lay-members and how, through them, Ciji is feminizing and by implication "civilizing" the public sphere.

The Lay Members

Ciji originally gained renown as a women's Buddhist charity organization, built up from the 1960s by Zhengyan, her nun disciples, and Ciji's women volunteers. In various times and places in Chinese history Buddhist monasteries sheltered victims of disaster; aided orphans, widows, the old, poor, sick and hungry; provided interest-free loans; and helped bury the dead.[31] As is well documented, a laywomen's Buddhist group undertaking charity also has historical precedent. Daniel Overmyer and Barend J. ter Haar have shown that "... many women assumed active leadership roles in Sung lay Buddhist societies and post-Sung popular religious sects."[32] Laywomen in the Song and Yuan dynasties "... carried out their Buddhist activities parallel to, but not subordinated under, the organized Sangha. They performed good deeds for society as well as ritual activities such as chanting sūtras...."[33] In late Imperial China (1550–1900), the animosity and censure voiced by Neo-Confucian moralists and some monks did not stop the public participation by great numbers of women in lay Buddhism when "... nuns became a familiar sight in the houses, and there was no lack of women in the mushrooming lay associations that organized such activities as *sūtra* chanting, temple visits, and pilgrimages."[34] In pre-1950s Taiwan, many women participated in *zhaijiiao* sects and some all-female *zhaitang* were headed by a woman.[35] But generally speaking, these traditional groups were more likely led by monks or local male elites than by nuns or laywomen, and the content and scope of their charitable and philanthropic missions cannot compare to the missions of a modern organization like Ciji.

By the mid-1990s, Ciji had developed far beyond a traditional laywomen's Buddhist group and was no longer only "a group of middle-aged Taiwanese housewives" doing good works. It had become "... instead a microcosm of multiple social statuses in Taiwan" with other subgroups such as the male faith corps, the teachers' association, the college students' youth corps, the entrepreneurs' club, and the police club.[36] These groups form the highly visible "volunteer" face of Ciji, yet Ciji also hires part-time and full-time professionals to work in general operations, medical and educational missions, broadcasting, publishing, public relations, and international relief; many of these professionals are male.

Ciji's changing membership over forty years is like a series of snapshots of the social and economic transformations in Taiwan over the same time period. It is crucial to highlight the differences in generations, class, and educational background of Ciji's lay-followers. Originally, the backbone of Ciji was composed of rural, small-town housewife volunteers and middle-class urban housewife volunteers (but often these "housewives" did piece-rate work, went to market to sell odds and ends, took odd jobs to add to household income, and especially, worked free of charge in small family businesses run from the home).[37] Men could be volunteers and aim to become commissioners. But in 1990, the Compassion Faith Corps (*Cicheng dui*) was established for men who were experienced Ciji volunteers and who were willing to follow the five basic Buddhist precepts of no killing, no stealing, no adultery, no lying, and no alcohol, as well as abstain from drugs, betel-nut chewing, gambling, and playing the stock market. Furthermore, the Faith Corpsmen are expected to be filial, soft-spoken, have a gentle expression, abide by traffic regulations, and must not participate in politics or social movements.[38] The following description speaks volumes:

> The Ten Precepts are like small wires that support and shape a bonsai banyan tree. They grow with each Cicheng Faith Corps Member, rectifying his bad habits and stubborn prejudices ... The men are as disciplined as soldiers, yet at the same time they are gentle and modest.[39]

Despite the men's "bad habits and stubborn prejudices," apparently the women welcomed the influx, "... because all the hard work could be done by the men. The male members emphasized organization and discipline and were strong and vigorous. Because of their participation, Ciji became more efficient and its public image was greatly elevated" and the organization could attain "the right balance of female compassion and male wisdom."[40] The tasks of the Faith Corps include night security duty, recycling center volunteering, hospital volunteering, situations involving transportation and traffic control, and disaster relief.[41] Males brought to Ciji new models of organization from the office, the university, and from their two-year military service experience, including the terms corps, battalion, company and platoons.[42]

Since the late 1980s Ciji increasingly called upon the expertise of paid professional men and women, as Ciji built its first hospital and expanded overseas, established a media enterprise (TV, journals, books), and built a complete school system from kindergarten to graduate school at their headquarters. Many of these professionals are active lay-members; some have left their former prestigious positions to work full-time for the Ciji organization.[43]

Laypeople join Ciji and other modern Buddhist groups in Taiwan for reasons similar to why laypeople supported Buddhism in Chinese history, for example, to seek guidance regarding soteriological questions, health issues, and personal problems with family and associates[44] and a conviction that undertaking charity and philanthropy not only relieves suffering but accrues merit for oneself and others in this life and the next. Thus, laypeople supported Buddhism for reasons ranging from pure compassion to carrying out devotional acts dedicated to parents or other family members; or from anxious intentions to "purify the social order."[45] As mentioned previously, a number of modern Buddhist groups in Taiwan, including Ciji, offer an "ethical-religious synthesis" based on Buddhist teachings and Confucian values. However, where the Ciji organization differs from the aforementioned groups, in addition to the unprecedented modern and global scope of its charitable and relief missions, is Zhengyan's interpretation of Buddhist compassion. Ciji promotes "great love" as corresponding to the "motherly" virtues of nurturance, selflessness, and self-sacrifice. Here the Ciji organization, more than other Buddhist groups in Taiwan, successfully taps into two deep wells within the traditional Chinese patriarchy: the "virtuous wife and good mother" (*xianqi liangmu*) ideal, and the cult of the Guanyin Bodhisattva.

Ciji and the Cult of the Guanyin Bodhisattva in Taiwan

"The Bodhisattva is continually smiling, calm and quiet, gentle and soft like a mother who never rests from her duties."[46]

The Buddhist practice of many contemporary temples in Taiwan draws upon a number of traditions, including Pure Land and various Chan schools, and includes the veneration of Bodhisattvas such as Kṣitigarbha (Dizang), Maitreya (Mile), Mañjuśrī (Wenshu), and Samantabhadra (Puxian). But it is the figure of Guanyin who stands out in the foreground at Ciji.

Zhengyan and her earliest followers grew up in the context of Taiwanese popular religion of central and east Taiwan including female and male practitioners of the indigenous *zhaijiao*, or "vegetarian religion," devotees of the Eternal Mother and Guanyin.[47] Guanyin is the Chinese name for Avalokiteśvara, often portrayed as the thousand-armed, thousand-eyed Bodhisattva of Compassion who hears and sees all and aids those in need. Chün-fang Yü chronicles the historical transformation of the representation and apprehension of Guanyin from a male or androgynous figure, to a female, and often maternal, figure in China. Of the many possible reasons Yü considers, the one most relevant to the present discussion is that since the Song dynasty, compassion has been associated with the feminine and the mother in Chinese culture,[48] related to popular notions like "father is strict, mother is kind and loving (*fuyan, muci*)." Also from the Song period on, the epithets "old women" and "grandmother" were used in Chan discourse "to refer to compassion, unselfishness, and kindness," and these epithets, which referred to pedagogical tales about humble but enlightened "old women," were used to praise spiritually-advanced Buddhist practitioners, both male and female. These stories may also have shaped the development of a feminine Guanyin in China.[49]

With the popularization of the *Lotus Sūtra* and Pure Land *sūtras* in China, Guanyin became known as a Bodhisattva who could appear in over thirty forms, seven of them female, promising salvation and granting petitions to both men and women.[50] Since the twelfth century, a representation of Guanyin as Chinese and female became popularized via the legend of the Chinese princess Miaoshan, daughter of a king with no sons. Due to her devotion to Buddhist faith, Miaoshan refused an arranged marriage and incurred the wrath of her father who attempted to kill her. While in the underworld freeing suffering ghosts, Miaoshan heard that her father was ill, as "karmic consequence" for his murder of Miaoshan's fellow nuns. Miaoshan cured him with a medicine made from her own eyes and hands, manifesting the ideals of both filial piety and the Bodhisattva.[51] Her father recognized her and "... Miaoshan miraculously grows new eyes and arms, becoming the thousand-eyed and thousand-armed incarnation of Guanyin."[52]

Li Yuzhen relates the great popularity of Guanyin/Miaoshan worship in Taiwan at least since the seventeenth century, attested not only by the number of temples dedicated to her, but also in the numbers of lay devotees both female and male in the *zhaijiao* tradition.[53] In Chinese Buddhist history, Guanyin/Miaoshan has been revered by both devout Buddhist women who resisted marriage[54] as well as those who, voluntarily or not, remained within the family structure.[55] Women prayed to Guanyin to relieve the suffering arising out of the karmic fate in being born female: marriage and family problems, menstruation and childbirth, and duty to bear sons.[56]

This Guanyin/Miaoshan fount is of central importance to Zhengyan and Ciji, to a far greater extent than to other Buddhist Masters in Taiwan. As we saw in the last chapter, Guanyin figured prominently in Zhengyan's early years and from the start of her Buddhist vocation in charity, medicine, and relief, Zhengyan dedicated herself to the fulfillment of the Bodhisattva vow to not rest until all are saved. She expects the same dedication from her followers: "We will become Guanyin's watchful eyes and hands, and the world can never call us Buddhists a passive group again."[57]

Zhengyan's advice presented in her *Still Thoughts* echo tracts of popular Buddhism such as the *Biography of the Guanshiyin Bodhisattva* available at Taiwan temples free or for a donation. Most of this book retells popular legends about Guanyin dating from the twelfth century, while the last section addresses contemporary family and emotional problems. It instructs women how to attain personal happiness as well as family peace and harmony (the two are inextricably intertwined) by adjusting and improving their own attitudes and behavior; the responsibility is one's own.[58] This type of popular tract, like Zhengyan's *Still Thoughts*, encourages "right speech" and voicing one's gratitude through words and deeds.[59]

> The advice can be empowering: A woman should take responsibility for herself and create her own happiness through positive words and thoughts. Or (this)... can be understood as calling for accommodation to an oppressive situation; she should not demand changes in her family situation but learn to cope with it.[60]

In a similar vein, Zhengyan does not advocate divorce as solution for women's marital problems such as a husband's adultery: "You need to cultivate a good relationship with your spouse every day. Even if the relationship turns sour, you must take one step backward to accept reality with an open heart. Love the person that your spouse loves, and it will be a great love."[61] "Don't call it an affair. You should view it as fate. It is part of your karma. You should accept it bravely. You should keep loving and thanking your husband. He has given you a chance to see that our lives are filled with changes."[62] Women should also display infinite patience and compassion with mothers-in-law, without exception.[63]

And as for household burdens, the solution is the age-old ideal of *ren*, forbearance:

> Q: Master, my husband doesn't want to take care of our family. I'm the one who has to look after the seventeen people in our household. I can't take it anymore.
>
> A: His family is also your family. Your husband does so because he knows you are very capable.[64] You are not tolerant enough if you regard responsibility as suffering. It's true that you have to look after seventeen people. But remember that I must look after even more people."[65]

Yet on the other hand Zhengyan's mission of realizing compassion through active social engagement departs radically from the style and method of popular tracts such as *Sacred Chant of the White-Robed Great Sage Guanyin*, which teaches the reader how to chant and to auspiciously arrange incense sticks to attain "family happiness," and describes petitions for divine intervention to honor specific requests like birth of sons, family members' health, or passing examinations.[66] Zhengyan goes far beyond traditional Guanyin worship and mobilizes the previously untapped potential of Taiwanese women. Furthermore, Zhengyan promulgates and expects of her followers, no matter if female or male, to manifest through concrete acts certain feminine qualities, seen as assets and strengths that will save the world. "Women's role attributes such as kindness, care, modesty, patience, and altruism are uplifted as the model manner in charity services. Maternal love is heightened to represent Buddha's boundless compassion."[67]

Says Zhengyan in *Still Thoughts*: "A loving, merciful, compassionate heart is the mark of a woman. It is a wife's duty to guide her husband in the right direction, and it is a mother's duty to do things that are beneficial to others."[68] And, "... one of the best things for a woman to have is the glory of the maternal instinct."[69] It is good for a professional woman to get ahead in her career, but she should not extinguish the glory of her maternal instinct. Furthermore,

> ... only when a housewife fulfills a housewife's duty will she qualify to become a Buddhist. A good housewife's contributions to her family and society are enormous. In fact, she has three different roles to play in order to become a good Buddhist. First, she must be a good daughter-in-law. She needs to embrace the concept of filial piety by serving her father- and mother-in-law well... Second, she must be a good wife. She should look after her husband and help society sweep away pornography... Third, she must be a good mother. She should increase her knowledge in every field, so that she can become a good teacher and guide for her children.[70]

As Confucian and Buddhist moralists have intoned for centuries, Zhengyan champions traditional ideas about the feminine and the ideal Chinese wife, mother, and daughter-in-law.[71] Yet when Zhengyan was asked if women have more karmic hindrances than men, she answered:

> Not necessarily. A woman's strength will become great if she is truly determined. Avalokiteśvara Bodhisattva is a good example. He often came into the world in the female form of the Goddess of Mercy. How compassionate a woman's heart can be! Compassion breeds wisdom, and you can then help promote the work of saving the world. A woman should not underestimate herself.[72]

It is striking to compare the case of women in Ciji to societies with Tibetan or Theravādin traditions, where the stress placed on negative female traits and female karmic hindrances found in Buddhist literature limit or even prohibit women from studying the *dharma*, let alone attaining enlightenment. In Bhutan, women cannot even touch *Thangkas*. Although Tibetan/Tantric Buddhism has a long history of famous female Buddhist teachers and practitioners, and the tradition of "divine female figures" like *Tārā* and *Dākinī* seem to convey powerful and liberating potentials for the "feminine principle," in fact, the reality for most Tibetan Buddhist women is harsh and bleak. "Tantric doctrine and imagery may valorize the female, but Tantric practice retains a puritan aversion to impurity. Although some Tantric doctrines and iconography appear to reverse the dominance of the male, much Tantric ritual practice reasserts difference."[73]

Generally speaking, Theravādin and Tibetan societies and their male Buddhist establishments propagate the stereotypes of women as spiritually and intellectually weaker, prey to the waxing and waning of emotions, more polluted, more bound than men are to material *samsāra* world due to women's reproductive role and "natural" inclinations to care for others.[74] The dominating message is that women can gain merit by supporting monks, by bearing sons who can become monks, and meanwhile pray to be born again in male form.[75] In Thailand, popular Buddhist texts laud women as mothers/nurturers in the literal social role of mother and symbolic role of mothers/nurturers of the monks.[76] But Thai Buddhist valorization of "mothers" is limited: This has not translated into support of nuns or organization of strong laywomen associations.

In contrast, as Chapter 1 discusses, over the past few decades a number of Taiwan's Buddhist leaders have stressed that the so-called feminine and motherly virtues of compassion, nurturance, empathy, selflessness, self-sacrifice, reconciliation, and warmth correspond precisely with Buddhist virtues. In their proselytizing, Taiwan Buddhist masters, including Master Zhengyan, have stressed phrases in the Buddhist tradition that compare the Bodhisattva's compassion to "a mother loving her child"[77] and have drawn upon the historical tradition of the female Guanyin in Chinese Buddhism. This to done to harmonize with and reaffirm Chinese gender roles and family norms to build a socially engaged Buddhism without overtly disrupting the *status quo*. Zhengyan has propagated Buddhist compassion (*cibei*) as Ciji's *da'ai* (great love) to mobilize women "... in the name of social utility, to leave the home and extend the benefits of maternity to society at large"[78] without directly challenging patriarchal norms. Two of Zhengyan's nun disciples confirmed that comparing Buddhist compassion *cibei* to *mu'ai* (mother's love) is an example of skillful means, by which Zhengyan communicates with and successfully mobilizes people unfamiliar with Buddhist terminology.[79]

Conclusion: Feminine or Feminist?

Ciji promotes and reproduces an essentialist notion of feminine nature, of the Bodhisattva Guanyin synonymous with Mother, as a self-sacrificing, infinitely forbearing, compassionate nurturer of others, and in doing so, has mobilized millions of people for good works and promoted a civic and global consciousness in Taiwan. How should we interpret Ciji's vision of and for women? Is it at heart conservative and reactionary, merely an expansion of women's traditional maternal role into the public sphere? Does Ciji's popularity in fact represent a backlash against feminism, routinely blamed in many societies for causing social problems like divorce, neglected and delinquent children, and abandonment of the elderly: in sum, general social chaos? It is probably most apt to characterize Ciji's popularity among women and the organization's power and influence in society as in great part due to Zhengyan's skillful utilization of women's improved social status over the past several decades in Taiwan.

Ciji's vision promotes values similar to those in the "relational feminism" predominant in the West before the twentieth century that championed "women's function in procreation and nurturing capacities ... It insisted on women's distinctive contributions in these roles to the broader society...." "Relational feminism" contrasts greatly with liberal feminism that de-emphasizes sexual differences and gender roles and works to attain human rights and equal opportunities for women as individuals and citizens.[80]

The spirit of relational feminism lives on in today's eco-feminism and feminist spirituality movements. "Feminine" traits of nurturance, community, communication, harmony-seeking, valuing relationship, and friendship, once criticized as inferior to the "masculine" values that have driven world history and civilization, are now celebrated as feminist values that should be promoted to save the world from isolation, aggression, alienation, and lack of communication: indeed, to save the earth, our mother.[81]

Ciji is certainly not promoting liberal feminism nor women's issues per se, but rather is dedicated to the universal relief of suffering and "purification" of the world, and upholds, if unconsciously, the values of relational feminism. Since many scholars have claimed that Ciji transforms and empowers women, it behooves us to examine this in more detail. Empowerment is a term liberally used in social science literature. It is instructive to know the background of this term and understand that "empowerment" is both a process and a goal.[82] "In the 1970s, when the concept was first invoked by women's organizations, [it] was explicitly used to frame and facilitate the struggle for social justice and women's equality through a transformation of economic, social, and political structures at national and international levels." But in more recent definitions, "women's empowerment is assumed to be attainable through different points of departure, including political mobilisation, consciousness raising, and education," as well as though changing the social and legal institutions that underwrite male control and privilege.[83]

If the women of Ciji are "empowered," it is on the individual level of "consciousness-raising" and self-development, as well as through the social influence gained through their Ciji collective identity. The nuns of Ciji, though unsung, contribute in many ways to the organization's missions both in Taiwan and overseas, though they have few if any opportunities to pursue further education, unlike nuns of other large Buddhist groups. Ciji lay-members report how much they learned in the areas of counseling, medicine and health care, publishing, media, and organization skills. Ciji gives women and men opportunities for foreign travel and volunteer experience, cross-cultural exchanges, foreign language training, mass media, and especially, skills in public speaking.[84]

Additionally, as Lu (1998) relates, Ciji women attest that joining Ciji brought them happiness, self-esteem, and even "rebirth." "Tzu Chi is a new social space for them in terms of self-development and enjoyment of self-autonomy as a result of carrying out socially visible projects."[85] Sometimes, Ciji saves women's lives: One woman attempted suicide seven times due to her husband's multiple extra-marital affairs and was saved by joining Ciji; while another woman with four daughters endured years of physical and mental abuse from her husband until she was assisted by the combined efforts of a women's domestic violence group, a government social service office, and Ciji.[86]

In sum, everyone is satisfied. Individuals feel empowered, while Ciji members contribute huge amounts of time, energy, expertise, and resources to Taiwan's society and do not question or critique injustices caused by government, the economy, or the family. Ciji's "free goods" are welcomed (except by other competing NGOs) by both patriarchal society and a government that encourages religious groups and the private sector to provide charity and medical care services.[87]

But, like "wires shaping a bonsai tree," there are limits to empowerment for Ciji women, who, like the men of the Ciji Faith Corps, should be gentle, modest, soft-spoken, and loyal to Ciji's collective identity. Will Ciji's vision of the Bodhisattva-as-mother continue to attract adherents in the next generation, especially among young professionals? Until now, Ciji's perpetuation of stereotypical gender characteristics have benefited their organization and Taiwan society, but continuing perpetuation of such stereotypes impedes current and future efforts by the government and many NGOs to rectify inequalities and injustices for girls and women. Is Ciji's interpretation of Buddhism and of nuns and laywomen's roles the exception or the norm among other Buddhist groups in Taiwan? In order to discuss these issues further, the next chapter will focus on the Xiang'guang (Luminary) Buddhist Institute, which is primarily dedicated to the education of nuns while also engaging in lay Buddhist education and social welfare projects.

Chapter 5

Jueshu renhua—
"Cultivating Buddhist Leaders, Awakening Humanity's Essence through Education"

The Nuns of Luminary Buddhist Institute

As discussed in Chapter 1, though fully-ordained nuns have out-numbered monks since the 1950s, it was primarily monks who held leadership positions and gave public *dharma* talks during the 1950s–1970s.[1] Li Yuzhen reports that before the 1980s, nuns at many mixed-gender temples in Taiwan were automatically relegated to kitchen duties and had few opportunities for study and giving *dharma* talks.[2]

To remedy this state of affairs, the nun Wu Yin (b. 1940) founded the Luminary Buddhist Institute in 1980 with the express goal of training nuns as spiritual leaders, while propagating the *dharma* through their missions of education, culture, and social service (Figure 5.1, next page). Their motto is "Vow of Compassion, *beiyuan;* Actualized Action, *lixing;* and Harmony, *hehe*."

This Institute of around one hundred nuns operates a number of organizations. The Luminary Buddhist Studies Institute, the Luminary Library, the nuns' main dormitory, and the Luminary Temple are located at the headquarters in a rural township outside of Jiayi city in southwest Taiwan; but now Luminary operates affiliated branches offering courses in Buddhist studies and meditation sessions, and other classes and camps for the public (children, youth, and adults) in Taipei (Yinyi Institute), Miaoli (Dinghui Institute), Taichung (Yanghui Institute), Jiayi (Anhui Institute), Fengshan (Zizhulin Study Center), and Taoyuan County (Xiang'guang Shan Chan retreat center).[3]

In contrast with other Buddhist monasteries and nunneries large or small in Taiwan, the Luminary Buddhist Institute's main mission is the training of nuns and lay outreach through education; its focus is on education and

Figure 5.1. Master Wu Yin and her disciples during the Vassa (Rains-Retreat). Ceremony at Buddha Hall, Luminary Temple (Shih Wu Yin)

scholarship rather than on the provision of charity or traditional Buddhist services like *sūtra* chanting and funeral rites. The Luminary nuns, many of whom hold post-graduate degrees, are actively engaged in teaching, writing, and publishing, and this has not escaped scholars' notice.[4]

After an overview of the Luminary Buddhist Institute's historical background and a description of their missions, this chapter will also discuss two of Luminary's social welfare missions: their post-earthquake reconstruction efforts and their work aiding foreign brides of local Taiwanese men. In comparison with Ciji, a look at the Luminary Buddhist Institute offers a different perspective from which to answer the questions: "How have women shaped Taiwan's Buddhism? How has Buddhism shaped the role and identity of Taiwanese women? How are Buddhist women shaping the future of Taiwan?" I agree with Wei-yi Cheng[5] that overall the Luminary phenomenon is feminist in its outlook and accomplishments, without having used the term "feminism," nor allying themselves with Taiwan's feminist movement. Yet this chapter will probe further into the questions of gender and feminism with regard to the Luminary nuns. The main "refrain" at Luminary proclaims equality, "all sentient beings are equal," "Buddha-nature has no gender," yet the nuns are expected to manifest the ideal of the male *da zhangfu*. At the same time, they speak of the individual and collective empowerment (*fuquan*) of women. Their transmission of Buddhist compassion is not articulated in terms of Guanyin or as mother's love as in Ciji. Yet among the Luminary nuns there persist some essentialist ideas of the feminine and a conviction that women's strength lies in difference. This androgynous balance has helped transform Taiwan's Buddhism, Taiwan's women, and Taiwan's society. First,

Taiwanese Buddhism gains well-trained female *dharma* masters. Second, at Luminary, Taiwan's women can become well-educated professionals, fulfilling both individual spiritual desires as well as expected social responsibilities. Third, Luminary is transforming Taiwan's traditional religious landscape, since laypeople who become Buddhist might cease to practice popular forms of worship. Finally, through their outreach programs in community education and their work with other NGOs, Luminary is building the horizontal links that are the sinews of civil society.[6]

The Luminary Buddhist Institute rose to prominence in Taiwan's Buddhist circles with the leadership and vision of Wu Yin, born Chen Xiazhu in 1940 in Taichung County. After graduating from high school she had hoped to enter college and become a teacher but her mother opposed her, saying, "Girls become someone's wife and wash diapers; it's useless for further study."[7] Thereupon in 1957 Wu Yin took the tonsure at Shipu Temple in Taipei, entered the Chinese Buddhist Tripiṭaka Institute, and in 1959 became ordained as a *bhikkhunī*. After graduating from this Institute in 1960, she continued in the graduate program there while teaching courses in the *weishi* ("consciousness-only") tradition and elementary English.[8]

Because she wanted to experience daily temple life, she went to Xinglongjing Temple in Kaohsiung to study with the esteemed Taiwanese nun Tianyi (1924–1980). Tianyi, educated in Japan and a lifelong advocate for a strong well-organized nuns' order in Taiwan, had a profound influence on Wu Yin and many other nuns, as Jianye (1999) relates. Tianyi, like Zhengyan's first teacher Xiudao, belonged to the crucial generation of Japanese-educated female Buddhists who bridged two eras: the Japanese era and the post-war era in which monastics from China re-established Chinese institutional Buddhism in Taiwan.[9] Tianyi did not leave works of scholarship, but her legacy lies in her experience and example of leading four different temples, teaching the *dharma* and the *bhikkhunī* precepts, serving as a senior ordination master (and the first female ordination master in Taiwan's history), and cultivating a generation of Taiwanese nuns : "Nuns should rely on themselves, not the laity or monks...Nuns should teach and lead nuns...Nuns must stand up and learn how to solve their own problems...be self-reliant...."[10] Her disciple Shi Conghui recalls that Tianyi was, to her nun disciples, the embodiment of a *da zhangfu*.[11]

However, it was at Xinglongjing Temple that Wu Yin had an epiphanic experience. One day when she and the other nuns labored barefoot in the rice paddies, she noticed at a nearby Catholic school a group of nuns dressed in white chatting between classes.[12] Wu Yin felt devastated and wondered disconsolately: We are all women religious, why can the Catholic nuns teach, but we Buddhist nuns, although educated, are spending our days doing heavy labor and chanting sūtras at funerals? She hoped that nuns could be more systematically educated to become *dharma* masters, while at the same time learn how to live communally and manage every aspect of a temple.[13] She envisioned a Buddhist institute whose primary mission was education of nuns and propagation of the *dharma* to the public, eschewing traditional temple functions such as provision of funeral services, constructing columbarium pagodas, and holding large-scale public Buddhist ceremonies "to eliminate disasters and pray for blessings."

Her opportunity came in 1979 when her classmate Xinzhi (b. 1939) asked Wu Yin, now a graduate of Chinese Culture University, to help manage the Xiang'guang Temple in a rural township outside of Jiayi. Xiang'guang (Luminary) was Xinzhi's choice of name for the extant temple with a hundred-year history called Yushanyan, renamed in 1943 as Jinlansi.[14] Yushanyan was a community temple dedicated to Guanyin and became a popular site of public worship and pilgrimage. But in 1943 an earthquake destroyed the main hall, and not until 1969 did the community begin full-scale reconstruction work. In 1974 the villagers asked the Buddhist Association of the ROC to send a professional religious leader to manage the temple, thereupon Xinzhi came and began a long and delicate diplomatic process of establishing an orthodox Buddhist institution while allowing local villagers to continue their popular forms of worship at the site, including sacrificial offerings of pigs, even though legally the Xiang'guang Temple lands belong to the Buddhists.[15]

Despite the challenges of this locale, in 1980 Wu Yin founded the Luminary Buddhist Institute and Library.[16] In contrast with other large Buddhist organizations in Taiwan that over-emphasize the leadership and charisma of their founder and his/her interpretation of Buddhism, Luminary's inspiration is first the Tripiṭaka (Buddhist canon), the vinaya (monastic rules) and meditation techniques.[17] Wu Yin wrote, "The teachings of the Buddha are the supreme essence of humanity's wisdom."[18]

While Wu Yin holds the chief position of abbot (*fangzhang*) and Luminary's founding and development reflect her ideals, Luminary's organizational structure and operations are based on modern methods of collective decision making, transparency, and accountability.[19] While both nuns and laypeople greatly respect Wu Yin as *dharma* master, scholar, and administrator, there is none of the pomp and circumstance surrounding her person, as with Zhengyan.

Luminary's Mission of Education

From the start, Wu Yin's design was that nuns study and live at the same institution, an institution governed and operated by the nuns themselves. The selection process at Luminary is more rigorous than other Buddhist institutions in Taiwan.[20] Luminary accepts as candidates women aged eighteen to thirty-five with at least a high school education, though many already have higher degrees and various work experiences.[21] A candidate is tested in various ways during a six-month trial period under the direction of a designated supervisor. The personnel department together with Wu Yin and other senior masters make the final decision of which novitiate is suitable to enter the two-year probationary period of study. Finally, another group decision process decides who can enter the five-year program (divided into Basic and Advanced curricula) at the Luminary Buddhist Institute.[22]

This program includes rigorous training in Buddhist studies, ritual practice, and temple management as well as "secular" courses in modern languages, psychology, philosophy, education, sociology, comparative religion, calligraphy, counseling and mediation, communications, administration and management, and computer skills.[23] The nuns also learn Vipassanā mediation as taught by the Burmese teacher S. N. Goenka, who lectured at Luminary Buddhist Institute in 1996. Some nuns continue their studies at graduate schools in Taiwan or abroad; at this writing, Luminary is planning its own graduate institute in Taoyuan. Luminary-trained nuns may choose to work within the Luminary organization, or may teach at other public or private schools and universities. Master Wu Yin and other nuns at the Luminary Buddhist Institute's contributions to scholarship include works on the *Bhikkhunī-Prātimokṣa* of the *Dharmaguptaka*, the compilation of a series of biographies of Taiwan nuns, collecting primary sources about nuns and nunneries, translations of foreign works, library information science, and research and seminars on Buddhist temple architecture.[24]

As is typical of many monasteries in Taiwan, the days at Luminary are long and busy. Monasteries are communities based on the *vinaya* Rules, each monastery's own Rules, and the principles of modern management; the timetables and schedules are a mixture of traditional and modern. They are not places for people seeking individual solitude and "communion with nature" or a quiet space for individual practice. With the sound of the wooden clapper and bell, the nuns rise before 4 a.m., if lucky, get a nap after lunch, and are busy again until around 10 p.m. or later.[25] Besides their classroom studies, the student nuns learn by participating in the daily ceremonies of the temple and dining hall and every aspect of a temple's management, including Buddha Hall preparation and upkeep, kitchen team, gardening (fruits, vegetables, pruning trees), laundry and sewing, cleaning and repairs, and other tasks.[26] Some of these administrative sections would have been found in traditional Chinese monasteries while others are modern: education, editing, computers, transportation, and so forth.[27]

The other main component of Luminary's education mission is public education. The original impetus came from Wu Yin's lay disciples who wished to understand the difference between Buddhism and their familiar popular religion. Since 1984 Luminary has developed a three-year curriculum (including their own teaching materials and pedagogical methods) on Buddhist studies and its application to daily life for adults ("purifying people's hearts through the *dharma*"). Luminary also holds camps, classes, and public lectures for polytechnic students.[28] Luminary sent qualified graduates from their adult education classes to teach in youth detention centers from 1990–1999 and in counseling in public primary schools from 1999 to the present.[29] Luminary also holds periodic seven-day Chan retreats and *sūtra* recitation and study retreats.

Mission of Culture

Luminary's mission of "Culture" includes a publishing house, books, journals, broadcasting, and a research library. Wu Yin is also a major advocate for *bhikkhunī* ordination for Buddhist women in the Theravādin and Tibetan traditions. At Bodhgayā India in February 1996, she gave a three-week session on the vinaya to Western women in the Tibetan tradition.[30] Wu Yin also participated in the May 2001 conference on *bhikkhunī* ordination held with the fourteenth Dalai Lama in Taiwan organized by the Buddhist Association of the ROC, and the First International Congress on Buddhist Women's Role in the Sangha, Hamburg, Germany in July 2007.[31]

Social Service

Though their contributions to Buddhism and society via their missions in education and culture would be enough to distinguish the Luminary organization, over the years they have also carried out small-scale social service projects such as assistance to local families, "adoption" of local parks, and provision of medical care. To meet the needs of Taiwan's increasingly older population, Luminary offers courses and lectures on various issues related to aging and end-of-life counseling.[32]

Luminary was also involved with post-earthquake local assistance projects (September 1999–October 2000). In the immediate aftermath of the earthquake, Luminary nuns held funeral services for the dead, brought relief supplies to victims in Taichung County and Miaoli and provided counseling and spiritual support to the survivors in Taichung and Nantou Counties. As a longer-term project, Luminary decided to "adopt" the children of Shigang Township whose schools were destroyed in the earthquake and whose parents were overwhelmed with daily chores and reconstruction work. Luminary nuns and lay volunteers ran a year-long program of study and enrichment activities for the children and also rebuilt homes in two remote aboriginal villages affected by the earthquake.

It is worth comparing Luminary's project with Ciji's Project Hope: Besides the obvious difference in scale, the Luminary's Shigang project did not aim for over-arching social reform as does Project Hope. Luminary's lesson-plans, activities, and guest lecturers did not dictate certain class or gender ideals. For example, parenting is presumed to be the responsibility of fathers and mothers together, not only mothers. Also there is no preaching of "the thought of Wu Yin," even no direct proselytizing of Buddhism, through the lesson plans included games and activities that explored expression of love, gratitude, mutual aid, and giving.[33] As for the reconstruction in the aboriginal villages, the nuns and other lay groups rebuilt houses and held classes in arts, crafts, and English. The nuns realized that serious problems such as land rights disputes, unemployment, and dwindling aboriginal population existed before the earthquake, and afterward, earthquake areas were vulnerable to landslides and road washouts. Thus, rebuilding homes is only the first small step in saving the aborigines and preserving their cultures. Luminary has ongoing contact with other NGOs specializing in aboriginal issues.[34]

Classes for Foreign Brides

Since 1990 the numbers of Taiwanese men marrying young women from Southeast Asia (Vietnam, Indonesia, the Philippines, Thailand, Burma, and Cambodia) and China have increased to the point that one in every five marriages is between a Taiwanese man and a "foreign bride," according to the most recent statistics of the Ministry of the Interior.[35] Some of the men have difficulty finding Taiwanese wives due to their jobs (truckers, farmers, and construction workers, for example), advanced age, poverty, or physical handicaps. This social trend involves issues such as whether this constitutes human trafficking, the phenomenon of false marriages to gain Taiwan residency, or even the spectre of female spies from China. Also, these women face serious language and cultural barriers, abuse and exploitation, social discrimination, and difficulties in raising bicultural children. Some voices in the media raise racist, xenophobic, and eugenicist fears about such couples and their children "reducing the quality of the Taiwanese population."[36]

Eden Social Welfare Foundation spokesman David Lee commented, "What is really needed is more education on the part of the Taiwanese men. We need to teach them that the bride is not just something you buy, that she is a person, not a thing."[37] Wang Chuan-ping puts it more bluntly: "Many Taiwanese husbands treat their Chinese wives as no more than dispensable baby-making machines and human punching bags."[38]

Five years before the government paid attention to needs of foreign brides, local foundations such as the Meinong Community Advancement Society in 1995 began Chinese literacy classes for these women. Now private groups and government agencies offer assistance concerning literacy, cultural adjustment, legal, health, raising children, and employment issues.[39]

In 1998 during a visit to a medical clinic, Wu Yin met a foreign bride from Indonesia and realized the extent of their language and cultural adjustment problems so she began planning a curriculum for them.[40] Due to the earthquake, the foreign brides' classes were postponed until February 2000; since then, nuns and their female lay-members of Luminary's branches in southern Taiwan have held classes in basic Chinese, local culture and customs, and legal issues.

Luminary nun Zichun has been involved with this program since its inception and believes this has empowered (*fuquan*) the new immigrant women in two ways: The classes not only educate them in Chinese for communication, but also give them an opportunity to interact with other women so that they can develop their own network outside of their husband's families. Zichun terms this "emancipatory education" (*jiefang jiaoyu*) and refers to these classes as a social movement. She speaks of not only personal empowerment but of collective empowerment: "We expect, in the empowerment process, program participants could start from self-empowerment, then would advance to collective empowerment and thus change their current situation."[41] However, Wu Yin confided to me: What if empowering these women encouraged them to run away? Therein lies the dilemma of empowerment—within are the seeds of rebellion. Though Luminary's intention is not to encourage runaways and rebellion, Zichun's belief that collective empowerment, since women can change the status quo, has advanced beyond Ciji's moral admonitions to individual women-as-mothers and may reach beyond the original intent of her master Wu Yin.

Another Luminary nun, Jianxian, points out that in fact Taiwan is and always has been an immigrant society and must transform its self-centered Han Chinese consciousness to a pluralistic and open identity in this age of globalization. Community education initiatives such as these are one step toward a more equal, just, and flourishing society.[42] This kind of argument is far more sophisticated and realistic than other proposals to reduce the number of foreign brides' visas in favor of encouraging immigrants with "high education and skills," or monetary incentives to increase the birthrate among Taiwanese women.

In another article about the goals of adult Buddhist education, Jianxian argues directly that Buddhist education is not only for one's own growth but should lead to social action; there should be a collective effort to undertake social reform, to change what is unfair and unjust. As a nun she asks herself,

How can I link my needs with the needs of society? Humans can create good conditions for good results, and, does "ultimate liberation" pertain to oneself only, or is there another meaning, in our modern society?

Here, Jianxian is arguing that Buddhists should go beyond *shehui guanhuai* (concern for society) and *shehui canyu* (participating in society) to social reform, *shehui gaige*, and like her fellow nun Zichun, argues that Buddhists should confront what is unfair and unjust and undertake social reform, a different approach than that of their master Wu Yin.[43] Perhaps, the next generation of Luminary nuns will take the path of activist social reform, or at the least, establish more links with NGOs and government bodies.

Luminary Nuns and Gender

Inspired by her master Tianyi, Wu Yin chose to stress the messages of equality in Buddhism such as "the Buddha-nature has no gender" and "all sentient beings are equal." Tianyi's interpreted the deprecatory and misogynist descriptions of women and women's nature in the Buddhist scriptures as admonitions to monks to guard against their own weaknesses, not attacks on women as such.[44] Tianyi was confident of women's equal abilities in learning the *dharma* and becoming Buddhist masters. In the monastic rules and during the tonsure ceremony led by one's master, the term *da zhangfu* is used repeatedly to describe the transformation of an ordinary man or woman, from one's worldly appearance, world desires and attachments, and worldly roles as man or woman, to a monastic who from then on dedicates his or her life to Buddhist cultivation, shouldering the great responsibility of guardian and propagator of the *dharma*.[45] The term *da zhangfu* implies a person of unusual moral greatness, via Mencius as well (see the discussion in Chapter 4), and is transcendent, of one's bodily limits and beyond: Nuns and monks vow to become a *dingtian lidi de da zhangfu* (a great man whose head supports the sky with feet planted on the ground, i.e., independent and indomitable).[46]

As for compassion, the Luminary speaks primarily of Buddha's compassion for the world[47] rather than the Guanyin Bodhisattva's mother-compassion, as does Ciji, even though Luminary was founded at Yushanyan, a temple dedicated to Guanyin.[48] In Mahāyāna Buddhism, "insight *(prajñā)* and compassion *(karuṇā)* are compared to two wings with which one flies to the island of enlightenment" *(bodhi)*.[49] Luminary often refers to *prajñā*; for example, its Chinese equivalent *hui* appears in three of their institutes' names. *Prajñā* in fact is not limited to academic knowledge, but refers to wisdom and "insight, discriminating knowledge, intuitive apprehension." This is the faculty that if cultivated will apprehend the truth of the *dharma*.[50] Luminary's mission, as summarized in this chapter's title, *jueshu renhua*, is twofold: the education and cultivation of nuns as *dharma* masters and transmission of the *dharma* via public education. "Packaging" Buddhism as an education process strikes two chords in modern Chinese society: High social status of well-educated and professional people, and a general consensus that religion should be of social benefit.

That the *dharma* masters are nuns and now enjoy a high social status is due in great part to the lifetime efforts of monastics such as Tianyi and Wu Yin. Previously it was difficult for women to learn about the *dharma* at all due to lack of materials and teachers or simply because family chains prohibited women's study. Even if women became nuns in the 1950s through the 1970s, they faced the social stereotypes of nuns as uneducated and superstitious—unwanted spinsters; escaping from failed romances; impoverished; in sum, social rejects.[51]

During the 1980s wave of young women graduates of polytechnical schools and colleges becoming Buddhist nuns, voices in Taiwan expressed shock and indignation: How and why do these well-educated women give up everything and become a lonely nun "with only an oil lamp for a companion?" How can they be so unfilial to their parents who have sacrificed so much for their education? How can they run away from women's "natural duties" of marriage and childbearing? How can they waste the great investment society has made in them?[52] It has taken another twenty years for Taiwan's nuns to finally enjoy high social status as professionals and spiritual leaders and for society to respect their choice to become nuns, though this choice is justified because the nuns are *serving society and humanity*.[53] It does not mean that Taiwanese people in general consider that becoming a Buddhist nun or monk is of inherent spiritual worth and merit for oneself or one's family, as is the case for monks in Theravādin or Tibetan traditions.

Nuns gaining high social status is due not only to the great efforts within the Buddhist community but was also sped by recent transformations in Taiwanese society and economy. Scholars and Buddhist masters alike note also that modernization and the end of the martial law period since the 1980s have opened up more opportunities and choices within Taiwan society. Women today enjoy the freedom to pursue higher education and a career.[54] When I asked newly-ordained nuns why they chose the monastic life, a standard answer was that, in this way, they can contribute their time, energy, and talents to far more people and to society at large, rather than devote themselves only to husband, children, and in-laws.[55]

Ven. Jianduan recalls asking her mother:

> Are you a happy person? Her mother answered: Yes, my husband takes good care of the family and respects me, you children are smart and obedient and don't make me worry... Jianduan then

asked: If Father didn't take care of the family and the children were bad and made you worry, would you still be a happy person? Her mother thought a bit and answered: No. Then Jianduan said: How strange! Why can't I determine my happiness by myself? Why is it others who determine whether I'm happy or not?

The Luminary Temple attracted her because of its credo of self-reliance: Nuns must cultivate and educate themselves, solve their own problems, and contribute to all aspects of monastic life, from studying and giving *dharma* talks to cooking and doing repairs. Jianduan pointed out how Luminary Temple differs dramatically from some of Taiwan's mixed-*sangha* monasteries where in accordance with socialized gender roles, nuns cooked, cleaned, and poured tea while monks gave *dharma* talks and did repair work around the monastery.[56]

One's first conclusion is that these nuns as *da zhangfu*, as tonsured *dharma* masters in their androgynous robes, have successfully transcended gender roles, or more precisely, have transcended the physical and social limitations of "being female." When one sees slightly built Taiwanese nuns, in the oppressive heat, cleaning filthy drainage ditches and water towers filled with slime, slicing lumber with power tools for fuel to be used in their kitchen ovens, or repeatedly lifting the super-sized pots, pans, steamers, and rice cookers in the hot kitchen; or when one sees the significant strength, stamina, and skills needed to play the drums and bells throughout long morning and evening temple services; the skill of nuns driving vans packed with people and goods through dusty country lanes and winding mountain trails and then doing repairs, construction and farm-work, traditional stereotypes about women as inherently frail, helpless, and permanently requiring male assistance to survive dissipate like incense smoke.

Yet some nuns retain essentialist notions of the feminine. When I asked why there are so many nuns in Taiwan, Ven. Mingjia answered that women are especially suited to undertake the rigorous path of Buddhist studies and training due to their patience, endurance, and attention to detail. She added that men in Taiwan are under more pressure to succeed in their career and continue their patriline, so fewer men than women choose the monastic life. Ven. Wu Yin contended that women by nature are particularly suited as caregivers, and excel in healing and counseling roles. Furthermore, she stated, women are more suited than men to live in communal groups due to their self-effacing and sacrificial nature; and nuns manifest the steadfast, persevering, hardworking character of Taiwanese women. Jianxian believes that "women's learning traits" of making connections, being concerned, and liking harmony, makes them good students and teachers. According to these female masters, nuns' strength also lies in their difference. As Zhengyan would agree, "feminine traits," for example, warmth, compassion, desire for harmony and peace, patience, endurance, and sacrifice, are claimed to correspond closely to Buddhist ideals. Like the nuns of Fuhu Temple on Emei Mountain in Sichuan, Luminary nuns manifest many characteristics: those of the *da zhangfu*; "feminine" compassion, harmony, and self-sacrifice; as well as those of a respected religious professional.[57]

Therefore, are the Luminary nuns feminist? As Cheng rightly notes, this term does not stand out in Luminary publications, nor do the nuns refer to themselves as feminist.[58] The Luminary nuns are dedicated to training nuns as *dharma* masters who can help purify hearts and bring peace and succor to Taiwan society. As Buddhist modernizers over several generations have argued, the goal is to understand the "true *dharma*" of orthodox Buddhism as opposed to the "blind and unthinking performance" [sic] of petitionary rituals. Yet during this process, they have cultivated a new generation of well-educated, articulate, and self-reliant women who enjoy high social status. From an outsider's perspective, this kind of empowerment is feminist and the nuns, like all women in Taiwan, whether they acknowledge it or not, benefited from the feminist movement's advancement of women's self-awareness and rights.[59]

Yet Luminary did not link up with the Taiwan's feminist movement in the 1980s because Wu Yin believed in the self-reliance of Buddhist women, and she did not think a direct confrontational approach would help her cause at that time.[60] However, younger nuns at Luminary are well acquainted with feminist history and theory, and as discussed above, Luminary nuns now work to assist foreign brides. Differences in attitudes between the older and younger generation of nuns are already apparent at Luminary with regard to the foreign brides' curriculum: Wu Yin's impetus to help these women was to help them carry out their responsibilities as mothers, wives, and caretakers of extended families, while her disciple Zichun says that she relates to them as women, seeing this curriculum as part of the larger project of improving all women's economic and political positions.[61] Luminary in the future may establish more connections with women's NGOs and government offices promoting women's issues.[62]

Another reason why Wu Yin took a non-confrontational approach to social reform is because Luminary is inspired by the basic principle that purifying hearts is the way to purify society: Teach the *dharma* to bring peace and happiness to both individuals and society as a whole.[63] On the one hand Wu Yin is not a disciple of Master Yinshun, but was educated at the senior monk Baisheng's Chinese Buddhist Tripiṭaka Institute and later went to Yushanyan Temple (Luminary Temple) due to Baisheng's arrangements.[64] Baisheng would also agree with Luminary's primary mission, that of training and cultivating *dharma* masters, which he believed is the first responsibility of

Buddhist monastics.[65] However, as we have seen, Luminary also serves society, endeavoring through propagating the *dharma* to create a "pure land on earth..." by "taking human beings as the root," which echoes the orientation of *renjian fojiao*.[66] Indeed, the reformist ideas of Taixu (1890–1947) "deeply stimulated" Wu Yin to undertake her own reforms.[67] Wu Yin attended classes taught by Yinshun in 1965 and published the history of Yinshun's Fuyan Buddhist Institute in 1994. Both Taixu and Yinshun's works are included in the Luminary Buddhist Institute's curriculum.[68]

Proponents of *renjian fojiao* stress that Buddhists serve and work to improve society. Yet to what degree does *renjian fojiao* challenge the status quo? How and to what extent is *renjian fojiao* supportive of nuns and laywomen, and what ideals and roles do the proponents of *renjian fojiao* prescribe for Buddhist women? Do socially-engaged Buddhists necessarily work for gender equality in the monastic world and in society at large? These are questions that the next chapter will explore.

Chapter 6

"Buddhism for the Human Realm" and Women

Every chapter of this book has mentioned "Buddhism for the human realm," *renjian fojiao*, the modernized form of Buddhism first formulated in early twentieth-century China and promulgated in Taiwan by a number of Buddhist groups.[1] Though certainly not all Buddhists or Buddhist groups in Taiwan claim *renjian fojiao* affiliation or inspiration, many do so, including the three main "mountain-tops of Buddhism" in Taiwan, as well as the radical activist and feminist nun Chao Hwei. The Luminary Buddhist Institute also, while not expressly founded as an organization promoting *renjian fojiao*, became one in the course of its development. Thus the question naturally arises: Is *renjian fojiao* especially supportive of Buddhist women, nuns and laywomen, and thus would this help to explain the predominance of women in Taiwanese Buddhism?

To answer this question, this chapter will first give an overview of the development of *renjian fojiao* and the links with, and differences from, global Engaged Buddhism.[2] Then the chapter discusses what the formulators of *renjian fojiao*, the monks Taixu and Yinshun, wrote about women in Buddhism. Does being "socially-engaged" necessarily entail working for women's rights and gender equality, including advocating for the nuns' order? We have already discussed Ciji's neo-traditional views on women and its nuns who labor anonymously in the shadow of Ciji's lay behemoth, contrasted with the "quiet feminism" of Luminary Buddhist Institute. This chapter will highlight Chao Hwei and Shing Kuang, the only Buddhist feminists, and among the few activist Buddhists, in Taiwan. Do Chao Hwei and Shing Kuang represent the wave of the future for Taiwan's Buddhism or will they remain the radical vanguard minority?

First, we turn to China in the transnational Buddhist Revival of the nineteenth and twentieth centuries.

The Chinese Buddhist Revival

Many scholars have discussed the Buddhist revival movements of Sri Lanka, Burma, India, China, Vietnam, Thailand, Laos, Cambodia, and Japan. It is remarkable to see how in each case the revival of Buddhism (whether state-directed, state-approved, or directed against the state) was seen as the way to assert each nation's "authentic" identity, toward the goal of unifying and strengthening the nation in the face of the Western onslaught, whether colonialism or modernization or both.[3] In a message similar to that of many reformers in the Buddhist Revival, Dharmapāla of Sri Lanka (1864–1933) urged that his compatriots "... should return to the Dhamma in order to solve the dual dilemma of [re]discovering their identity and responding to the modern context."[4] And in Sri Lanka as in other countries with Buddhist traditions, "(i)n response to ... [Western and Christian] criticism that Buddhism lacked a social ethic and social concern, some Buddhist organizations began social service agencies."[5]

Besides the stimuli of nationalism and modernization in the late nineteenth century, there was the influence of a "reverse Orientalism" as works by Western scholars in Hindu and Buddhist studies were translated into the languages of South, Southeast, and East Asia, also stimulating domestic revivals in a number of Asian nations.[6]

In China:

> (t)he Buddhist revival, I believe, began as an effort by laymen to reprint the *sūtras* destroyed in the Taiping Rebellion [1860s]. It gathered momentum as the discovery of Western Buddhist scholarship stimulated the need for Chinese Buddhist scholarship, and as the invasion of China by Christian evangelists and missionaries led to the idea of training Buddhist evangelists and sending missionaries to India and the West.[7] Up to this point only laymen were involved ... But in the last years of the Ch'ing dynasty [late 19th–early 20th c], when moves were made to confiscate their property for use in secular education, the monks began to organize schools and social-welfare enterprises as a means of self-defense.[8]

Holmes Welch believed that three threads ran through the Chinese Buddhist revival: The need to secure religious identity by the laypeople; the need for economic self-preservation on the part of monastics;[9] and the need to gain international status, by both lay and monastics. Speaking of the Buddhist reformers in early twentieth century China:

> The need for status—intellectual status—led to the necessity of meeting the challenges of science and Western philosophy, of

Marxism, and of Christianity. It helped to bring about the revival of interest in Dharmalaksana (*Faxiang zong*, Consciousness-only school), the birth of Buddhist scientism, and participation in modern, Western forms of social welfare.[10]

The major figure in the Chinese Buddhist Revival was the monk Taixu, born in Zhejiang Province in 1890. His reform program was forged in the late Qing intellectual environment of debates about religion and the relevance of Buddhism to the modern world, engaged in by Kang Youwei, Liang Qichao, Zhang Taiyan, Wu Zhihui, Xiong Shili, Cai Yuanpei, Ji Zizhen, and Ouyang Jian.[11] Confucian scholars, Westernized Chinese intellectuals, and lay Buddhists alike immersed themselves in Tiantai, Faxiang, and Huayan studies, while some eminent Buddhist monks, like Taixu, were "Confucian exemplars in thought and behavior."[12]

Taixu was a modernizer but not a secularizer; he was a restorationist, aiming to reorient Buddhism toward world engagement and focus more on the human realm, less on gods and ghosts. Taixu often lectured on the *dharma* common to all five Buddhist vehicles or conveyances of rebirth among human or spiritually-advanced beings[13] while emphasizing that "the most efficacious path for those pursuing bodhisattva-hood is not through some celestial realm or distant pure land. Rather, it takes our common, ordinary experience on this plane as its starting point...." *Rensheng*, the "human vehicle," is homophonous with *rensheng*, "human life": to take the bodhisattva path is to manifest the bodhi-mind and relieve the sufferings of oneself and others, to enlighten oneself and others, in the here and now.[14] Taixu's mission was to promulgate what he believed to be the essence of Chinese Buddhism, "the essence of wisdom and compassion, embodied by the bodhisattva, [which] was for Taixu the hope of all sentient beings."[15]

Holmes Welch found the Buddhist revival of the late Qing and early Republic noteworthy for the growth of lay organizations and lay teachers of the *dharma*; clinics, orphanages, and schools; a radio station in Shanghai; proselytizing in prisons; and the effort to start an ecumenical movement with Buddhists abroad. Also, the modern revival saw Buddhist publishing houses, newspapers, and journals; modernized seminaries for Buddhist monastics; and modern Buddhist associations. All of the above innovations were directly or indirectly indebted to the vision and reforms of Taixu.[16]

Taixu's political stance is not easily categorized. He came of age during the heady years of the 1911 revolution and his friends and colleagues included revolutionaries, anarchists, and socialists. At first he admired socialism because it, like Buddhism, he claimed, advocated human equality and social welfare. He liked socialism's message "from each according to his abilities; to each according to his needs."[17] Over the course of World War II, he came to believe that state-directed capitalism, a limited welfare state such as Roosevelt's New Deal government, could curb the excesses of individualism as well as monopolies and large corporations that exploit national and international markets and create growing disparities between rich and poor.[18]

However, for Taixu, to "save the world," political and economic restructuring alone was not sufficient. Using the language typical of the "clash of civilizations East and West" debates of the first half of the twentieth century, he believed the Western civilizations were sick, due to their overly individualistic and aggressive orientation of *zongwo zhiwu*, "an unrestrained self, conquering nature," leading to imperialism and war. Though not explaining why, he held that other Asian nations (especially Japan who had imitated the West and become an imperialist aggressor) cannot offer effective means to deal with these calamities, and he concludes that Buddhism, together with the Chinese spirit of *keji chongren* (overcome the self, esteem compassion), are the best remedies for this civilizational sickness.[19]

After 1925, Taixu rejected Communism's call for violent class conflict and over-emphasis on the material and the collective, while neglecting the mind, the body, and the individual. His political stance became situated "right of center"[20] partly for pragmatic reasons (to obtain political imprimatur for his plans to reform and modernize Buddhism, and to proselytize abroad) and partly for ideological reasons.[21]

Taixu's relationship with the Nationalists was fraught with contradictions. Taixu liberally borrowed from Nationalist vocabulary and ideological categories, and received material support: money, means of transport, use of diplomatic channels and state-related associations abroad. But whenever the Nationalists made one of their numerous attempts to confiscate temple properties, then Taixu and others publicly opposed the government.[22]

With the end of World War II and the restoration of the Nationalist government in Nanjing, as Taixu and other Buddhists struggled to maintain Buddhist control over property and other interests, Taixu articulated his idea of the relation of Buddhists and Buddhist groups to the state, as expressed in the phrase *yizheng bu ganzhi*—to participate in political debates is the right and duty of any citizen in a democracy, but not to hold formal political office. This idea was premised on Sun Yat-sen's distinction between *zhiquan*, holding political/administration office, and *zhengquan*, democratic rights of any citizen including freedom of speech and debate, the right to participate in public affairs, i.e., civil society. However, this stance met with opposition from other Buddhist leaders, who preferred that Buddhists remain "above-politics."[23] Nevertheless, in July 1946 Taixu founded a Buddhist political party, "Awakening the Masses Society," and was nominated by Bishop Yu Bin to serve as a representative to the National Assembly, though Taixu was not elected.[24]

Unfortunately, Taixu was unable to fully realize his plans and ideals for Chinese Buddhism; Taixu died prematurely from a stroke in March 1947 and, from 1948 to 1949, China was engulfed in the chaos of civil war and the collapse of the central government in Nanjing and its retreat to Taiwan.[25] A decade earlier, Taixu had already deemed his attempts to inspire "a revolution in Buddhism" to be a failure, due to both his own "weaknesses and failures" as well as the strength of his opponents.[26] He was too self-critical.

Though the sociopolitical and economic environment of the early twentieth century placed severe limits on the Buddhist Revival within China, Taixu spent much time and energy attempting to transform Buddhism into a global movement that would transcend the limits of nation, political faction, and Buddhist school. Toward this end, Taixu traveled to Taiwan, Japan and Hong Kong (1917–1925), then to France, England, Belgium, Germany, and the United States (1928–29), as well as to Myanmar, Sri Lanka, India, and Malaysia (1939–40).[27] In Sri Lanka, homeland of the great Buddhist revivalist Dharmapāla, Taixu spoke at length with the Buddhist scholar G. P. Malalasekera about forming a world Buddhist federation; in 1950 this plan came to fruition when Dr. Malalasekera founded the World Fellowship of Buddhists.[28]

Taixu did not use the current Chinese term for "globalization," *quanqiuhua*; rather we find *quanqiu* as a noun, "the whole world," *shijiehua*, "globalization," and *shijie zhuyi*, "world-ism." Taixu, a fierce Chinese nationalist during World War II, was also a staunch proponent of globalization and "world-ism" as those terms were understood earlier in the twentieth century, especially at the close of the Second World War, when many people hoped that transnational bodies such as the United Nations could transcend nationalist interests and conflicts and prevent future wars. But even more fundamentally, when Taixu spoke of *shijiehua* and *shijie zhuyi* he was referring to the potential of Buddhism and the need to propagate Buddhism worldwide. Taixu believed that Buddhism was the one international force, of all religions, "isms," and sociopolitical systems that could lead to true one-world-ism, a broad and tolerant worldview, and true world peace.[29]

Besides being the inspiration for several leading Taiwanese Buddhist organizations (to be discussed later in this chapter) decades after his death in 1947, Taixu, unbeknownst to both him and modern Chinese scholars, had a great influence upon the Vietnamese Buddhist Revival in the 1920–40s, which set the stage for Vietnamese Engaged Buddhism in the 1960–70s.[30]

From Taixu to Yinshun

Taixu did not live to see the fate of Buddhism in China after 1949. All religions were strictly controlled by the Communist party-state; Buddhist monasteries and monastics suffered under land reform and counterrevolutionary campaigns from 1949–1953, and again in the 1957 anti-Rightist campaign.

If possible, monks and nuns fled to Hong Kong or Taiwan but as Don Pittman relates, some disciples of Taixu who remained in China hoped, however naively (and for pragmatic reasons, to survive under Communism), that the violent changes might lead to long-term reform in institutional Buddhism, clearing the path to realize Taixu's original blueprint, which included advocating a self-sufficient monastic economy based on agriculture, commercial, and handicraft production.

Taixu's student Juzan (1908–84) allied with other Buddhists, monastic and lay, to form the new Chinese Buddhist Association in 1953 and pledged to help the Communist party-state build a collective economy and rid society of "superstitions," Pure Land worship, and popular religion in general; some monks even argued for a secularization of the *sangha*, to do away with the precepts, allow the monastics to marry, eat meat, wear lay dress, etc.[31]

During the Cultural Revolution 1966–76, all religions were nearly eliminated: Buddhist monasteries were destroyed or greatly damaged, properties were confiscated, monastics were persecuted and forced to return to secular life. After 1979, the atmosphere for the officially-controlled religions such as Chinese Buddhism (Tibetan Buddhism is another story), Daoism, Islam, and Christianity has improved somewhat.[32]

Scholars in China are currently interested in Taixu and the Buddhist Revival, after a long period of neglect.[33] Chen Zimei writes that the Hebei-based monk Jinghui (b. 1933) promotes *renjian fojiao* but Jinghui's is not the mainstream tradition.[34] However, in Taiwan, Taixu's student Yinshun (1906–2005) is highly esteemed for his rationalization of Buddhist doctrine and historiography; applying academic standards to the study of Buddhism," and articulation of the idea of *renjian fojiao*, "Buddhism for the Human Realm."[35]

"Taixu's legacy is most clearly visible in Taiwan."[36] The struggle within the Buddhist Association in China in the 1930s and 1940s between traditionalist monks *versus* monks who supported Taixu in his reformist efforts continued after 1949, via each one's disciples and their circles in Taiwan.[37] Yinshun was Taixu's student, a graduate of one of Taixu's seminaries in China, chief editor of Taixu's *Complete Works*, and Taixu's biographer. During his long life, Yinshun produced a large and sophisticated body of scholarship on Buddhism for the Human Realm, early Indian Buddhism, Madhyamaka studies, and Chan. By his own admission, he in no way resembled Taixu the organizer, administrator, and internationalist.[38]

But politics played a crucial influence on Yinshun's career in Taiwan. After 1949 Yinshun left China for Hong Kong. In his *New Treatise on the Pure Land* of 1951 Yinshun roundly criticized, from scriptural, historical, and methodological perspectives, Pure Land practices as reductionist and full of errors. Though his was certainly not the first critique of Pure Land

Buddhism, it led to great political trouble for Yinshun.[39] In 1952 Yinshun left Hong Kong to become abbot of the important Shandao Temple in Taipei. He was invited by disciples of Taixu in Taiwan, who were engaged in a political struggle over the leadership of BAROC and of the future direction and scope of Buddhism in Taiwan.[40]

Yinshun became caught in the fray; he was criticized publicly and privately. This took place, of course, in the Cold War context of the 1950s, as the Nationalist government newly transplanted to Taiwan carried out repression of the native Taiwanese elite establishment as well as suspected Communist influences. "(S)ome within BAROC even used their influence with the government to have certain Nationalist Party officials issue a statement that Yinshun's writings were infected with the poison of Communism...."[41] Yinshun resigned from his post at Shandao temple, wrote a "self-criticism" asking pardon, and devoted the rest of his life to scholarship, monastic education, and publishing.[42]

Both Taixu and Yinshun in their propagation of *renjian fojiao* are considered to be the major reformers in twentiety-century Chinese Buddhism but the theory and practice of *renjian fojiao* was first articulated by Taixu.[43] In 1930, Taixu discussed the idea of constructing a Pure Land in the human realm in his "*Jianshe renjian jingtulun*."[44] Then, in his 1933 "*Zenyang lai jianshe renjian fojiao*" [How to establish renjian fojiao], he wrote:[45]

> *Renjian fojiao* is not a Buddhism in which you leave the human realm and become a god or ghost, or for everyone to take monastic vows, go to a temple, or become an eremite in the forest. It's a Buddhism which, in accordance with Buddhist teachings, reforms society, helps humankind to progress, and improves the whole world.[46]

As for Yinshun, he wrote that Buddhism should stress "Here, now, this person...." He stresses the path of taking the Bodhisattva's vow, *pusa yuan xing*, which their students and those inspired by them put into practice as *serving society*, in various forms, in order to create a Pure Land on earth.[47] Yinshun agreed with Taixu that one taking the Bodhisattva path "should undertake works that benefit others... that benefit humanity"; this itself is an intrinsic part of one's individual cultivation.[48] The forms of each mission will vary but all should start from a heart filled with wisdom, compassion, and emptiness, toward the goals of helping others and propagating the *dharma*.[49] But Yinshun did not elaborate upon the details; he did not (like Taixu) outline a blueprint for action for the contemporary Bodhisattva: The "heirs" of Yinshun made their own interpretative and methodological leaps from Yinshun's thought to its actualization in Taiwan society.[50]

"Heirs" of Taixu and Yinshun: Foguangshan, Ciji, and Dharma Drum Mountain

Some scholars have used the term "Engaged Buddhism" to describe the orientation of a number of prominent Buddhist organizations in Taiwan because they are socially engaged in numerous missions to promote charity, medical care, education, environmentalism, and so on.[51] There is still no complete and precise account of the evolution of the term "Engaged Buddhism," though scholars conventionally trace its earliest use to Thích Nhất Hạnh,[52] who adapted Sartre's term, *engagé*, in his own way.[53] According to my investigation, Vietnamese-language Buddhist periodicals and books of the 1960s, including those of Thích Nhất Hạnh, explored the existential ideas of Sartre and Camus, as well as the activities of Gandhi and his successor Vinoba Bhave and the Indian *Sarvodaya* rural development movement.[54] By 1967 Thích Nhất Hạnh employed the English term "Engaged Buddhism" to describe his many activities during Vietnam's Buddhist Struggle Movement, such as the School of Youth for Social Service, his new Buddhist "Order of Inter-Being," and his efforts in peace negotiations abroad.[55] The term "Engaged Buddhism" is also used to describe Buddhist sociopolitical movements in modern Sri Lanka, Thailand, and India, and more broadly, the contemporary global phenomenon of socially and/or politically engaged Buddhism.

"Some say... the distinctive new feature of Engaged Buddhism is to challenge the present system with a new paradigm of activities and programs, not merely an activity that cleans up social problems without confronting their roots" in structural violence.[56] However, not all engaged Buddhists openly challenge the status quo; and all Buddhists, including Taixu, Yinshun, and Thích Nhất Hạnh would agree that the roots of all outer conditions lie in the mind, and through practice and discipline one must first quell the "poisons" of craving, anger, ignorance, arrogance, and others in order to end both personal and social suffering.

This is the approach taken by the leaders of Foguangshan, Ciji, and Dharma Drum Mountain. Xingyun, for example, stresses how cultivation of wisdom, morality, virtue, and conscience can cure the ills of modern society, rather than through political mobilization or by opposing the political or economic status quo.[57] In a similar vein, Zhengyan believes that individual and social suffering have primarily moral and spiritual causes. In fact, Ciji organization forbids its nuns, members, and employees from participating in formal politics or sociopolitical activism. "Fighting for the downtrodden and shouting about justice will make the situations [*sic*] even more complicated and confused ... (a) sense of responsibility is more important than a sense of justice."[58] Akin to Foguangshan and Ciji, Dharma Drum aspires to "protect the spiritual environment, uplift the character of humanity, and build a pure land on earth."⁵⁹ In sum, Foguangshan, Ciji, and Dharma Drum advocate a process of peaceful evolution, with emphasis on the individual transformation prerequisite for wider social change.

Thus, in contrast with the Engaged Buddhisms of Sri Lanka, Thailand, Vietnam, and India, "[Buddhist leaders in Taiwan] have developed neither a comprehensive perspective on political economy nor a detailed social doctrine."⁶⁰ All three groups refrain from a critique of the larger structural causes of violence, inequality, and waste. Yet, Ciji supporters argue that their approach is in fact "radical" and in full accordance with fundamental Buddhist teachings, because Zhengyan calls for a total and holistic reorientation in values and psychology that aims to eliminate suffering, and thus would transform the individual and society far beyond what schemes for sociopolitical reform could accomplish.⁶¹ However, a broader structural critique is not totally absent from Taiwan's engaged Buddhism, as will be discussed below.

Paradigm Shift?

Taiwan's environmental movement began in the late 1980s and several major Buddhist groups like Ciji and Dharma Drum Mountain have done good work promoting environmental awareness. This was the first shift in the paradigm wheel, according to Jiang Canteng.⁶² Yet Jiang points out that these Buddhist groups are inspired by traditional Chinese attitudes of *husheng, xifu* (protect life, lead a frugal life/not waste resources) and do not criticize the source of environmental problems within industry, government policy, capitalism, etc. Jiang categorizes this kind of approach as *biedu*: case by case, individual salvation, an approach that assumes the root of social problems lies in curbing desires within oneself.

Yinshun's student Shi Chuandao of Miaoxin Temple in Tainan continues to shift the paradigm wheel, and in Jiang's phrase, has progressed to the level of *pudu*, universal salvation, as he critiques the collusion of government and big business. The message of Chuandao's writings and films is break the myth of Taiwan's "Economic Miracle," and rectify biased government development policies. Chuandao has called for the passage of laws to end manufacturing of styrofoam and plastic, though these are huge enterprises in Taiwan, as evidenced by the conglomerate Formosa Plastics. Chuandao has taken to the streets to oppose construction of the Fourth Nuclear Power Plant, as has Chao Hwei (Figure 6.1, next page). Chao Hwei also founded the "Caring about Life Association" to promote animal protection and animal rights in Taiwan (more below) for she believes that *renjian fojiao* is not exclusively human-centered; it is for the liberation of all sentient beings.⁶³

Figure 6.1. Master Chao Hwei at anti-nuclear rally (Shih Chao Hwei)

The Post-Yinshun Generation[64]

In Taiwan today, only a few monastics such as the nun Chao Hwei, her student Shing Kuang,[65] and the monk Chuandao (mentioned above) are radical activists.[66]

Chao Hwei (b. 1957) founded the Hongshi Buddhist Institute in Taoyuan in 1998, though she has been a Buddhist activist since the late 1980s (Figure 6.2). She regards her social activism as the "testing ground" for Yinshun's exhortation to undertake the Bodhisattva's path in the present world. She is a brilliant debater and lecturer, teaches at several universities, has produced many books and articles, has hosted innumerable academic conferences and press conferences, and also is an indefatigable worker for a number of social causes. She first gained public notice as a spokesperson for the positive portrayal of monastics by the media, especially to counteract the negative stereotypes of nuns previously common in Taiwanese society.

Chao Hwei and her colleagues[67] have published many books, including explications of Yinshun's works and *renjian fojiao*; *vinaya* studies; and works on Buddhist normative ethics with regard to such issues as organ transplant, surrogate motherhood, abortion, stem cell research, euthanasia, suicide, the death penalty, Taiwan's adultery law, human rights, animal rights, environmen-

Figure 6.2. Master Chao Hwei (Shih Chao Hwei)

tal rights, and aboriginal hunting practices. Chao Hwei has also founded the Research Center for Applied Ethics at Hsuan Chuang University, a Buddhist university in Taiwan.

Why is Chao Hwei a radical activist, unlike most Buddhists in Taiwan? Chao Hwei feels that Buddhists, according to the *dharma* and also as citizens in a democratic society, have the powers and duty to speak out and act, to protect the weak and silent, especially animals, and to work for a fair and just society (Figure 6.3, next page). "A silent people in a democratic society is just like empty air." The Hongshi Institute's "Caring about Life Association" has tackled the serious problem of stray dogs in Taiwan's cities and the abuse of laboratory animals and animals in circuses. One of the fruits of their efforts is the passage of wild animal protection laws and a law to forbid horseracing in Taiwan.

In addition, Chao Hwei and Shing Kuang are the only Buddhist monastics that have voiced opposition to the death penalty and have assisted those on death row whose sentences are controversial.[68] Chao Hwei believes that the three major Buddhist groups in Taiwan have made great achievements in charity and relief, education, and culture, but should do more regarding

Figure 6.3. Nuns of the Hongshi Institute at rally to save the Lo Sheng Leprosarium (Shih Chao Hwei)

issues of human rights, animal rights, and environmental protection. Charity and relief is not enough to relieve suffering, she asserts, for much of this arises from flaws in government policy and law, and from the collusion of money and power. Thus she believes that non-governmental organizations in civil society should play crucial roles as watchdogs by analysis, advocacy, and lobbying.[69]

She says that Buddhists should not sit back, and "... cool themselves in the shade of trees that others planted." Where were the Buddhists, she wonders, while others took to the streets during the previous decades of social movements in Taiwan? She continues by saying that now Taiwan is an open and free society yet many Buddhists shun social activism, for fear of alienating their followers and donors.[70]

Chao Hwei has praised Zhengyan for her achievements in welfare, relief, education, and medical services. But she has also written that charity is a Band-Aid that does not necessarily bring spiritual growth or structural change... claiming "neutrality" may in fact at times contribute to social problems and the sum of human suffering.[71] "Sometimes the cause of human suffering is political. What good is going to be accomplished if we feed the hungry without addressing the causes of their hunger...."[72] In turn, Chao Hwei has been criticized by some Buddhists for her activism. Members of Ciji, for example, criticized Chao Hwei (a major activist for animal rights in Taiwan) for showing a videotape of a pig slaughterhouse, for this would give bad publicity to pig farmers, disrupt the economy, and thus disrupt social harmony in Taiwan. "But I [Chao Hwei] think the harmony this person and others speak of is illusory. From my [Buddhist] perspective eating pork is not only causing the pig to suffer but also humans... *Renjian fojiao* is not just about human society, but all living creatures. I want to address the areas of inequality and injustice that affect all beings."[73]

She says that Taixu inspired her stance regarding politics: Buddhists should be concerned with politics but not become directly involved in its administration, or run for office, etc. Chao Hwei works to raise the public's consciousness and lobbies to change laws if necessary. In Taiwan's polarized political environment, where every issue tends to be reduced to partisan politics, Chao Hwei believes that NGOs (including Buddhist groups) should act like a "permanent opposition party," and keep the focus of debate on critical issues common to all citizens. Regarding issues such as protecting the dignity and reputation of monastics, environmentalism, human rights, animal rights, and other ethical issues, Chao Hwei has many supporters, both Buddhist and non-Buddhist. However, the most radical aspect about Chao Hwei and her disciples is that they are the only self-proclaimed "Buddhist Feminists" in Taiwan.[74] To expose, denounce, and demand change in the patriarchal hierarchy in the Buddhist *sangha* is to challenge the status quo maintained and reproduced not only by monks but also by nuns themselves.

Chao Hwei and Feminism

Does being "socially-engaged" necessarily entail working for women's rights and gender equality, including support of the nuns' order? Earlier chapters discussed Zhengyan's neo-traditional views on women's social roles and her primary emphasis on mobilizing laywomen rather than education and development of nuns; moreover, Ciji usually does not work with other Buddhist groups or NGOs.[75]

In fact, Engaged Buddhists, whether in Asian or Western countries, did not especially highlight Buddhist women's issues or pay attention to concerns with the nuns' order until the 1980s when feminism intersected with international Buddhism.[76] The first International Conference on Buddhist Nuns organized by Karma Lekshe Tsomo at Bodhgayā India in 1987 "... was the first Buddhist conference ever to address the problems faced by Buddhist women... Socially-engaged Buddhists need to recognize that

Buddhist women are among the poorest, least educated and most neglected sectors of society...."⁷⁷ Out of this historical conference came the Sākyadhitā International Association of Buddhist Women, dedicated to promoting the *bhikkhunī* order, gender equality in Buddhist institutions, and the welfare and rights of global Buddhist women.

Though conditions have improved for many Buddhist women in the world over the past decades, in terms of education, ordination and leadership opportunities, and economic and social standing, Santikaro writes that the discourse on Engaged Buddhism still mostly involves male voices, despite the fact that "the majority of Buddhists ... still live in Asia, and are women. And that will be the case for many years to come. Their lives, their concerns, their actions must not be marginalized just because the textual record on them is sparse."⁷⁸

The feminism of Chao Hwei and her colleagues derives in part from the ideas of Master Yinshun's explication of *renjian fojiao*, but more from the modern feminist movement. As mentioned earlier in this chapter, Taixu was a modernizer, full of "May Fourth" reformist spirit in many ways, but did not advocate radical change regarding women in Buddhism and women in Chinese society, though he supported the modern education of women. His *sangha* institutional and education reforms were primarily intended for monks.⁷⁹ Believing that women have more karmic hindrances than men, Taixu encouraged women to remain lay-practitioners and through their traditional roles as wife and mother, cultivate Buddhist families and good citizens.⁸⁰ Yet he also envisioned that Buddhist laywomen would study Chinese medicine and proselytize abroad, like Christian medical missionaries; and become nurses, doctors, kindergarten and primary school teachers, to proselytize in China as well.⁸¹

Yinshun later commented that one of the main reasons why Taixu's Buddhist reform movement failed was because Taixu underestimated the force of women in Buddhism; he did not value them or win their support.⁸² But certainly if Taixu had lived longer and in stable, peacetime conditions, with access to more resources, his reform plans for monks, nuns, and laypeople would have had better chance for success. It is interesting, however, to note that Taixu's promotion of Tibetan Buddhist studies among Chinese Buddhists helped nurture "... the most outstanding *bhikkhunī* of the contemporary era" in China, Longlian (1909–2006), via Taixu's reformist colleague Nenghai (1886–1967), Longlian's master, who pioneered a new Sino-Tibetan Buddhist tradition in China.⁸³

When Chinese monks relocated to Taiwan in the late 1940s, as mentioned in Chapter 1, they relied heavily on Taiwanese Buddhist women as they established themselves in a new environment and developed their institutions, and were never able change the fact that in Taiwan, Buddhist women, both ordained and lay, have always outnumbered men. Master Yinshun in particular stressed the doctrines in Buddhism that advocate gender equality. Pragmatic acknowledgment of nuns' talents, hard work, and devotion to Buddhism may be one reason why Yinshun supported the nuns' order, in addition to his broad-mindedness and his intensive inquiry into early Buddhist scriptures. He wrote that in Buddhism, there is little to no difference between men and women in faith, morality and conduct, and wisdom; and their biological and physical differences will not matter much regarding men and women's quest for enlightenment.[84] He also wrote: "For two thousand years, the *dharma* has been in the hands of the monks and thus Buddhism could not manifest its spirit of gender equality, could not support Buddhist women, on the contrary it was slanted to male chauvinism, to the point of scorning and detesting women, saying women cannot be taught the *dharma*. This is truly a distortion of the *dharma*!"[85]

In promoting "Buddhist feminism," Chao Hwei is inspired by Yinshun's egalitarian interpretation of Buddhism but even more by modern feminism in its critique of structural gender inequalities in society and culture, as well as its methodologies for activism and change.[86] Chao Hwei and her disciples support efforts by the government and NGO circles to work toward gender equality in Taiwan, and often debate and work with feminist groups. Chao Hwei's 2002 Chinese book, *Intonation for Thousands of Years: Buddhist Feminist Thought for a New Century,* has one section called "Deconstructing Buddhist Male Chauvinism" and a second section on "Building a Space for Gender Equality in Buddhism."[87] With their call to "say farewell to tradition," they have tried to rally Buddhist circles to abolish "the Eight Special Rules" that uphold the subordination of nuns to monks and to end "Buddhist male chauvinism." In fact, Chao Hwei from 1991 had already begun to criticize as "*bhikkhu* chauvinists" several monks in Taiwan who had insisted upon nuns' strict observance of the Eight Special Rules and who had demanded their nuns to memorize the "eighty-four ugly gestures of women" listed in the *Mahāprajāptī-bhikkhunī sūtra*.[88] Then, on March 31, 2001, during the opening ceremony of the Second Annual Conference (organized yearly by Hongshi Institute) on the theory and praxis related to Yinshun's works, Chao Hwei, together with seven other monastics and laypeople, first read out the Eight Special Rules and then tore them up, declaring that "Mahāprajāptī's Second Revolution" had begun, and immediately launched a full-blown "storm" of controversy.[89]

But the most surprising reaction came from Master Yinshun himself, who on June 3 responded to the Buddhist Association of the ROC's earlier letter of "concern." In his brief letter, Yinshun stated that the Eight Special Rules were "... laid down by the Buddha. If the Eight Special Rules are no longer compatible with our time and social context, we need the consent of the elders and the resolution passed through a grand council."[90] As Wei-yi Cheng points out, this reply was used by both supporters and critics of Chao Hwei's movement. Taken at face value, Yinshun's statement sounds like a repudiation of Chao Hwei's actions; however, his message is ambiguous.

In fact, since 1945, there had been no consensus regarding whether and how to uphold the Eight Special Rules; as in many other temple matters, this was left to the discretion of each temple to decide upon. In general, there have been three stances in Taiwan Buddhist circles: the first, *laissez-faire*—neither abolish them nor force nuns to observe them;[91] the second—strict observance of the Rules, including those pertaining to the rainy-season retreat; the third and most recent—to advocate for the Rules' abolishment.[92] As is well-known in Buddhist circles, Yinshun had spent a lifetime taking a historical and critical approach to Buddhist texts, including the Eight Special Rules, about which Yinshun had previously questioned both their historical authenticity "... and the necessity to observe the Rules in contemporary contexts." Thus, the door is open for Chao Hwei and any others to question and criticize Buddhist texts.[93]

Chao Hwei's call to abolish the Eight Special Rules received a mixed response: full and open support from a minority, and various degrees of opposition from the majority.[94] The reaction from many nuns can be summarized in this way: Since the nuns' order is strong and flourishing, the degree of gender equality is high in Taiwan, and in Taiwan the "Eight Special Rules" are not universally observed and have not limited or posed a burden on nuns' spiritual cultivation or educational and professional development, why sow discord and division in Taiwan Buddhist circles?[95]

According to Cheng Wei-yi's fieldwork findings, in fact "... there is a negotiation between the Eight Special Rules and convenience, the normal social code of conducts, and the increasingly gender egalitarian or feminist awareness . . . ;"[96] nuns of different ages and from different temples hold a wide variety of opinions regarding the Eight Special Rules. Some see paying homage to distinguished monks as signifying their request to receive the monks' teachings, and is a practice by which nuns can "... liberate themselves from both arrogance and conventional idea of hierarchy."[97] Another nun commented that some nuns in Taiwan follow the Eight Special Rules and automatically bow to or kneel in front of monks, but she would not, unless she met an older nun, or if she was receiving a teacher or Chan Master in the Main Hall. On other occasions and places, upon meeting a monk, she would, at the most, join her palms in greeting.[98]

However, Chao Hwei cannot accept any kind of rationalization of or accommodation to the Eight Special Rules, and she insists that the perpetuation of gender inequality in Buddhist institutions cannot be justified or compensated by reiterating the doctrines on spiritual equality in Buddhism.[99] Chao Hwei wants nuns to face the fact that the Eight Special Rules perpetuate arrogance and pretensions to special privileges among monks (who are the minority in Taiwan), while continuing tendencies of self-deprecation and deference to male authority among nuns,[100] despite the nuns' numerical supremacy, decades of hard work, study, cultivation, and contributions to Taiwan's Buddhism. The nun Yikong writes about a "... joke in the Buddhist community" describing monks "as being 'VIP, middle, and front,' referring to the *bhikkhu's* preference for VIP seats during *dharma* functions and activities; *bhikkhus* sitting in the middle of the front row when photos are taken, and, walking in front of others."[101] She might have added that in Buddhist audiences or meditation sessions, laymen often are seated in front of laywomen, due to the traditional misogynist belief that women are spiritually and intellectually deficient. To Chao Hwei, these are not joking matters; and Jiang Canteng agrees with Chao Hwei that true gender equality in Buddhism will not be realized without abolishment of the Eight Special Rules and that Taiwan Buddhists could seize this opportunity to set a historical precedent for the rest of the Buddhist world.[102] Despite the fact that nuns have always outnumbered monks in Taiwan, the Eight Special Rules act like a glass ceiling and ultimately bar them from top leadership positions in national Buddhist organizations.[103]

However, though Taiwan's Buddhist monks and nuns have not reached a consensus, let alone taken further action regarding the abolition of the Eight Special Rules,[104] Chao Hwei points out that her movement seems to have influenced BAROC to allow nuns for the first time to serve as standing board members and Secretary-General, while the Taipei Buddhist Association allowed nuns for the first time to be elected for board chairperson. At a November 2001 meeting of BAROC, the board chairman, the senior monk Jingliang, invited Chao Hwei to deliver an address "representing nuns," also an unprecedented event.[105] Furthermore, the controversy caused by her movement to abolish the "Eight Special Rules" did not hinder her from being invited to lecture on the *bhikkhunī* precepts at ordination ceremonies and monastic summer retreats in Taiwan and in China.[106] Thus her movement did lead to reforms in the monk-led Buddhist leadership in Taiwan, and has forced open the door to long-needed discussion and debate about the Eight Special Rules, gender equality in Buddhism and Taiwan's Buddhist leadership.

In conclusion, Chao Hwei has transformed Yinshun's "modern Bodhisattava" at the service of society, into a social activist, ceaselessly questioning the status quo, working for structural change, and fearless of controversy. Her inspiration is not only from Buddhism but also the theory and practice of global social movements such as human rights, environmentalism, animal rights, and feminism. Her critics may disapprove of her tactics, but no one can deny the effectiveness of her strategy, which results in actual change.[107]

Due to her books, lectures, and conferences she is becoming known in Hong Kong and China; the Hongshi Institute might find it beneficial to translate their publications into foreign languages and establish more connections with like-minded Engaged Buddhists in Asia and throughout the world.[108] Taiwan's *renjian fojiao* groups, especially Chao Hwei and her colleagues, could work more with the International Network of Engaged Buddhists (INEB) founded by Sulak Sivaraksa of Thailand in 1989.[109] High on his list of priorities are human rights, social justice, environmentalism, and a critique of consumerist society, and he has been censored and jailed for his activism. INEB is a loose non-hierarchal network comprised of a few, "very small marginalized Buddhist NGOs and activists."[110] Groups from Taiwan (Foguangshan, Ciji), Korea, and Japan did not send participants to INEB annual meetings until recently. This was not due to regional (Southeast Asia, Northeast Asia) or doctrinal differences (Theravāda, Mahāyāna) but to the organization structures of INEB (small grassroots, marginalized from the government and national *sangha* establishments). For even the large NGO *Sarvodaya* in Sri Lanka did not attend INEB meetings until the last few years.[111]

The emergence of engaged Buddhism over the past century, and its radical activism from the mid-twentieth century on, is one strand among many in contemporary Buddhism practice.[112] And within Engaged Buddhist circles there is no consensus about what degree of engagement defines one as an engaged Buddhist. Ken Jones distinguishes between two types of Engaged Buddhists as:

> "... Soft-enders who trust in the ripple effects of one-to-one influence in launching a peaceful society, and the hard-enders who are committed, quietly or militantly, to influence public policy and create new institutions."[113]

Radical Buddhist activism is new in Taiwan; it is unclear whether in the future a younger generation of Buddhist women will follow this path, as well as stand together and call for the abolition of the Eight Special Rules. Chao Hwei herself wrote that though she and Zhengyan take very different approaches to social action, both are Buddhist nuns who hope to improve Taiwan society; each employing skillful means to good ends.[114] Diverse Buddhist interpretations and practices together can contribute to the growth of a vibrant and pluralistic society.

Conclusion

Buddhism, Women, and Civil Society in Taiwan

To conclude, we return to the three focalizing questions of this book.

How Have Women Shaped Taiwan's Buddhism?

Over the past half-century, ordained and lay Buddhist women, together with monks and laymen, have built up modern Chinese institutional Buddhism on the foundations of *zhaijiao* and Japanese-era institutional Buddhism.[1] Taiwan's Buddhism is unique in the world for several reasons: Taiwan has the largest number of nuns in the world; nuns outnumber monks three to one; and, among nuns in Taiwan are leaders in the fields of education, charity, the arts, normative ethics, and human rights. Finally, Taiwan's Buddhists have to a great extent transformed negative depictions of "women" and "the feminine" into positive traits worthy of emulation by both genders; in the case of Ciji, Zhengyan strives to reform Taiwan and the world through a feminized Buddhism. To my knowledge, this particularly strong propagation of positive feminine traits as making "women especially suited for Buddhism" is only found in Taiwan, not in the Mahāyāna Buddhism circles of China, where the monks' order is more numerous and powerful, with privileged access to resources, education, and positions of leadership and where negative ideas about women's "pollution" and "karmic burdens" still prevail.[2]

Nor is this kind of argument found in Korean Buddhist circles, though more than half of the monastics are nuns and eighty percent of lay Buddhists are women.[3] In Vietnam, the female image of Guanyin is also very important to Mahāyāna Buddhists, as in Taiwan, but according to my observations, monks or nuns do not regard *từ bi* (compassion) as being particular associated with women or "the feminine," rather, *từ bi* is one of the great Buddhist virtues to be cultivated by all. Though it is claimed that now nuns outnumber monks in Vietnam,[4] and many nuns seek higher education in Vietnam and abroad, monks and nuns still have unequal status. Only monks are called "Teacher/ Master," *Thầy*, while nuns are called *Sư Cô*, "Teacher-auntie"; also, monks' names begin with *Thích* while nuns add the word for "woman," *Thích nữ*. Monks in Vietnam, as they have throughout history, have higher social standing and power, have privileged access to lay disciples and resources, and are in command in all areas of Buddhist circles except the monastic kitchen.

Due to the hard work and achievements of nuns such as Zhengyan, Wu Yin, Chao Hwei, and their disciples, a form of socially-engaged Buddhism, Buddhism for the Human Realm, flourishes in Taiwan. Monastics in Taiwan are now perceived as educated professionals, and the Buddhist religion is now respected for its achievements in many fields. Taiwan also plays a key role in developing global Buddhism through its overseas branches in many countries, and is helping to revive Buddhism in China, with Taiwan's nuns and monks officiating at ordination ceremonies, giving lectures and holding retreats, and disseminating Buddhist publications, as well as with Taiwan's Buddhists' generous donations. Master Xingyun deserves great credit for his support of the nuns' order in Taiwan and around the world, and Foguangshan has sponsored full ordination ceremonies for nuns of Tibetan and Theravādin traditions, such as in February 1998 at Bodhgayā India, which helped restore Sri Lanka's *bhikkhunī* order after a lapse of nine centuries.[5] Taiwan has become a center for female Buddhist novitiates, Asian and non-Asian, from all Buddhist traditions (Theravādin, Tibetan, Zen) to receive training and full ordination. For over fifteen years, the Dalai Lama has called for full ordination for nuns in Tibetan Buddhism and sent a special team to Taiwan in 1997 and in 2001 to investigate the Taiwanese system.[6] All these accomplishments have proven wrong Zhang Mantao's gloomy prediction that: "Relying on women [in Taiwan's Buddhism] probably will make it impossible to obtain perfect results."[7]

How Has Buddhism Shaped the Role and Identity of Taiwanese Women?

We have seen that there are many types of Buddhist groups in Taiwan besides those advocating *renjian fojiao* and not every temple chooses active social engagement. Taiwan offers many choices for women and men regarding Buddhist doctrine and practice, including whether to remain a lay practitioner or become a monastic, and this is one strong point about Taiwan's Buddhism.[8] Women can choose to become Buddhist nuns and in doing so satisfy their intellectual and spiritual needs and professional aspirations. Buddhism in Taiwan has produced women leaders in education, culture, and social service and has empowered women on an individual level as in Ciji's level of self-strengthening, *ziwo peili*, where women gain a new voice, new knowledge, worldview, and skills, and are saved from despair, abuse, and death. Furthermore, Ciji promulgates the world-saving Guanyin as "mother" and in the process has extended women's nurturing and healing role from home to society, with benefits to women, the Ciji organization, and society.

Luminary nuns endeavor to empower women, first as self-reliant, well-trained *dharma* masters, and also empowers women through Luminary's community outreach programs in post-earthquake relief and their classes assisting "foreign brides." And the feminist Chao Hwei endeavors to work toward gender equality for all women, whether nuns, lay Buddhists, or non-Buddhist women.

As Taiwan's Buddhists stressed Buddhist doctrines on gender equality and also championed positive "feminine traits" such as compassion, nurturance, peace-making and communication skills, Taiwan's Buddhists have cultivated women's heretofore "hidden" or disparaged potentials and mobilized women and men to great good for the commonweal. Tapping into Taiwan society's gender essentialism has served the Buddhists well, but will Ciji's ideal of Guanyin-as-mother appeal to the next generation? As for Dharma Drum's Shengyan, though he lectured on the doctrines in Buddhism that advocate gender equality, he also held essentialist concepts about gender: "Women are restricted due to their family and child-bearing responsibilities...the fact that women are willing to sacrifice [their potential for self-development] for the sake of the family, it's in their nature...in the animal world, this is also true."[9]

Buddhists' perpetuation of gender essentialism seems to be at odds with the strenuous efforts by NGOs and the government to realize gender equality in Taiwan, not to mention the calls for gender equality in Buddhism. Su Qianling criticizes the myth of "woman as wife and mother" and the tendency to abuse the notion of "mother's love," when a woman is defined as mother and wife in both private and public spheres, and her "natural" role as nurturer, healer, and service-provider supercede her humanity, her self, and her potential to develop other aspects such as the intellect and other talents. Moreover, Su believes that this abuse of mother's love is not beneficial for society, that the Taiwanese will never become independent mature people if they are always hiding beneath a mother-figure's wings.[10] But Lu Hwei-syin reminds us that at least for now, women in Taiwan can accept gender differences and "celebrate" gender complementarity, as long as they can successfully obtain the resources, power, self-fulfillment, and social status they want by maneuvering and negotiating among their domestic roles as mother, wife, daughter, and their "outside" roles as worker, professional, and other non-family-based identities.[11]

The ambiguous discourse in Taiwan's Buddhism about "women's nature" can perpetuate Buddhism's attraction as it can weaken its appeal. Ultimately, the long-term success of Buddhism in Taiwan will depend considerably upon the way women themselves in Taiwan define their role and identity.

How Are Buddhist Women Shaping the Future of Taiwanese Society?

Among Taiwan's Buddhists are those who professed no previous religious belief, but others are converts from Christianity and above all, the popular religious tradition. Thus Buddhism is altering Taiwan's traditional religious landscape, also in a literal sense when one sees the proliferation of Buddhist temples and mega-structures in city and countryside alike. Taiwan's Buddhists have also helped to shape the current public discourse on illness, dying, and death through publications, community classes, and public advocacy.[12] As one example, Ciji's medical center is a pioneer in the field of hospice care in Taiwan.

But perhaps most intriguing is the question of *if* and *how* Taiwan's Buddhists are contributing to the making of civil society, and scholarly opinions can be divided into those who hold a broad definition of civil society and those who prefer a strict, activist definition. In the broad neo-liberal definition that has taken shape since the 1980s, "... civil society consists of associational life—a non-profit, voluntary 'third sector'—that not only restrains state power but also actually provides a substitute for many of the functions performed by the state ... Civil society ... is the realm between the state, the market, and the family, but it is a realm of stability rather than struggle, of service provision rather than advocacy, of trust and responsibility rather than emancipation."[13]

Robert Weller's (1999) is an example of a broad definition of civil society: Ciji "... is a classic civil organization in the sense that it is an intermediate institution between the private world and the state ... It is insistently apolitical, yet politically vital as a central field for the redefinition of self and morality."[14] As evidence to support Weller, we can point to the power of changing consciousness. As mentioned above, Ciji has mobilized women as mothers to make great contributions to Taiwan and the world, while both Ciji and Fagushan [Dharma Drum] have been very effective in educating people about basic environmental issues. In addition, these *renjian fojiao* groups have led the family-oriented Chinese to think beyond family unit to neighborhood, other regions, and other countries, to extend care and resources universally, in other words, developing a public consciousness that is crucial for a true civil society. To take another example, the Ciji organization worked strenuously to overcome popular taboos against blood and bone marrow donations; now, their bone marrow bank is the largest in Asia and third-largest in the world.

Moreover, the crux of Weller's argument is that Taiwan has manifested an alternate form of civil society development. Western ideas about civil society took as the norm the notion of the autonomous individual in his or her search for identity, while the Chinese did and still do "... maintain strong links to the bonds of local community, kinship, and religion," dismissed by classic sociologists as "premodern."[15] Civil groups multiplied so quickly after 1987 because they grew out of the numerous extant informal groups based on ties of community, local politics, religion, and kinship. This informal sector, rooted in community and family life, includes such phenomena as rotating credit associations, the environmental movement, and Ciji. In each of these, women play a large and active role, while men, past and present, have dominated the formal sectors of society.[16] Studies by David Schak and Hsin-Huang Michael Hsiao of six socially-engaged Buddhist groups in Taiwan similarly conclude that these groups have, through their missions of education, culture, philanthropy, and environmental protection, created social capital and have contributed to Taiwan's growing civil society.[17]

However, a number of scholars in Taiwan hold a strict, activist definition of civil society. "For the activist version, the inhabitants of civil society can be roughly equated with civic-minded or public-spirited groups. Those active in civil society would be those concerned about public affairs and public debate."[18] Mary Kaldor defines civil society "... as the medium through which social contracts or bargains between the individual and the centres of political and economic power are negotiated, discussed and mediated."[19]

Lin Yusheng, for example, cannot call Ciji an example of a public organization in Taiwan. Like Chao Hwei, Lin believes NGOs should supervise, critique, advise, and proactively shape the public discourse, which so far Ciji shies from doing.[20] As another example, Gu Zhonghua employs the definition of the term civil society dating from the global democratic movements of the past twenty years especially against the authoritarian states in Eastern Europe and Latin America. As Gu Zhonghua describes it, the possibility for civil society (*gongmin shehui*) in Taiwan began with the abolition of martial law in 1987, initiating a period of spontaneous social movements and public demonstrations that culminated in a series of large multigroup public marches in spring of 1997. Then, in the period from 1997 to the present, social movements crystallized into NGOs and NPOs (non-profit organizations). NGOs and NPOs comprise "the third sector," together with government and business, in a triangular balance of power. This "third sector," as it exercises citizens' civil rights, participates in public discourse, and influences public policy (for example, education reform groups, the local community movement, women's rights groups, environmental groups, aboriginal rights groups) has the potential to evolve into "civil society."[21] But Gu points out that the large Buddhist NGOs in Taiwan like Ciji, Fagushan, and Foguangshan, as we saw in Chapter 6, "... due to various concerns, have a strong 'apolitical' orientation, unwilling to challenge the powers that be" and thus are not yet "public" organizations.[22]

Finally, Ting Jen-Chieh and Zhan Sujuan comment that with the "9.21" earthquake and Project Hope, Ciji could have seized the opportunity to help build a Habermasian public sphere, "where public opinion is formed," but did not, due to Ciji's perennial claims to be apolitical, always seeking consensus and harmony, above and beyond the polity, avoiding debates and confrontation.[23] Ting Jen-Chieh argues that though Ciji has developed into a large, modern, international NGO, the group still retains characteristics of a *Gongde hui*, a traditional Chinese charitable association based on the spirit of *keji chongren* (overcoming the self, esteeming compassion), whose members, by meeting the needs of their community, (for example, in famine relief or financing local educational and infrastructure projects) accumulate both personal and family merit; such merit associations were uninvolved with upper-level state policymaking.[24] In contrast, Chao Hwei and her colleagues as well as the Luminary Buddhist Institute, through their work with other NGOs, are building the horizontal links that constitute civil society.

In closing, we can ask: By becoming nuns, have Taiwanese women found their "Peach Blossom Spring," their Utopia, their freedom from patriarchal bonds, gender discrimination, and power games?[25] This is the question the novelist Chen Ruoxi explores in her two novels *Huixinlian* [The Story of Taiwan's Nuns] (2000) and *Chongfan taohuayuan* [Return to Peach Blossom Spring] (2001).[26] Chen Ruoxi asks piercing questions such as: Do women simply go from a lay environment, serving father, husband, son, to the Buddhist environment, serving other Buddhist masters and serving society, without changing the traditional image and self-image of women as "gentle and yielding... able to endure hardships and ceaseless work?" In addition, Chen wonders if Buddhism for the Human Realm risks becoming secularized, valued only for its utilitarian aspect in serving society, not for its intrinsic spiritual value. Furthermore, she fears that high levels of education and training do not necessarily lead to high levels of self-awareness and powers of critical reflection. Chen also ventures into the taboo subjects of emotional attachments, sex, power, and gender inequality in contemporary Taiwan's religions, including institutional Buddhism.[27]

The novels offer no definite answers but, precisely because they raised such sensitive topics, Chen Ruoxi's novels had a cool reception among the Buddhist community. For example, in her terse review of *Huixinlian*, the nun Xinghe sympathized with the novel's description of the pain and guilt involved as women leave their families to become nuns, however Xinghe rejected the novel's "stereotyped" description of Buddhism as a refuge of last resort for broken hearts and victims of broken homes. Xinghe refrained from discussing the other controversial issues raised in the novel. Sensitive or not, Chen Ruoxi's questions still await wide discussion in the Buddhist community.[28]

Regarding the future, as the older generation of nuns who were ordained from the 1960s to the 1980s age and become less active, the younger generation of nuns might cooperate more with NGOs and government initiatives. However, another scenario may unfold: As Taiwan's society undergoes further liberalization, it may become socially acceptable to remain as an unmarried laywoman.[29] In that case, there would be no need to make the sacrifices required by the monastic life.

The sudden increase in numbers of young women who became nuns in the 1980s may simply have been a passing phase, akin to the surge of new Catholic nuns in the decades of 1960 through the 1970s, inspired by the "Vatican II" reforms and Liberation Theology, youth movement ideals such as the imperative of social engagement, and the rise of feminist consciousness.[30] In Taiwan, some young women and men felt a personal spiritual bond with the charismatic Buddhist masters and nuns who propagated *renjian fojiao* in Taiwan: These masters are now aging and must increasingly delegate tasks and responsibilities to the younger generation. But Mingjia predicted that in the future, young people drawn to the monastic life will not do so due to the compelling charisma of any master, but due to the appeal of living and working in a Buddhist community, as a member of a collective team. She or he will have to be drawn first for religious and spiritual reasons, because in modern society, the enticements and pressures of the secular world are ever-increasing. Mingjia stated that the number of newly ordained nuns is steady, and she feels the Buddhist community should continue to emphasize comprehensive and professional education and training for nuns to meet the challenges of socially-engaged and globally-oriented Buddhism.[31]

When asked is there equality in Taiwan between the *bhikkhus* and *bhikkhunīs*, Wu Yin answered: "The leadership rests with the *bhikkhus*.[32] But concerning their presence and what is given back to society, the *bhikkhunīs* do much more than the *bhikkhus* . . . [The *bhikkhunīs*] are much more engaged in studying and propagating the Dharma."[33] Even without absolute equality with monks, the state of the nuns' order in Taiwan today surpasses even the best times for Chinese nuns over the past seventeen centuries, and far exceeds the situation for most Buddhist nuns in the world. To note but one poignant example, the Tibetan nuns of Labrang in China, because they are female, are greatly limited in their scope of ritual and merit-making activities. One way Labrang nuns can gain lay support is by practicing the grueling ritual of fasting and ritual silence called *smyung gnas*. However, the time spent and bodily hardships endured "severely limit" the nuns to "improve themselves beyond [the ritual's] scope," and thus nuns are "constrained [by the monks] to collude in their own silencing."[34]

Nuns in Taiwan possess the power to speak, write, and publish, and have been instrumental in the in development of civil society. On par with monks, nuns can pursue studies, lead and administer temples, perform a variety of rituals and officiate at ordination platforms, and teach the *dharma* to nuns, laypeople, and other monks. Nuns enjoy high social status and material welfare[35] and can travel abroad to study, lecture, transmit the precepts to new nuns, and to advance global Buddhism.[36] Taiwan's nuns have fought for and secured voice, space, and power that no person or institution can take away from them. These are infinite worlds, *tiankong*.

> Tianxia mingshan shei shi zhu
> Kongzhong wuwo xin ji fo

> Who is master of the famed mountains all under Heaven?
> [Dwelling] in emptiness, ego-less, the mind is Buddha.[37]

Notes

Introduction

1. I have been told the following estimates, from a scholar who wishes to remain anonymous until the figures can be proven: 1,500 fully ordained nuns in China; 9,805 fully ordained nuns in the world, excluding Taiwan. See Chapter 1 for more information about nuns in China, past and present. Korea has a long history of fully-ordained Buddhist nuns, beginning in the fifth century AD; Vietnam has had a tradition of fully-ordained nuns since the twelfth century. Both countries since the twentieth-century have experienced growth in education opportunities for nuns, and have seen the development of socially-engaged Buddhism in recent years. See Batchelor and Son'gyong Sunim 2006 and articles on Korean Buddhism in Tsomo 2006; Thich Nu Dong Anh, "A Survey of Bhikkhunis Sangha in Vietnam," in Tsomo 2004a: 51–54. In Japan, the first ordained monastics were three young girls who were sent to the Korean peninsula for ordination in 590 AD, while ordination for monks in Japan was not established until the mid-eighth century. However, due to Meiji government policies of the late nineteenth century, male "monks" in Japan have married and raised families; alcohol and meat are not prohibited to them. Japan has a long and varied tradition of Buddhist nuns, many of whom were celibate, were fully or partially tonsured, and were scholars, teachers, administrators, and ritual specialists. Some lived in convents, some remained at home, some were itinerant. Full ordination never became the norm in Japan; nuns instead have taken Bodhisattva or novice vows or were "self-ordained." Since the late nineteenth century, Japanese nuns, particularly from the Sōtō Zen sect, have fought to establish schools and institutes to provide Buddhist and secular education to nuns, and have succeeded in changing their sect's regulations to allow nuns access to higher ranking, administration posts, and the right to perform certain rituals, all from which nuns were previously barred. However, lay models of Buddhist practice are more popular and numerous in Japan. See Arai 1999, Ruch 2002, and Faure 2003. In Theravādin countries and in Tibetan Buddhism, although many Buddhist laywomen, ten-precept nuns, and novice nuns practice devoutly and diligently, they suffer from limited resources, limited access to education, limitations in the ritual sphere, and low social status. Unless they are able to seek full ordination based on the Chinese *vinaya* of the *Dharmaguptaka* tradition, they practice as novices their entire lives. Due to the efforts of many Buddhist women and men (including Taiwan Buddhists) over several

decades, the Buddhist authorities in Sri Lanka restored *bhikkhunī* ordination in Sri Lanka in 1998; the order had disappeared in the tenth century AD.

2. Li Yuzhen (2000: 354. In this book, "Li 2000" refers to Li Yuzhen's English doctoral dissertation, unless otherwise indicated.

3. Ibid.

4. Li, 2005: 6, quoting Ven. Chao Hwei. A representative at BAROC told me that there are around 30,000 monks and nuns in Taiwan at present. If nuns comprise about 75 percent, then the number would be 22,500. Phone call, May 7, 2008.

5. See Clart and Jones 2003 and Jordan in Harrell and Huang 1994.

6. According to the numbers reported by Buddhist organizations to the Ministry of the Interior, the number of Buddhists in Taiwan increased from 800,000 followers in 1983 to 4.9 million in 1995, and at the end of 2002 had reached 5.48 million believers, out of Taiwan's total population of 22.5 million, while the number of "Buddhist temples" rose from 1,157 in 1983 to 4,037 in December 2002. See www.moi.gov.tw/stat, accessed on April 2, 2008. However, a strong caveat is in order: These numbers do not clearly specify what qualifies as a "Buddhist believer" or a "Buddhist temple," and are probably inflated. As Yü 2003: 267 notes, a person may claim to be "Buddhist" without having formally taken the "three refuges" with a Buddhist master. To complicate matters further, when I phoned the Ministry of the Interior for the latest numbers (as of December 2006), I was told that this time the Ministry of the Interior asked cities and counties, instead of Buddhist organizations, to provide numbers of believers (165,049) and temples (2,262), numbers which the MOI representative admitted were too low. Phone call to MOI, Office of Statistics, April 3, 2008. A representative at the Buddhist Association of the Republic of China told me that they do not know the total number of Buddhist believers in Taiwan, but estimated that there are around 2,000 temples in Taiwan. Phone call May 7, 2008.

7. For example, Jiang 1992 and 1997; Heng Ching 1995; Chao Hwei 2002; Yang and Zhang 2004; and all by Chern Meei-hwa and Li Yuzhen.

8. See Li 2002: 1–2; 7–10; 14–16.

9. Kan Zhengzong's history of the development of Taiwan's Buddhism since 1945, *Re-Reading Taiwan's Buddhism* (2004), is a thoroughly androcentric study. Five-hundred pages of text, though well-researched and full of useful information, narrate the story of a minority, monks and laymen, while the majority, nuns and laywomen, are dismissed in a few pages. When Kan does mention nuns and women in Taiwan's Buddhism, he is often quoting other authors' derisive views of women in Taiwan's Buddhism, and does not make a great effort to counter these biased accounts or offer his own interpretation. See pages 75; 285–88; 407–15; 467. Jones 1999 has brief but insightful remarks about nuns in Taiwan on pages 51–52; 62–63; 152–56.

10. As for doctoral dissertations about Taiwan's nuns and/or laywomen, see Chern 2000, Li 2000, Crane 2001, Huang 2001, and Foy 2002; as well as Shi Jianye's biography (1999) on the pioneering nun Shi Tianyi. Notable essays on nuns and/or laywomen include: Huang and Weller 1998, Li 2004a, b, Lu 1998, Cheng 2003, Travagnin 2004a, b, and Lu Hwei-syin's works. The subject of Qin's 2000 dissertation is Buddhist nuns on Mt. Emei in Sichuan, China.

11. Cheng 2007 is a comparative work in Buddhist studies about Buddhist nuns in Taiwan and Sri Lanka. Her book tests the "Western feminist critique on

Buddhism" by showing how nuns variously interpret certain ideas and strictures about women and gender in the Pāli and Chinese scriptures, especially in light of the nuns' life experiences and religious practices and their various contexts. See my review in *Journal of Chinese Philosophy* 34:4 (December 2007), pp. 606-11.

12. Yikong 2004: 67.

13. Li Xueping 2000: 3; 17.

14. Huang and Weller 1998: 391.

15. Chinese reformist monk Taixu (1890-1947) first developed *renjian fojiao* to answer the critiques of and challenges to Buddhism in the modern world. For more details see Pittman 2001 and Jones 1999. As Chapter 6 will explain, the "three mountaintops" of *renjian fojiao* in Taiwan include Zhengyan's Ciji (Compassion-Relief) enterprise, founded in 1966; Xingyun's Foguangshan (Buddha Light Mountain) enterprise, founded in 1967; and Shengyan's Fagushan (Dharma Drum Mountain) enterprise, founded in 1989.

Chapter 1

1. Earlier forms of this chapter appeared in the *Taipei Ricci Bulletin* 3, 1999-2000: 79-89, and in Karma Lekshe Tsomo ed. *Buddhist Women and Social Justice* NY: SUNY Press, 2004: 219-31; reprinted with permission.

2. Luminary Publishing Association, 1997b: 86-122. For this chapter I interviewed Master Wu Yin, head of the Luminary Buddhist Institute, Jiayi; Ven. Mingjia, former second-in-command of the Luminary Buddhist Institute; Ven. Heng Ching, professor of philosophy emerita at National Taiwan University; Ven. Jianshen, professor of education, Hsuan Chuang University; Ven. Shanhui of the Qianguang Temple, Jiayi; Vens. Guang'guo and Xianyue of Lingjiu Mountain Monastery, Jilong; Ven. Lianchan of the Wuyan Association, Taipei; Ven. Jingxin at Benyuan Temple, Kaohsiung, and Ven. Man'guang, Foguangshan, Kaohsiung County. I am especially indebted to Ven. Chao Hwei of the Hongshi Buddhist Institute for generously speaking with and writing to me countless times. Many thanks to Prof. Dominique Tyl who organized and carried out a phone survey of all officially registered Buddhist monasteries in Taipei, August 1999. These interviews are one source for the section of this chapter called "Why Become a Nun?" I also thank Dr. Jiang Canteng and Dr. Li Yuzhen for their generous help and guidance.

3. Qin 2000: 223-26; 239-31; 265; 437-39. Qin illustrates how hard the nuns on Emei Shan have struggled to shape their own path as female religious practitioners. They have recently gained lay support and access to ritual and financial powers traditionally monopolized by monks. But nuns, she points out, still remain in a state-determined inferior position to monks. "The continuing male dominance over women in the Buddhist monastic tradition is justified by the patriarchal administrative structure set up by the state," including a state-determined quota system to guarantee more monks than nuns. 226, 239-40.

4. Li 2000: 22-23.

5. As stipulated by the *vinaya*, the monastic rules, a male Master can take both monks and nuns as disciples, but a female Master can only take nuns. At mixed-*sangha*

temples in Taiwan, monks and nuns are housed separately and honor all monastic precepts including celibacy. A comparison of all-nun and mixed-*sangha* communities might reveal different institutional patterns and teaching and leadership styles, as well as the problems special to mixed-gender celibate communities. According to Wei-yi Cheng's findings, some Taiwanese nuns believed that the female-only *sangha* was a more empowering environment overall for nuns, while others felt that mixed-*sangha* environment provided more opportunities for education and preaching. Cheng 2007: 149–66.

6. Kan 2004: 22–23.
7. Cheng 2007: 36.
8. Hs'ing 1983: 6.
9. Ibid., 5.
10. Ibid., 11–16.
11. Kan 1999 and 2005; Shi Huiyan 1996.
12. Kan 2005:24.
13. Hs'ing 1983: 14–15; Kan 1999.
14. Jones 1999: 9. "Wild frontier" is a typical term used in colonialist discourse and the validity of this term should be scrutinized in that context. See Emma Jinhua Teng, *Taiwan's Imagined Geography: Chinese Colonial Travel Writing and Pictures, 1683–1895*. Cambridge, MA: Harvard University Press, 2006.
15. Jones 199: 13, 30. Jones here relies on Chen 1974 and the *1971 General Gazetteer of Taiwan Province*, published by the Nationalist government on Taiwan.
16. Kan 2005: 26, 30. Kan is quoting from Shi Miaoran, ed. *Minguo fojiao dashi nianji* [Annual Chronicle of Important Events in Republican-Era Buddhism]. Taipei: Hai Chao Yin Magazine Publishers, 277.
17. Goossaert 2002: 42, note 21. The argument that links a lack of ordination center to a weak or inferior Buddhism in Taiwan is made by Chen 1974: 10–11.
18. Goossaert 2002: 42; Personal communication, July 11, 2007.
19. Goossaert 2002.
20. David K Jordan and Daniel L. Overmyer, *The Flying Phoenix: Aspects of Chinese Sectarianism in Taiwan*. Princeton: Princeton University Press, 1986. Wan-li Ho of Emory University studies the recent phenomenon of female Daoist clergy in Taiwan, including the celibate ordained clergy of Daode Yuan in Kaohsiung, whose practice combines the rituals of the Zhenyi sect with the ideas regarding "inner alchemy" from the Quanzhen traditions.
21. Li 2000: 73. For more information about *zhaijiao* in Taiwan, see Jiang and Wang 1994; Jiang 1997: 49–60; and Jones 1999: 14–43.
22. Cheng 2003: 41.
23. Topley 1978: 67–88. Marjorie Topley studied women's "marriage resistance" and women's vegetarian houses in the Pearl River Delta, Hong Kong, and Singapore. In some areas of Guangdong, women's refusing or delaying marriage was related to their desire (or that of their family) for wages earned in the local silk industry.
24. Li 2000: 75; Jiang 1997: 113–24.
25. Li 2000: 77.
26. Zhang Kunzhen 2003. *Taiwan de lao zhaitang*. Taipei County: Yuanzu Wenhua, 156–61.

27. Li 2000: 74, quoting Lin Mei-Rong.

28. Jiang 2001b: 59.

29. Goossaert suggests that regional variation found among clerical groups (monks, nuns, Buddhist, Daoist) is related to patterns of master-disciple succession of temple properties and management positions as well as the cultic and liturgical needs of the local communities that supported these groups. Thus, he argues, traditions evolved in certain areas, where it was "standard and honorable" (and economically pragmatic) to send or permit one's son or daughter to join the Buddhist *sangha*. Goossaert 2000: 16–18.

30. Jiang 1997: 49–60; Jones 1999: 153.

31. Taiwan Shukyō Chōsa Hōkokushō [Report of the Investigation into Religion in Taiwan]. Taipei: Taiwan Sōtokufu, 1919; Shi Huiyan 1999: 263–64. Jones also claims that at the end of the Qing, there were no nuns in Taiwan. Jones 1999: 153, quoting Cheng Ruitang 1974: 11.

32. Chen Wenda, ed. 1958. *Taiwan wenxian congkan*, Type 103, "Taiwan County Gazetteer, Geography, Customs." Taipei: Economic Research Office, Bank of Taiwan, Oct., 60.

33. Lian Heng 1977. *Chuan* 11, "Education Record," and *Chuan* 22, "Religion Record." *Taiwan tongshi* [General History of Taiwan]. Taipei: Tatong Shuju. Lian Heng's (1876–1936) first edition of the *Taiwan tongshi* was published in Taipei in 1920–21.

34. In the early twentieth century, the monk Jueli accompanied his nun disciples to Yongquan Temple in Fujian to pursue Buddhist studies and become ordained, see section below.

35. Li 2000: 87–88.

36. Li 2005: 42.

37. Jones 1999: 86.

38. In November 1919, Chinese monks at Kaiyuan Temple held the first ordination for nuns in Taiwan, following its 1917 ordination for monks. Shi Huiyan 1999: 263–64.

39. Jones 1999: 35; 83–92.

40. The Japanese authorities intensified their efforts to control Buddhist personnel and activities after the 1915 "Xilai An Incident." A plot to overthrow the colonial government was mapped out at Xilai An, and among those later arrested and punished for intent to insurrection were lay Buddhists practicing the "vegetarian religion."

41. The complicated interactions among Chinese Buddhist temples and monastics in Taiwan, the various vegetarian sects, Japanese Buddhism, and the Japanese colonial administration during the period 1895–1945 are beyond the scope of this chapter. See Chen 1992, Jiang 1996: 100–243, Jiang 2001, and Jones 1999: 33–96.

42. The five great Chinese Buddhist temples of the Japanese period included Lingquan temple in Jilong; Fayun Temple in Xinzhu; Kaiyuan Temple in Tainan; Chaofeng Temple in Kaohsiung County, and Lingyun Chan Temple in Taipei.

43. Shi Huiyan 1999: 261–64.

44. Travagnin in Tsomo 2004a: 87–88.

45. All three nunneries still exist but are now small institutions and their influence has greatly diminished.

46. Li 2000: 92–93.
47. Kan 1999: 58.
48. Ibid., 13.
49. Li 2005: 50–52.
50. Ibid., 43–46.
51. Li 2000: 91–95.

52. Jianye 1999: 11–12; Chuandao 2004a: 63; Travagnin 2004a: 83–96. The nun Tianyi is one such example, discussed in Chapter 5.

53. It is unclear how many nuns from China came to Taiwan at that time. Li 2005: 64.

54. Jianye 1999: 7, 9; 23–32. See Jiang 2003: 3–246 for more details on this crucial transitional period, as well as Luminary Publishing Association 1997b: 93. Also, Li 2000: 97 stresses the important role that the nun Yuanrong played in the 1953 ordination, as she negotiated between the indigenous Taiwanese monastics and the Buddhist Association of the Republic of China.

55. Li 2000: 109. Three leading Chinese monks of the Japanese era had already died: Jueli in 1933, Shanhui in 1945, and Benyuan in 1947. For more information about the "fate of *zhaijiao*" during and after Japanese colonial rule, see Jones 1999: 88–92.

56. Li 2000: 83–85.
57. Li 2005: 64–65.
58. Li 2002: 3.
59. Kan 2004: 287.
60. Cheng 2007: 155.

61. Of course, these teachings were not completely absent, for most nuns learned about (and may have interpreted literally) females' "Five Hindrances" (from the *Lotus Sūtra*) restricting them from attaining Buddhahood, and, the "Eighty-Four Kinds of Women's Ugly Gestures" a list of negative "feminine traits" such as narrow-mindedness, bad-temper, insolence, ignorance, jealousy, etc. that nuns should overcome; this tract also teaches nuns "correct" body movements and body language, to avoid attracting attention to herself and to avoid "distracting" the monks. "To a great degree, these eighty-four requirements are very similar to the Confucian parameters of a humble lady." Li 2000: 112–13. Another example among many that could be cited is that of the monk Guangqin, who "required his nun disciples to spend the first seven years in the kitchen..." not only, as required of most new monks and nuns, to fulfill one's duties as part of the monastic community, but also because to Guangqin, "cooking is the best way to repay the karma of being born in the female body." Additionally, Wei-yi Cheng writes that nuns in Taiwan have been usually prohibited from leading ghost rituals, apparently due to the popular belief in "women's polluting nature and inferior karma" (2007: 65–66) and that the misogynist "Blood Bowl *Sūtra*" used to be narrated at women's funerals in Taiwan. Crane (2001) studied one temple in Taiwan, led by a monk, with monk and nun disciples, whose nuns are especially determined to overcome "the negative qualities of females," "female pollution," and the "heavier karma and bad fate of women," all of which hinder their spiritual path, so that they practice in every way to become "men in spirit" in this life, with the hope of being reborn in a man's body. Yet both Li Yuzhen and Wei-yi Cheng also found in their research that some nuns agreed that there are extra burdens and difficulties of being

born in a woman's body, but interpreted these in a positive light, as challenges to overcome, thus manifesting women's powerful spiritual sensibility. Li 2000: 11, Cheng 2000: 67. Furthermore, Taiwanese women refute the idea of "women's inferior karma" by stressing that Bodhisattvas can and do appear in female form. Cheng 2007: 68.

62. Li 2000: 112. Sukdham Sunim writes that Korean nuns had been excluded from obtaining formal monastic education from the fifteenth century until 1956. In an interesting parallel with Taiwan's case, "... Korean monk masters in the 1950s played a major role [in] educating Korean nuns, with the hopes that nuns would play vital roles to rebuild Korean Buddhism," because institutional Buddhism had been oppressed under the Choson Dynasty from 1400–1910, then suffered under Japanese colonial rule and its Buddhist policies, and has had to compete with Christianity for followers and funds. "Crossing Over the Gender Boundary in Gray Rubber Shoes: A Study on Myoom Sunim's Buddhist Monastic Education," in Tsomo 2006: 218–27. Quotation is from page 221.

63. Li 2000: 117–18; Jianye 1999: 30; Travagnin 2004b: 196.

64. Li 2005: 70.

65. Li 2000: 113–14.

66. To ordain a female candidate, most *vinayas* state that ten nuns are required for the first ceremony in the nuns' *sangha* and ten monks for the second ceremony in the monks' *sangha*. Li 2000: 341–42.

67. Ibid., 107–20.

68. Ibid., 125–29.

69. Ibid., 209. Though Ven. Heng Ching and many other senior nuns support dual ordination, Ven Chao Hwei, in the spirit of monastic gender equality, suggests that a committee of ten qualified nuns is sufficient to ordain nuns, without the second ordination by monks. Chiu Min-chieh, "Fojiao dui nuxing zhuyi de sikao: yi Zhaohui fashi de fojiao nuxing zhuyi lunshu weili" [Buddhist Thinking on Feminism: Taking Venerable Chao-hwei's Exposition of Buddhist Feminism as an Example]. Paper presented at the International Conference on Religious Culture and Gender Ethics, Hsuan Chuang University, Nov. 24–25, 2007: K8–9.

70. Travagnin 2004b: 186–87. Translation is by Travagnin.

71. Jiang 1992: 84–85, citing an exchange of letters between the two masters. Shengyan had sought Yinshun's guidance about his (SY's) plans to found a new Buddhist organization but what to do about the large number of nuns? Bingenheimer 2004: 160–61. "The ordination of Mahāprajāpatī, the first *bhikkhunī* . . . is said to have been conferred by the Buddha only upon the nuns' acceptance of the eight special rules. . . ." Traditionalists invariably point to this to justify gender hierarchy in Buddhist institutions. But recent "textual analysis reveals that these discriminatory passages have been artificially embedded in earlier texts" and could not have been uttered by the Buddha. As one glaring example, the "nuns' assemblies" did not exist yet at the time of Mahāprajāpatī's ordination. (Tsomo, "Mahāprajāpatī's Legacy," in Tsomo 1999: 27–28. The eight *garudhammas* are 1. A nun must always show deference to a monk, however junior in age or experience the monk is. 2. A nun should not spend the rain-retreat in a place without monks. 3. The monthly ceremony of *vinaya* reading should be led by a monk. 4. At the end of the rain-retreat, a nun must report on actual or suspected breaches of discipline before the assemblies of monks and nuns. 5. If a nun commits

a serious offense, she must confess before the assemblies of monks and nuns. 6. After the two-year period as a novice, she must be ordained by the assemblies of both monks and nuns. 7. A nun must never offend or insult a monk. 8. A nun cannot admonish a monk, but a monk may admonish a nun. Keown 2003: 99–100. See Chapter 6 for more discussion of the Eight Special Rules in Taiwan.

72. Adopting out daughters, whether to relatives, or to non-kin for a price, was a common practice in Taiwan from the Qing dynasty up to the 1970s. Some young girls who were adopted into non-related families later married their adopted brothers and became daughters-in-law, called *tongyangxi*. During the Japanese era, the commoditization of *yangnu* increased, with a variety of formal and detailed contracts in the transactions. Gates 1996: 127; Lin Manqiu et al. *Taiwan xin nuren* [Portraits of Women in Taiwanese History]. Taipei: Yuanliu, 2000: 161–63. However, it is as yet unknown how many *yangnu* became nuns in Taiwan. Ven. Zhengyan is one example; see Chapter 2 for more details.

73. *Xin juesheng*, vol. 12, no. 3, Dec. 15, 1965, p. 5. Kan 2004: 410–11.

74. Kan 2004: 289; 412.

75. Ibid., 279–80; 409–10.

76. Kan 1999: 229–30.

77. Kim Gutschow's brilliant study of Tibetan Buddhist nuns in the Zangskar region of the Indian Himalaya clearly details "the economy of merit within which nuns and monks operate [albeit, in different and unequal ways] on behalf of their village clients to produce merit and other ritual effects." In this exclusively Buddhist economy of merit, "... frequent and ongoing village and household rites rely on extensive reciprocities and networks between the monastic and lay spheres." Gutschow 2004: 83–89.

78. See Li Yuzhen's "Fojiao lianshe..." (2000) on laywomen's vital participation in Pure Land Buddhist Lotus Societies in twentieth-century China and Taiwan. During the martial-law era, the Nationalist party-state forbade any open religious proselytizing in public schools, and religious personnel of any religion were rarely allowed to lecture in public schools, etc. Thus, Buddhist student groups on campus registered with their schools as "study" or "culture" groups. Kan 2004: 465–511, especially 482, 489–90.

79. Ibid., 466–68.

80. Jianye 1999: 9.

81. See Appendix Two of Li Yuzhen's doctoral dissertation for biographical capsules of fifteen eminent nuns in Taiwan.

82. Luminary Publishing Association 1997b: 100.

83. Cheng 2007: 48–49, and Shi Tzu Jung, "The Development of the Bhikkhunī Order" in Tsomo 2004a: 77. "Haven't you heard of the 'five dragons of Foguangshan'? Without these five dragons [the five senior *bhikkhunī* disciples of Xingyun], Foguangshan would be nothing." Cheng 2007: 48–49. Dragons in Chinese culture are positive and auspicious symbols.

84. Jiang 1992: 77–85.

85. Interview with *fangzhang* Ven. Jingxin, Aug. 5, 2000, Kaohsiung.

86. Li Yuzhen, "Bodhisattva Kṣitigarbha and Buddhist Nuns in Contemporary Taiwanese Bhikkhunīs," in Tsomo 2006: 190–96.

87. Jiang 1992: 77–85; Li Yuzhen 2004a: 98–99.
88. Interviews with Shi Rongzhen, May 11–12, 2007, Hong Kong.
89. Interviews with Shi Lianchan, Dec. 2001 and June 2002, Taipei.
90. Interview with Shi Shanhui, Sept. 4, 1999, Jiayi.
91. Faure 2003: 40–51.
92. Tsai 1994: 2.
93. The validity of these earlier nuns' ordinations was debated at the time. "All the *vinayas* indicate a minimum number of monks and nuns to be present at the ordination ceremony. To ordain a male candidate, ten monks are needed in the [monks' *sangha*]. In border regions, a group of five monks is sufficient. To ordain a female candidate, most *vinayas* state that ten nuns are required for the first ceremony in the [nuns' *sangha*] and ten monks for the second ceremony in the [monks' *sangha*]. In border regions, five nuns and five monks can presumably carry out the ordination." Ann Heirman, "Chinese Nuns and Their Ordination in Fifth Century China," in *Journal of the International Association of Buddhist Studies*, vol. 24, no. 2, 2001: 275–304. Quotation is from pages 294–95.
94. Tsai 1994: 2, 5–6; Ranjani de Silva, "Reclaiming the Robe: Reviving the *Bhikkhunī* Order in Sri Lanka," in Tsomo 2004: 121; Chikusa Masaaki, "The Formation and Growth of Buddhist Nun Communities in China," in Ruch 2002: 12.
95. Chikusa Masaaki, Ibid., 3–20. Also see Tsai 1994.
96. Hinsch 2006: 16–17. At the same time, *Lives of the Nuns* praises the nun Fasheng for adopting and caring for an elderly widow, thus extending "filial piety" beyond the boundaries of one's own family into "an expression of universal Buddhist morality," of universal compassion. Ibid., 23. See also Cole 1998.
97. Hinsch 2006: 16.
98. Li 1989; Levering 1991, 1992, 1998, 2000; Hsieh 1991; and Grant 1996.
99. Shi Zhenhua. 2005. *Xu biqiuni zhuan* [Lives of the Nuns, Continued]. Beijing: Xianzhuang shuju.
100. It is premature to conclude, (as do Faure 2003: 27 and Susan Mann, *Precious Records: Women in China's Long Eighteenth Century*. Stanford: Stanford University Press, 1997: 10) that Confucian anti-clerical literature and anti-clerical laws of the late Imperial period effectively and consistently prevented women from becoming nuns in the Ming and Qing eras. See Goossaert 2000 and 2006.
101. Zhenhua's findings will help correct the false hierarchy often drawn between "Chan-mediation-monastic" *versus* "Pure Land-devotional-lay." See Qin: 2000, Chapter 5, for a sophisticated interpretation of Pure Land meditation practice as a means to transform the body and mind.
102. Economic production is another under-explored aspect in the history of nuns. Some Jiangnan nunneries in the Song dynasty specialized in silk weaving, and according to nineteenth-century foreigners' reports, nuns (though unclear what kind) engaged in various economic activities such as tea-picking (Sichuan), embroidery, sewing, spinning, and weaving, and raised orphans to become workers and potential ordinands (Chaozhou). Gates 1996: 50; 194.
103. In 1927, Taixu suggested that China should have 20,000 nuns, by which he meant, of high quality. "Sengzhi jinlun" [On the monastic system today]. *Hai Chao*

Yin [Sound of the Tide], vol. 8, nos. 4–5. The Chinese Buddhist Association estimated that in 1930, China had 225,700 nuns, but it is unclear what type of nun this referred to. Goossaert 2000: 11–12.

104. Looking at examples of existing scholarship, Holmes Welch's *The Practice of Chinese Buddhism, 1900–1950,* excludes the subject of nuns. Chün-fang Yü's *magnum opus* (2000) includes many scattered references to Buddhist nuns, but has more sustained discussion on various aspects of "domesticated religiosity" in late Imperial China. Likewise, Zhou Yiqun's 2003 article on female religiosity in late Imperial China focuses on laywomen, not nuns.

105. Tsung 1978; Chern 2000.

106. Li 2000: 266, 287–89; Appendix 2.

107. Ibid., 284–85.

108. Chandler 2004: 151–52; Li, "Religiosity and Leadership Among Taiwanese Buddhist Nuns," in Tsomo 2004a: 104, note 12.

109. Jianxian, "Fojiao nuxing de tiaozhan yu weilai" [The challenge and future of Buddhist women]. *Xiang'guang zhuangyan,* vol. 84, Dec. 20, 2006.

110. Li Lijun. 2006. "Shi Jianduan fashi" [Master Jianduan]. *Renlai lunbian yuekan* [Renlai Monthly: A Chinese monthly of cultural, spiritual, and social concerns], Oct., 44–45.

111. Each temple has a different training and selection process, but most require that potential members obtain their family's consent. Buddhist circles in Taiwan are especially sensitive to this issue due to the "Zhongtai Chan Temple Incident." In 1996, at the end of Zhongtai's Buddhist summer camp for college students, 129 female students decided to be tonsured, without informing their families, leading to frantic parents rushing to the temple and physically forcing their daughters home, some trussed up with rope. Most observers in Taiwan, Buddhist monastics included, criticized Zhongtai for their irregular and non-transparent recruitment process and charged both Zhongtai and the students with violating the strictures of filial piety. See Li 2000: 260–65.

112. Though each monastery must obey the *vinaya* for general guidance, the details about daily operations, fiscal and personnel administration, and long-term missions are decided by each Master and disciples. Monastic education and training is also based on the *vinaya,* but the actual courses of study, length of novitiate period, selection process, etc., are also decided by each monastery. Each monastery is an autonomous authority unto itself, according to the principles of self-regulation and self-examination. Each monastery forms its own customary laws as well as Constitution and by-laws, ideally reached through group consensus.

113. During the course of my fieldwork I was unable to find out information about the numbers or rates of nuns returning to lay life. David Chandler compared monastic community numbers at Foguangshan, 1988 and 1997, and found an overall dropout rate over these nine years of thirty-seven percent, with a much higher dropout rate among monks than among nuns. Chandler 2004: 206–12.

114. Influenced by Western feminism, former Vice-President Annette Lu pioneered the women's movement in Taiwan from the early 1970s, despite the dangers involved in organizing sociopolitical movements during the martial law years. See Chapters 12 and 16 in Farris, Lee, and Rubinstein 2004.

115. See the many books edited by Karma Lekshe Tsomo, who in 1987 pioneered this movement by founding "Sākyhadhitā: International Association of Buddhist Women" with other concerned Buddhist women. On the founding of Sākyadhitā, see Karma Lekshe Tsomo, *Sākyadhitā: Daughters of the Buddha*. Ithaca, N.Y.: Snow Lion Publications, 1989, and "Mahāprajāpatī's Legacy: The Buddhist Women's Movement, An Introduction," in Tsomo 1999: 1–44.

116. See also Li Yuzhen's dissertation 2000: 12–14 and Cheng 2007: 190–91.

117. Interview with Shanhui, Sept. 4, 1999, Jiayi.

118. Yikong 1992: 1.

119. Interview with Jingxin, August 5, 2000, Kaohsiung.

120. Chao Hwei 2001: 4. Ven. Chao Hwei "... promotes such female characteristics as 'gentleness,' self-respect and self-worth, and a 'spirit of giving.'" Chiu Min-chieh, "Fojiao dui nuxing zhuyi de sikao: yi Zhaohui fashi de fojiao nuxing zhuyi lunshu weili" [Buddhist Thinking on Feminism: Taking Venerable Chao Hwei's Exposition of Buddhist Feminism as an Example]. Paper presented at the International Conference on Religious Culture and Gender Ethics, Hsuan Chuang University, Nov. 24–25, 2007: K2, K10.

121. This book takes issue with Hillary Crane's assertion that "(r)ather than built on physical difference, gender is correlative and built on relationships . . . A Chinese woman . . . is only a woman insofar as she is performing the role of a woman (as daughter, mother, wife, etc.) in relation to others" (Crane 2001: 237). I argue that gender in Taiwan is constructed, built on perceived "essential" sex differences, as well as correlative, built on relationships; far from being contradictory, these are mutually reinforcing concepts. Crane's thesis that ". . . nuns work hard at constructing and performing a masculine gender they expect will in turn produce a masculine body" (Ibid., 241) is primarily based on observations of one atypical Buddhist monastery and seems to have over-relied on the constructivist arguments of works like Zito and Barlow, eds. 1994. *Body, Subject, and Power in China*. Chicago: University of Chicago Press.

122. In contrast, nuns on Mt. Emei, according to Qin Wenjie's findings, approach their struggle to reconstruct their Buddhist practices having been "ingrained" with Chinese Communist ideals of gender and social equality. These nuns look to Buddhism to realize the ideals of equality and liberation that Communism had promised but failed to achieve. Qin 2000: 465.

Chapter 2

1. An earlier form of this chapter was published in DeVido and Vermander, eds., *Creeds, Rites, and Videotapes: Narrating Religious Experience in East Asia*. Taipei: Taipei Ricci Institute 2004: 75–103.

2. Huang and Weller 1998: 391. There are numerous works on the Ciji organization, see Jiang 1997; Huang and Weller 1998; Ding 1999; Weller 1999; Huang 2001; Laliberté 2004 and the many works of Lu Hwei-syin. I am indebted to Dr. Lu Hwei-syin for the time and insights she has given me.

3. As claimed by the Ciji Foundation. C. Julia Huang has written a number of articles on Ciji and globalization, such as Huang 2003 and "Sacred and Profane?

The Compassion Relief Movement's Transnationalism in Taiwan, the United States, Japan, and Malaysia," in *The European Journal of East Asian Studies*, vol. 2, no. 2 (Autumn 2003): 220–25.

4. Chapter 3 will address the nuns of Ciji. Ciji bears some resemblance to Japan's Sōka Gakkai (Value-Creation Society, with exclusive devotion to the *Lotus Sūtra*). Both are large, hierarchical, wealthy, international Buddhist groups with millions of lay-members; both carry out missions of education, relief work, culture, and environmentalism. But unlike Ciji, Sōka Gakkai is directly involved in domestic politics and international diplomacy and holds an anti-war stance. Daniel Mertraux, "The Soka Gakkai: Buddhism and the Creation of a Harmonious and Peaceful Society, in Queen and King 1996: 365–400.

5. See C. Julia Huang's doctoral dissertation 2001 for a detailed and insightful study of Zhengyan and the Ciji organization. The observations and conclusions in this book regarding Zhengyan and Ciji are my own, unless otherwise cited.

6. *Taishō Tripiṭaka*, CBETA Project, T09n0276_p0384b17 (02), T09n0276_p0384b18 (02), to T09n0276_p0384b19 (03). "Their minds are calm and clear, profound and infinite. They remain in this state for hundreds and thousands of kotis and kalpas, and all of the innumerable teachings have been revealed to them. Having obtained the great wisdom, they penetrate all things." Ting Jen-Chieh, "Renjian Buddhism and Its Successors: Toward a Sociological Analysis of Buddhist Awakening in Contemporary Taiwan," in Hsu et al. 2007: 229–67. Quotation is from p. 248. For more explanation, see Shi Zhengyan, *Wuliangyi jing: Zhengyan shangren jiangshu* [An Explanation by the Shangren Zhengyan on the *Sūtra* on Immeasurable Meanings]. N.D. Taipei: Ciji Culture.

7. Shi Zhengyan 1996: 43, 174–75, and Shi Zhengyan 1993 (Trans. Lin): 160.

8. Jones 1999: 213. See Chapter Three for more discussion on teaching *Still Thoughts* in Taiwan's schools. On Ven Hiuwan, see Chen Xiuhui, *Xiaoyun fashi jiaoyu qinghuai yu zhiye* [Master Hiuwan's education sentiments and mission], Taipei: Wanzhuanlou, 2005, and on Ven. Xingyun, see Chandler 2004: Chapter 8.

9. "Still Thoughts Abode" in Chinese is *Jingsi Jingshe*.

10. Though other Buddhist and religious groups in Taiwan have their own logos, uniforms, songs, etc, for lay-members, only Ciji places such exacting emphasis on group and subgroup identity.

11. *Shangren*, literally "The Supreme Person," is one of several respectful titles for a distinguished Buddhist master in modern and pre-modern Chinese Buddhism. See Huang 2001 for more discussion on the interactions and bonds between Zhengyan and her followers.

12. Ciji values and encourages expressing one's emotions, and broadcasts the virtue of being *ke'ai*, lovable and cute, to dispel the stereotyped image of Buddhism as a solemn and repressive religion. Like performance art, emotional expression can be genuine while at the same time choreographed. On the "text and context" regarding the expression of emotions through crying and silent melody by both women and men in Ciji, see the analysis by Huang 2001, Chapter Five.

13. Shi Zhengyan 1993 (Trans. Lin): 156.

14. This topic, how and why Buddhist groups such as Ciji use the latest media technology, deserves further study informed by visual culture studies, to probe whether this obsession to literally *capture* "moments of being" on film (and written form) is

contrary to Buddhist teachings on impermanence, practice of right concentration and right mindfulness, etc.

15. At our evening small-group session, a senior member of the Ciji Teachers' Association confessed his feelings of pressure and guilt because he felt his "small" efforts could not begin to compare with other members' accomplishments, and how his fear of not living up to the *Shangren*'s expectations and high standards makes him sweat with anxiety.

16. Sangharakshita 2000: 31. Ciji does not focus on this central aspect of Buddhist teachings.

17. Sign language is used not only to communicate with the hearing impaired but also, I was told, to create an atmosphere of quietness, grace, and peace. See Huang 2001 Chapter Five for an analysis of sign language and silent melody.

18. See also Huang 2001: 46–48. But not everyone finds Zhengyan's voice and *dingning* style (like a teacher with young children) appealing; a nun from another Buddhist group told me that Zhengyan's voice is too light and high for a Buddhist master, not *zhuangyan* (solemn and dignified) enough.

19. Lu Hwei-syin, in a number of essays, remarks that Zhengyan combines the "traditional" qualities of the strict father and gentle mother, *fuyan, muci*. Stuart Chandler says the same about the monk Xingyun of Foguangshan. Chandler 2004: 37.

20. The Master urged me to stay in Taiwan and "continue to help Taiwanese society."

21. Sōka Gakkai members ". . . often speak of a 'Soka Gakkai' spirit, referring enthusiastically to the ways that this Buddhism has changed their lives." Daniel A. Metraux in Queen and King 1996: 274.

22. See Huang 2001 Chapter Five for a complete exploration of crying in Ciji. She discusses different types of crying such as confessional; redemptive, being shocked/embarrassed (being reproached by senior members); cathartic; sorrowful/empathetic upon seeing pain and suffering; ritualistic; ecstastic in meeting Zhengyan; and a contagious group response.

23. See also Huang 2001, Chapters Four and Six.

24. Pan 2004: 427.

25. Ibid., 428. Here I am reminded of how the Chinese Communist Party described the moral authority and power of the masses as a wave or tide, though of course the notion of violent class struggle couldn't be more alien to Zhengyan's philosophy.

26. Huang 2001: 137.

27. Ibid., 83.

28. Ibid.

29. See Huang 2001 Chapters One and Two for a theoretical discussion of charisma with regard to Zhengyan and the Ciji organization.

30. As mentioned in Chapter 1, adopted girls, *yangnu*, were a common phenomenon in pre-1970s Taiwan. The popular belief that an older daughter can hopefully "summon" the birth of younger brothers is called *zhaodi*. Zhengyan's younger brother Wang Duanzheng is a top lay administrator in the Ciji organization.

31. Liu 1997: 32.

32. Shi Zhengyan (Kao, ed.), 1993: 211. In a similar vein, the official hagiography of Xingyun claims that from his earliest years on, Xingyun displayed many acts of spontaneous generosity and compassion. Chandler 2004: 41.

33. Shi Zhengyan (Kao, ed.), 1993: 211.
34. Shi Zhengyan (Kao, ed.), 1993: 211–12.
35. Li 2000: 261.
36. Liu 1997: 33; Shi Zhengyan (Kao, ed.), 1993: 212.
37. Li in Tsomo 2004: 99. Shi Baochang's *Lives of the Nuns* extol Buddhist women paragons who first fulfilled their Confucian obligations to their families, often displaying exceptional and consistent filial piety from a young age, then surpassed these obligations with Buddhist practice. Hinsch 2006: 9.
38. Xiudao is a good example of a nun whose career spanned the transition in Taiwanese Buddhism before and after the 1950s. Upon her return from Japan, Xiudao, who later received the *bhikkhunī* precepts in Taiwan, founded the Ciyun temple in Fengyuan.
39. Shi Zhengyan (Kao, ed.), 1993: 212–13. It is unclear how much of this text is based on direct quotations from Zhengyan and how much is the editor's historical imagination.
40. Unless otherwise noted, this section on Zhengyan's early life relies on Chen 1983; 1984; 1989.
41. After a time in Hualian, Xiudao returned to Ciyun temple in Fengyuan and has continued as Temple head to the present, now over 80 years old, as I discovered when I called the temple and Xiudao herself answered the phone. In May 2008, after the massive earthquake in Sichuan, China, Xiudao donated NT $ 6 million (approximately US $194,000) to the Ciji organization to help with their relief efforts in Sichuan. http://www.newdaai.tv/?view = detail&id = 42003, accessed May 31, 2008.
42. There are a number of interesting parallels between the lives of Zhengyan and the Chan master Zhiyuan Xing'gang (1597–1654): Both were famed as exemplary filial daughters; neither relied on donations for their own livelihood; both are well-known as popular lecturers on the *dharma*; both have nun and lay (both female and male) disciples; and both are praised for their ceaseless charitable undertakings. Grant 1996: 54; 58–59.
43. For Zhengyan, since true compassion is more profound than words, consolation must amount to more than words and involve active physical interventions. *Fuwei* means to console using a range of expressions including tone of voice, facial expressions, and actions such as stroking or patting as a mother would comfort a child. Zhengyan often describes soothing and comfort as a type of "coolness," see the metaphor where Ciji is alluded to as an unlimited forest of Bodhisattvas-as-Bodhi trees in which "... everyone who is experiencing difficulties or feeling insecure can have a part of the coolness of Bodhi." Shi Zhengyan (Kao, ed.), 1993: 210. And to humans, suffering in this polluted world, "the people of Ciji are like a vast and cool breeze." Ibid., 208. The "Universal Door" chapter of the *Lotus Sūtra* speaks of the Bodhisattva's compassion that can transform the fires within humans into a cool, clear, lotus lake. "The 'cool and pure' is a Buddhist technical term." Miriam Levering in Cabezón 1992: 156, n. 61.
44. For years, the nuns at the Still Thoughts Abode produced small red "tearless" votive candles, especially designed to burn for ten hours without a drop of wax: instead the wax slowly melts to form a protective "skin."
45. In a sad turn of events forty years later, in 2003 the family of the doctor in question sued Ciji for defamation (though neither Zhengyan nor Ciji publications

had ever mentioned the doctor's name) and in September the Ciji organization was ordered by the court to pay NT $1.01 million (about US $30,000) to the plaintiffs; Zhengyan decided not to appeal. The activist nun Chao Hwei publicly supported Zhengyan throughout the whole trial and media frenzy, see *Hongshi Buddhist Institute Bimonthly*, vol. 61 Feb. 2003, Special Issue: "The 'Pool of Blood Incident': The Truth Comes to Light Eventually."

46. Though initially Zhengyan's mother had vehemently opposed her decision to become a Buddhist nun, she did donate money, "as if she were marrying her off," to help finance land and construction costs of the Still Thoughts Abode, and to purchase raw materials used in the nuns' handicraft endeavors. Liu 1993: 38. A Buddhist monastic is supposed to have "left home," but Chinese Buddhists for centuries have argued for the compatibility of Buddhist monasticism with filial piety, see Cole 1998. Shi Baochang [in *Lives of the Nuns*, 517] "... reconciled Buddhism with filial piety by showing how the two could be practiced simultaneously. Even after a woman had 'left home' [*chujia*] for a religious life, she could still try to honor her moral obligations to her parents." Hinsch 2006: 12. Zhengyan has had close contacts with her family over the years and her brother is the executive director of the Ciji foundation. See Li Yuzhen's dissertation for many examples of nuns' continued interactions with their natal families, including nuns' widowed mothers living with their daughters at the temple. Many Taiwanese nuns in Wei-yi Cheng's study revealed that they supported themselves through natal family and/or personal assets. Cheng 2007: 141-42. Stuart Chandler discusses the particular emphasis at Foguangshan to "include biological families [of the monastics] as part of the Foguang extended family." Chandler 2004: 238-48, quotation from page 242. Qin 2000: 200-1 and 454 also writes that most of the nuns she studied at Fuhu Temple in Sichuan maintained ties with their natal families.

47. Jones 1999: 209. However neither Zhengyan nor Ciji voice support of any political party, nor are they radical nativists intent on "de-Sinicization"; on the contrary Ciji actively promotes Confucian values. See Chapters 3 and 6.

48. See Chapter 4 for more discussion on the nuns of the Still Thoughts Abode.

49. Lu 1998: 545-46, 548-49.

50. However, a nun at another Buddhist temple described Ciji members as insecure and immature in their over-reliance on Master Zhengyan as an omniscient parental figure.

51. Ting 2007: 249-51; Brook 1993: 105-7; 185-88.

52. Shanhui Shuyuan, 1999: 300-1.

53. From the movie "Walking Across the Wounded Earth" 2001, shown to members of the Ciji Teachers' Association, April 28, 2001. To take an especially dramatic case, the force of the earthquake caused massive landslides on Chiuchiu Mountain, denuding the peaks of its upper-level vegetation.

Chapter 3

1. Besides written sources, this chapter is based on the author's notes from a fieldtrip taken with the Ciji Teachers' Association to visit Fengdong Middle School,

Xinshe Primary School, Dongshi Primary School and Dongshi Middle School, Taiwan, April 28, 2001, and the author's visits to Jiji Primary School, Jiji Middle School, Yanping Primary School, Zhongzhou Primary School, Sheliao Primary School, and Sheliao Middle School, August 5–6, 2007. An early form of this chapter was published in Chinese, "Xiwang gongcheng: Fojiao Ciji jijinhui 9.21 zaiqu xuexiao chongjian gongzuo," [Project Hope: Ciji's Post-921 Earthquake School Reconstruction Plan] in Lin, Ting, and Chan, eds. 2004: 439–60.

 2. See the works referred to in Chapter 2, note 2. There are also many theses and dissertations from Taiwan's graduate schools on Ciji's organization structure and philosophy, identity, and function as a non-governmental organization (NGO) or non-profit organization (NPO); contributions to community and civil society, etc.

 3. A few Chinese works mention Ciji's Project Hope, namely, Yao 2003, Luo 2004, and Zhang 2005, but only Yao's work takes Ciji's Project Hope as its focus.

 4. This was the most destructive earthquake in Taiwan since 1935. See Lin, Ting, and Chan 2004: 151.

 5. Reforms in education and school design were initiated by these private groups such as the Humanistic Education Foundation and concerned architects in the 1990s. See Luo 2004.

 6. See Zhang Kaiping 2005 for more details. "Project Hope" constituted in fact the third stage of Ciji's post-earthquake relief and reconstruction work, after its immediate emergency relief and medical efforts, psychological counseling, and building of temporary pre-fabricated housing and school-rooms.

 7. Yao 2003: 82.

 8. In three years, Ciji also rebuilt five schools in Bam, Iran, where 26,000 people died in the 2003 earthquake. The Filipino architect convinced the skeptical mayor to accept the schools' design, an ingenious integration of the Ciji "Still Thoughts Abode" sloped-roof with Islamic and Persian styles, by referring to Bam's historical links with the Silk Road and global networks. The schools' exteriors vary in shades of red, yellow, and green, not sombre gray like Taiwan's Ciji schools, but some schools display the Ciji logo of the Boat of Compassion, *cihang*, within lotus leaves. *Tzu Chi Monthly*, no. 484, March 25, 2007, pp. 11–27. Ciji also has completed five "Project Hope" schools in Yogyakarta, Java, Indonesia. For a Buddhist group like Ciji to successfully complete school projects in Islamic Iran and Indonesia attests to the group's superb diplomatic skills, particularly in the case of Iran, without a local Chinese community to assist in the mediation process with the government.

 9. Laliberté 2001.

 10. Guo Yiqin, Graduate Institute of Building and Planning, National Taiwan University, phone interview, August 13, 2004. Also see Yao 2003 and Zhang 2005.

 11. Taixu, "Xiandai rensheng duiyu foxue de xuyao" [Modern life's need for Buddhism]. *Hai Chao Yin* [Sound of the Tide], (May 1931), vol. 12, no. 11.

 12. The foundation states, "Humanistic Education refers to an educational philosophy that believes humans are, by nature, self-developing creatures. An educator's primary responsibility is to create an environment in which students can do their own growing."

 13. Taixu, "Fu Zhu Duomin jushi shu" [Letters to Layman Zhu Duomin]. *Hai Chao Yin* [Sound of the Tide], n.d., vol. 37, no. 67. See Chapter 6 for more discussion of *renjian fojiao*.

14. Of course, in all pre-modern societies, the individual could hardly live outside a web of family and social obligations. In the Pāli canon, the Sigālaka Sutta addresses lay ethics, and explains the six directions in terms of six primary social relationships and their mutual obligations: parents (the east); teachers (the south); wife and children (the west); friends and companions (the north); servants and workpeople (the nadir); and religious teachers and Brahmins (the zenith). Damien Keown. 2003. *Dictionary of Buddhism*. Oxford: Oxford University Press, p. 267. But Project Hope does not refer to this text.

15. The NGO "Humanistic Education Foundation" was the first to call for education reform in Taiwan and continues to lead initiatives for education reform and community revitalization. Sergiovanni 2000 addresses related trends in the United States. Xu Shirong 1999 discusses NPOs (nonprofit organizations) and the rise of community consciousness in Taiwan, while Huang Liling 1999 probes the topic of community reconstruction after the 9.21 earthquake.

16. For details see Republic of China, Ministry of Education 2004 and Zhang 2005.

17. Luo 2004.

18. Zeng Zhilang, 2004. "Yi 'xin xiaoyuan yuandong' zuowei zaiqu xiaoyuan chongjian de qidian" [Take the 'New Campus Movement' as the starting point for rebuilding of schools in the disaster area]. Zhonghua Minguo Jiaoyubu. ed., "Introduction." Also Zhang 2005.

19. Luo 2004: 176–87; Zhang 2005: 75–157.

20. Yao 2003: 137.

21. For example, at the Jiji Primary School's request, their new Activities Center, though built with concrete, was designed to recall their school's former wooden auditorium built in the Japanese era.

22. Shi Zhengyan, "Yuanyi zuo, jiu neng gaichu zhide guanmo dadi yishupin" [If we want to, we can build great works of art worthy of emulation by others], July 17, 2000. http://news.tzuchi.net/HopeProject.nsf, accessed on August 18, 2007. Luo Rong claims that Project Hope's standards for use of steel-reinforced concrete exceeded the requirements set by the government for the New School Campus Movement. Luo 2004: 161–62.

23. See Lin Minchao 2000 and Lin Huiwen 2000.

24. Yao 2003: 126 ff.

25. When asked, teachers used the adjectives open and broad, stable and firm, spacious.

26. He Youfeng, "Bosa jianzhu liangxin zhongzi" [Spread the seeds of architecture conscience]. http://news.tzuchi.net/HopeProject.nsf, accessed on July 5, 2007.

27. Shi Zhengyan, "Jiaoyu de yuanquan" [The Fount of Education], Jan. 18, 1990. http://news.tzuchi.net/HopeProject.nsf, accessed on July 5, 2007.

28. Shi Zhengyan, "Si wu xie, junzi wusuozheng" [With no evil thoughts, the gentleman has no conflicts], Jan. 18, 2001. http://news.tzuchi.net/HopeProject.nsf, accessed on July 5, 2007.

29. Ciji Cultural Mission Center, 2002. *921 Building Projects*, vol. 7, Yanping Primary School, Introduction.

30. Luo 2004: 160–61. But, one teacher remarked to me that there is enough color outside the school, with the luxurious green foliage, flowering trees, and blue sky

of rural Taiwan. Another teacher welcomes gray as a calming influence because children already have too much stimuli in their lives from television, computers, etc.

31. Yao 2003: 128.

32. Guo Shusheng 2002. "Shejishi yu shiyongzhe (xuexiao), yezhu (Ciji) jian de hudong xinde" [Reflections on the interaction among the designer, user (school), and client (Ciji)]. Ciji Cultural Mission Center, ed. *921 Building Projects*, vol. 12, Zhongxing Middle School.

33. Interview with a Project Hope architect, July 27, 2007. His last point is very important, and would take another book to fully explore, but the central Buddhist virtue for Ciji is compassion, so for Ciji, a large well-organized collective body is the best "vehicle" to undertake compassionate works. For a detailed study of the interactions among Ciji, the schools, and the architects/builders involved in Project Hope, see Yao 2003.

34. Luo 2004: 162.

35. Sheliao Primary School in Nantou uses solar energy for a part of its power needs. Taiwan, with its sub/tropical climate, could develop solar power but has not done so; the national electric company relies on nuclear power and fossil fuels.

36. Guo Shusheng 2002. "Shejishi yu shiyongzhe...," *921 Building Projects*, vol. 12, Zhongxing Middle School.

37. Zhengyan could have been inspired by these books, or by popular religious texts such as the *Dimu jing*, Earth Mother Scripture, as well. She seems informed about current debates on global warming, carbon footprints, the greenhouse effect, etc. Shi Zhengyan, "Yuwang shao yidian, ai diqiu duo yidian" [Have fewer desires, and love the Earth more]. *Tzu Chi Monthly*, no. 484, March 25, 2007, 6–9.

38. Shanhui Shuyuan, ed. 1999: 300–1.

39. Shi Zhengyan, "Yuwang shao yidian, ai diqiu duo yidian" [Have fewer desires, and love the Earth more]. *Tzu Chi Monthly*, no. 484, March 25, 2007, 9.

40. Shi Zhengyan, "Renhuo you xin qi, aixin qunji cai neng meihua shehui" [Human disasters arise from the heart: amassing loving-hearts is the way to improve society], July 17, 2000. http://news.tzuchi.net/HopeProject.nsf, accessed on August 12, 2007. Shi Zhengyan, "Huanhui qishijian de huimiequ" [Reverse the current course toward world destruction], October 9, 2001. http://news.tzuchi.net/HopeProject.nsf, accessed on August 12, 2007.

41. Former Vice-President Annette Lu was heavily criticized for her proposed solution to the perennial problem of severe erosion and flooding in the central mountain regions: Allow the over-cultivated mountain areas to rest by encouraging local residents, many of whom are non-Chinese aborigines, to emigrate to Fiji and Central America. Lin Chieh-yu, "Annette Lu again says emigration can help Aborigines." *Taipei Times*, August 5, 2004: 3. The betel-nut industry is also controversial due to first, the proven link between betel-nut chewing and incidence of oral cancer, and second, the popular phenomenon of "betel-nut beauties," scantily-clad young women who sell betel-nuts, cigarettes, and drinks from roadside sheds.

42. "You li ze an" [If there is courtesy, there is peace], *Tzu Chi Monthly*, no. 484, March 25, 2007, Editorial. Zhengyan might be aware that to Buddhist reformer Taixu, Confucius' *keji chongren* (overcome the self, esteem compassion) conveyed the fundamental spirit of Chinese culture. "Zenyang lai jianshe renjian fojiao" [How to

establish *renjian fojiao*] Taixu 1956; 1970, 47: 453. For Buddhist reformer Taixu, *keji chongren* (overcome the self, esteem compassion) conveyed the fundamental.

43. Shi Zhengyan, "Shishi xin cun haonian, heli jiu shi hao dili" [At all times have a good year in your heart, 'rationality' is good geography], Sept. 14, 2001. http://news.tzuchi.net/HopeProject.nsf, accessed on July 23, 2007. However, two school administrators told me that they consulted *fengshui* masters anyway during the building of their schools.

44. Shi Zhengyan, 1989, 184. To Zhengyan, a scientific outlook is compatible with apocalyptic ideas.

45. Shi Zhengyan, "Huanxi gan'en de yingjian wenhua: yi xiwang gongcheng gongdi wei li" [A Joyful and Grateful Construction Culture: The Example of Project Hope's Construction Sites], Feb. 10, 2001. http://news.tzuchi.net/HopeProject.nsf, accessed on July 23, 2007. C. Julia Huang calls drinking, smoking, and betel-nut chewing markers of normative Taiwanese masculinity, 2001: 234–35, but did not discuss the variations in performance of and attitude towards these habits according to social class.

46. See McCarthy 1990: 11–12; Mintz 1995; and Pascoe 1990.

47. Huang and Weller 1998: 392–95; Weller 1999: 96–102.

48. Lin Huiwen 2000:109; Yao 2003: 125–29.

49. However *nuqiangren* may also connote a positive aspect, when appealing to yearnings for upward mobility. Farris 2004: 363 relates the popularity of the 1984 novel *Nuqiangren* about a high school graduate who failed the national college entrance examination but who became a successful businesswoman.

50. Yao 2003: 83; 132–42.

51. As one Taiwanese scholar lamented to me about Ciji, "The Taiwanese were forced to submit to Japanese culture and then, during the Nationalist era, were suppressed under the weight of 'Greater Chinese culture.' When can the Taiwanese be free to be themselves?"

52. Luo 2004: 237.

53. One primary school teacher told me he selects quotations from *Still Thoughts* that students can understand, excluding Buddhist teachings on liberation, the Pure Land, etc, which he felt were beyond students' comprehension.

54. Ciji Wenhua Zhiye Zhongxin [Ciji Cultural Mission Center] 2002. *921 Building Projects*, vol. 7, *Yanping Elementary School*; Introduction. The principal of Yanping primary school views the Buddha Hand not as a religious symbol per se, but as part of "Chinese traditional culture." August 6, 2007.

55. Luo 2004: 48–50.

56. Basic Education Law: ROC Legislative Yuan, June 4, 1999. "Article Six: Principle of Neutrality and Religious Freedom. Education should be based on the principle of neutrality. Schools must not allow proselytizing on the part of any specific political or religious organization. Education administrative offices and the schools must not compel school staff, teachers, or students to participate in any political or religious activity." In addition, Luminary Buddhist nuns (see Chapter Five) have provided counseling in Kaohsiung public schools since 1999.

57. Huang and Chen 2002.

58. There are too many of these studies to list here, but they can be found easily on Taiwan's academic databases.

59. C. Julia Huang relates that due to recent education reforms, teachers had to find their own materials to teach required courses on life studies and ethics, and *Still Thoughts* seemed an apt choice for many teachers. Huang 2007: 278. "Buddhist Education and Civil Society in Modern Taiwan: Notes from The Buddhist Compassion Relief Tzu Chi Foundation's Mission of Education," in Hsu, et al. 269–83.

60. Ciji teaches in schools abroad, as well. Furong Primary School, a school for Chinese students in Seremban, Malaysia since 1997 has held a weekly *Still Thoughts* assembly where students learn Chinese moral values of propriety, justice, honesty, and shame (*li, yi, lian, chi,* the values of Chiang Kai-shek's New Life Movement, values formerly propagated in Taiwan schools); the value of maintaining order, and learning to keep silent as much as possible. The students also donate money from their recycling program to needy students. "Furong Primary School," *China Press,* (Malaysia), July 2, 2007: 5. Also see Huang 2001: 311 and 315, about Ciji Malaysia teaching in local Chinese high schools. In Fang County, Chiang Mai, Thailand, Ciji has built bilingual (Chinese-Thai) primary and secondary schools. The schools' principals are Chinese, the teachers were trained in Taiwan and *Still Thoughts* is part of the curriculum.

61. School visits, August 5–6, 2007.

62. In fact, the Still Thoughts Abode and the Still Thoughts Hall were the models for Project Hope schools, but there was room for some variation upon the main theme.

63. Kang Liwen 2002. "Chongjian xiaoyuan chengle qiye wenhua tuteng?"[Has rebuilding schools become the totem of "enterprise-culture?"], *Ziyou shibao shenghuo yiwen,* Sept. 16, p. 2.

64. Huang 2007: 282.

65. Some criticize the Ciji organization for lack of transparency about their finances, membership rolls, and decision-making process, while others resent the help Ciji gives to China and other foreign countries, without first assisting all the needy in Taiwan. Huang 2001: 255–60.

Chapter 4

1. Pan 2004: 516.

2. Huang 2001: 99.

3. "Empowerment" in Chinese is a recent neologism, variously rendered as *fuquan* (bestow-power); *chongquan* (to be full of power), *zengneng* (increase-ability/power), or *ziwo peili,* (self-strengthening). I have not yet seen these terms used in Ciji's literature, however the last two renderings are closer to the spirit of Ciji members' testimonies. They would probably reject the term *quan,* power, a politically-saturated term.

4. Zhou 2003: 121, note 31.

5. "Biology is destiny": Men and women are born with essentially different physical, mental and spiritual natures that *predetermine each sex to certain behaviors and certain social roles.* The danger is that upholding these as "natural" differences was and is a means to justify male control over women or otherwise limit women's

autonomy and choice. Essentialism also limits males' full human expression. In contrast, recent social science theory focuses on the cultural construction of gender, how the definitions of "male" and "female" are "... inculcated as part of the process of socialization...." Richman in Cabezón 1992: 112. See Sherry B. Ortner and Harriet Whitehead, eds. *Sexual Meanings: The Cultural Construction of Gender and Sexuality*, (Cambridge: Cambridge University Press, 1981) and Sherry B. Ortner, *Making Gender: The Politics and Erotics of Culture*, Boston: Beacon Press, 1996.

  6. My main sources are Huang 1999: 52–75, and my observations from several visits to the Still Thoughts Abode. On May 19, 2005, I interviewed the nun Shi Defu at Ciji University, and the nun Shi Deni and one novitiate-in-training, Lisa Shih, at the Still Thoughts Abode. Li Yuzhen's dissertation (2000) has a few pages, 316–19, on Ciji's nuns.

  7. Huang 1999: 69.

  8. From 2004, Zhengyan employed a new metaphor: The Ciji organization as a series of concentric circles, with Zhengyan at the center and layer upon layer of Ciji members going out into the world, all with hearts as clear as crystal. See Pan 2004.

  9. Either five or six, according to different Ciji sources. Huang 2001: 35

  10. Huang and Weller 1998: 385, note 7.

  11. Jones 1999: 212.

  12. Huang 2001: 66; 126–29.

  13. Huang 1999: 70.

  14. Zhengyan 1996: 209–10.

  15. Compare with Mao Zedong's self-reliant production movement in Yan'an and its use by the CCP as their symbolic capital, as a wellspring of revolutionary moral authority. See Apter and Saich 1994.

  16. Huang 1999.

  17. Interview with Ven. Deni, May 19, 2005.

  18. Interviews with Vens. Deni and Defu, May 19, 2005.

  19. Huang 1999: 61, 75.

  20. Ibid., 65.

  21. "The *locus classicus* in the Mencius states ... 'To dwell in the wide house of the world, to stand in the correct seat of the world, and to walk in the great path of the world; when he obtains his desire for office, to practice his principles for the good of the people; and when that desire is disappointed, to practice them alone; and to be above the power of riches and honor to make dissipated, of poverty and mean condition to make swerve from principle, and of power and force to make bend—these characteristics constitute the great man, (*ta-chang-fu*).'" Levering 1992: 143–44.

  22. Ibid., 142.

  23. Ibid., 142–43.

  24. Levering in Cabezón 1992: 115; Hsieh 1991; Grant 1996. The "... idea that extraordinary women are worthy of the title of *zhangfu* is ubiquitous in Ming-Qing literati writing...." Grant 1996: 63.

  25. Chen 1989: 6–7. For Zhengyan and many women in history, becoming a nun was the only relatively respectable way to transcend the socially-dictated roles of wife and mother, confined to the domestic sphere.

26. Interviews with Vens. Defu and Deni, May 19, 2005.

27. These nuns, like other monastics and laypeople I have interviewed in Taiwan for this book, hold stereotypical beliefs about male and female "characteristics." Similar to nuns in Taiwan, nuns at Fuhu Temple in Sichuan China report that the *da zhangfu* should cultivate the qualities of courage, strength, tolerance, and wisdom, still defined in Chinese culture as masculine qualities. Qin 2000: 312–16; 431.

28. Cheng 2007: 190; Li (dissertation) 2000: 14–16, respectively.

29. Chapter 5 discusses nuns and the *da zhangfu* ideal at the Luminary Buddhist Institute. Crane 2001 gives a detailed and helpful discussion about *da zhangfu*, a great man, and what this Buddhist ideal means to the nuns and monks of one temple in Taiwan. She argues that as nuns at this temple embrace the *da zhangfu* ideal they reject their female gender, as defined by Confucian moralists and Chan misogynists. As nuns internalize this ideal of the *da zhangfu* in behavior and thought, she claims they become men in spirit and even in physical reality (loss of feminine body shape and cessation of menses). Her dissertation is problematic because she draws conclusions about "Buddhist nuns in Taiwan" based primarily on her observations of one temple; she refers to culture, society, and gender in "China" when in fact she is describing Taiwan; she provides very little historical and social context; she uses no Chinese sources; and the English ethnographical sources are out of date.

30. Qin 2000: 319–20.

31. Hs'ing 1983: 38–40.

32. Hsieh 1991: 180, citing Overmyer in Shinohara and Schopen 1991: 105–9, and Barend J. ter Haar, *The White Lotus Teachings in Chinese Religious History*, Leiden: E. J. Brill, 1992: 31–43.

33. Yü 2001: 337.

34. Zhou 2003: 113.

35. Zhao 2003: 157.

36. Huang 2001: 104.

37. An important part of any economy that may not be measured in the GNP. Moon 2002: 480, note 7.

38. Huang 2001: 103.

39. Yeh, http://taipei.tzuchi.org.tw/tzquart/99fall/99fall.htm, accessed on July 2, 2007.

40. Liu 1997: 133, 26. These are regular gender norms in Taiwan and Ciji members do not regard these statements as sexist.

41. Yeh, http://taipei.tzuchi.org.tw/tzquart/99fall/99fall.htm, accessed on July 2, 2007. Overseas disaster relief is mostly undertaken by males, who are deemed, according to Taiwan's gender norms, "more suitable" to face the rigors of such overseas assignments.

42. C. Julia Huang 2001: 150, 184–85, made fascinating comments about the organizational and programmatic influence upon Ciji by the Nationalist Party's (KMT) China Youth Corps.

43. From 1992 the Ciji Youth Corps has endeavored to mobilize the student population through camps and volunteer training opportunities. But it remains to be seen whether young people can identify with and propagate the Ciji's code of behavior, appearance, and values and whether young people will join Ciji and be fully dedicated members like their parents' generation.

44. Wang Fansen, "Mingdai xinxuejia de shehui juese—yi Yan Jun de 'Jijiu xinhuo' weili" [The Social Role of the 'School of the Mind' Followers—The Example of Yan Jun's 'Emergency Treatment for the Heart's Fire']. In *Zheng Qinren jiaoshou rongtui jinian lunwenji* [Essays in Honor of Professor Zheng Qinren's Retirement]. Taipei: Daoxiang, 1999: 249–66.

45. Brook 1993: 185–203.

46. Yang 2002: 62.

47. Jiang 2001 and Jones 1999: 14–30.

48. Yü 2001: 414. Barbara Reed similarly writes, "... The Chinese since the Sung Dynasty have 'seen' Buddhist compassion as female: female figures surrounded by female symbols." Reed in Cabezón 1992: 164. But neither Yü nor Reed can explain why this is so.

49. Hsieh 1991: 178.

50. Reed in Cabezón 1992: 160. The cult of Guanyin is popular throughout East Asia and Vietnam; the Chinese regard Mount Putuo as her "residence." "Since the later third century... Buddhists have gone on pilgrimages to Mount Putuo [an island off the Zhejiang coast] to worship Guanyin's relics. During the Tang dynasty... a sacred Buddhist altar... was founded at the island, and has remained a focal point for cult worship of Guanyin there for more than a thousand years." Zhao Hongying and Xu Liang, "Putuoshan guanyin xinyang de lishi, chuanshuo ji qi yingxiang" [History, Legend and Influence of the Cult of the Bodhisattva Guanyin at Mount Putuo]. In *Min-su ch'ü-i* [Journal of Chinese Ritual, Theatre, and Folklore], no. 138: 112.

51. Yü 2001: 338–39.

52. Li, "The Religiosity and Leadership of Taiwanese Buddhist Nuns," 2004a: 100.

53. Ibid., 97. Also see Li Yuzhen's dissertation 2000, Chapter Five.

54. See Topley 1975, Sankar 1978, and Sangren 1983.

55. Yü 2001: 335–36. To older laywomen on Emei Mountain in China, Miaoshan's story affirms that laywomen can attain spiritual independence while still fulfilling familial responsibilities. Qin 2000: 328–29.

56. Reed in Cabezón 1992: 159–61; 176.

57. Reed in Clart and Jones 2003: 199.

58. Reed in Cabezón 1992: 171–72.

59. Ibid., 172.

60. Ibid.

61. Shi Zhengyan 1996: 29, 169–70, 172.

62. Ibid., 173. Mei 1998: 168 points outs Zhengyan's acceptance of the sexual double standard in Taiwan society: it is inconceivable to imagine the same advice being directed at a husband regarding a wife's affair.

63. Shi Zhengyan (Trans. Lin) 1993: 171–72, 1996: 2, 179–80.

64. The Chinese word for "capable" is *neng'gan*, one of the greatest compliments paid to Taiwanese women, and means much more than "capable," but omni-competent and super-efficient, anticipating others' needs and fulfilling them, without question or hesitation.

65. Shi Zhengyan 1996: 167.

66. Reed in Cabezón 1992: 175.

67. Lu 1998: 539.

68. Shi Zhengyan 1996: 26.
69. Ibid., 171.
70. Ibid., 174–75.
71. Older Buddhist laywomen on Emei Mountain in Sichuan sing folksongs lauding similar ideals. Qin 2000: 321–33. These songs belong to the *fumu en nan bao* genre [it is difficult to repay the debts of gratitude owed to one's parents] in Chinese Buddhist literature. See Cole 1998.
72. Shi Zhengyan 1996: 259. Zhengyan says "compassion breeds wisdom," probably alluding to the course of the Bodhisattva path, which "begins with giving rise to the 'aspiration to enlightenment (*bodhicitta*).' " Through cultivation of compassion, through the vow to liberate all sentient beings, the Bodhisattva also aspires "... to attain the wisdom and skill-in-means necessary to teach." Levering 2000: 190. But as José Cabezón has discussed, the Indo-Tibetan Mahāyāna texts describe "wisdom" as the mother of all types of "spiritually-accomplished individuals" who then need male "compassion" and "altruism" to possess full Mahāyāna "paternity." Cabezón in Cabezón 1992: 181–99. Rita Gross 1993: 11 reminds us that the imagery in Vajrayāna Buddhism "... portrays all the Buddhas and Bodhisattvas as partners—male and female—in sexual union. The fundamental pair consists of discriminating awareness (*prajñā*), which brings insightful liberation, and her partner, compassion (*karuṇā*). Though she represents the epitome of realization, she is not isolated, but is joined in male-female union with compassion, understood as activity to save all sentient beings." It is important to note these qualities of "feminine" insight/wisdom and "masculine" compassion are qualities to be cultivated within each person, and are not referring to actual or ideal social roles.
73. Gutschow 2004: 16–19; 224–25. Quotation is from page 218. Also see Faure 2003: 126.
74. But Cheng 2007: 57–83 found that many Sri Lankan *bhikkhunī* and ten-precept nuns "dismiss the idea of women's inferior karma" and firmly believe that women can become arahants.
75. Sponberg in Cabezón 1992: 3, 13, 18.
76. Keyes 1984: 227–30. Kate Crosby's study of a wide range of Theravāda texts (not limited to the Theravāda canon) finds examples of the valorization of feminine embodiments of compassion, wisdom, and other female-inclusive symbols therein, based however, on "... two aspects of motherhood: protective nurturing and procreation." However, Crosby concedes that such symbolic valorization of motherhood cannot "be taken as a historical valorization of women as human beings," though mothers and motherhood were both culturally valued and mother-related symbols were vital to the spiritual practice of celibate males. "Gendered Symbols in Theravāda Buddhism: Missed Positives in the Representation of the Female." Paper presented at the International Conference on Religious Culture and Gender Ethics, Hsuan Chuang University, Nov. 24–25, 2007. Quotations are from pages D: 13–14.
77. See, for example, the *Ekottara Āgama*, 32, 0725c07.
78. This quotation refers to Western women active in nineteenth-century reform movements such as prohibition, poor relief, anti-prostitution, public hygiene, etc. Duby and Perrot in Pantel 1992: xi–xii.
79. Interviews with Vens. Defu and Deni, May 19, 2005.

80. Hughes and Hughes 1997: 153–56.
81. Gross 1993: 264–65. On eco-feminism, see Plant 1989; Diamond and Orenstein 1990; and Adams 1993. On feminist spirituality, see Sered 1996: 205–6.
82. Bisnath 2002: 2–3.
83. Ibid.
84. As reported to me by Ciji's lay followers.
85. Lu 1998: 544.
86. The woman in the first case (whose throat and stomach are permanently damaged by the suicide attempts) did not get divorced while the second one did. Fan 2001: 1 and Lai 2001: 2.
87. Laliberté 2003: 176–77. The Taiwan's Government Information Office Web site's section on "social welfare" discusses government efforts together with Ciji's contributions.

Chapter 5

1. Li 2005: 66–68.
2. Li argues however that many nuns viewed cooking as part of their Chan spiritual practice, and making the most of their limited voice and segregated space, built social networks different from the monks,' via female bonding with other nuns and laywomen. Furthermore, Li writes that nuns' cooking (for ritual celebrations and visiting pilgrims, etc) was "... essential for monastic finances." Additionally, for many nuns, success in the kitchen was crucial to their promotion to positions related to temple finance and administration. Li (dissertation) 2000: 300, 336–37.
3. Reflecting the many talents of the nuns and in response to lay interests and backgrounds, classes (besides Buddhist courses) include music and the arts such as at Yanghui, which has produced a CD of Luminary songs; while in stressful Taipei, the Yinyi branch holds classes in yoga, aromatherapy, organic food and healthy eating, psychological health, Buddhist camp for college students, and reading Buddhist works in English, one by Thích Nhất Hạnh.
4. See Ding 1996; Shi Jianye 2001and 2004; Shi Zichun 2002; and Cheng 2003 and 2007. Chün-fang Yü of Columbia University has a forthcoming monograph on the nuns of the Luminary Buddhist Institute. I thank Dr. Yü for sending me her paper on Luminary's outreach programs entitled "Bringing the Dharma to the People: The Adult Education Classes on Buddhism in Taiwan." See also Yü 2003. In addition to the works just mentioned, for this chapter I have relied on publications from the Luminary Buddhist Institute, their Web site, www.gaya.org.tw, and my visits to Jiayi and to their Taipei Yinyi Institute. Also I conducted interviews with Ven. Wu Yin (*fangzhang* means "head monk") in 1999 and 2002, and with Ven. Mingjia, formerly with the Luminary Buddhist Institute in 1999.
5. Cheng 2003: 44, 49–50; Cheng 2007: 47.
6. The central government hopes religious groups will take on even more social welfare work, as evidenced by two lectures given by the Director of the Department of Social Affairs, Xiao Yuhuang, on April 29 and June 17, 2007 at the Luminary Buddhist Institute.

7. Shi Zichun et al., 1992: 126. Yü Chün-fang adds that Wu Yin's father so vehemently opposed her becoming a nun that he swore never to see her again. Before his death ten years later, Wu Yin saw him once, when she returned home for a visit. Yü 2003: 274-75. Yet, Wu Yin recalls that both her parents sobbed terribly when she told them she would become a nun, and her mother told her to wait until she (her mother) saved enough money to give her so (Wu Yin) wouldn't' suffer so much. Wu Yin declined her mother's offer, preferring to be self-reliant. Wu Yin, "Chujia de yiyi" [The meaning of 'becoming a monastic'] speech at ordination ceremony, May 12, 1996, Luminary Temple, Jiayi.

8. Shi Jianye 1999: 323.

9. Rare for females of her generation, Tianyi received both high school (Pingdong Girls' High School, a Japanese school) and university education (Showa University in Tokyo). Shi Jianye 1999: 38-39.

10. Shi Jianye 1999: 148-50; Shi Zichun et al. 1992: 128-29; Cheng 2003: 46. In honor of Tianyi, Wu Yin named Luminary's Taipei branch, *Yinyi*, Tianyi's other *dharma* name.

11. Shi Jianye 1999: 396. Tianyi told her disciples that nuns were not secular women anymore and should rid themselves of girlish attitudes, *nu' er tai*, and secular women's looks and behavior, *nuzhong xiqi*. Li 2005: 68.

12. Compare with Zhengyan (b. 1937) who decided to become a Buddhist nun when she was working with her nun friends in a rice-paddy. Later, a conversation with Catholic nuns was one reason Zhengyan devoted her life to provision of charity and medical service.

13. Ding 1996: 425; Shi Jianhan et al. 1992: 11-12; Shi Zichun et al. 1992: 127-28.

14. *Xiang'guang zhuangyan* (literally, *xiang* is fragrant; *guang* is bright, and *zhuangyan* denotes the splendid sublime qualities of the Buddha) are four characters displayed in Luminary's Guanyin Hall and is the name of one of Luminary's journals. The phrase is taken from the *Śūraṅgama Sūtra*, fifth fascicle, *Dashizhi pusa nianfo yuantong zhang* [The Bodhisattva Mahāsthāmaprāpta Recites the Buddha's Name and Attains Perfect Inter-Penetration], a well-known Pure Land text. *Xiang* conveys being clean and pure, *bright* conveys wisdom. Those who recite the Buddha's name can attain the purity and wisdom of the Buddha, the sublime qualities of the Buddha. Shi Jianhan, "Ran xinxiang, xu foguang" [Light the heart's incense, continue the light of the Buddha] *Xiang'guang zhuangyan*, vol. 89, Dec. 31, 2004.

15. Ding 1996: 420-23; Cheng 2003: 43; *Xiang'guang zhuangyan*, no. 49. 1997a: 2-93. The relationship between the Luminary nuns and the villagers has had its ups and downs, such as in 1996 when a group of townspeople, seeing Luminary's new construction projects and growing social influence, insisted that part of the land still belonged to the community and attempted by force to seize the Luminary Temple, leading to violence against the nuns, police intervention, and a law case. See the sources mentioned for more details about "The Feb. 18th Incident."

16. The Luminary Buddhist Institute's library has 31,000 books and 481 journals and each affiliated branch has a library. Luminary also publishes a *Buddhist Library Journal* and is a leader in the field of digital information management for Buddhist libraries in the Chinese. Their achievements in this and other areas

have been accomplished without the vast resources of Dharma Drum Mountain or Foguangshan.

17. Shi Zichun et al. 1992: 14, 25; Shi Jianhan et al. 1992: 34, 41.

18. "Introduction to the Director," http://www.gaya.org.tw/hkbi/visit/c_teacher1.htm, accessed on February 10, 2008.

19. Ding 1996: 426,433,435; Shi Zichun et al. 1992:129.

20. Ding 1996: 426.

21. Ibid., 439, 447; Shi Zichun et al. 1992: 200; Shi Jianhan et al. 1992: 23-24.

22. Interview with Ven. Mingjia, Sept. 1999; Shi Zichun et al. 1992: 24-28. Ordination can take place after two years of study at the Institute. Luminary also accepts ordained nuns as students.

23. Ding 1996: 443-44.

24. See Luminary's Web site, www.gaya.org.tw.

25. During my first visit to the Luminary Institute, during morning chores, a nun placed a toilet brush in my hand and asked me if I knew how to use it. I noticed that the bathroom lacked mirrors, to avoid *vanitas*, I was told. Also I read in the toilet stalls the Chinese verse: "When relieving oneself, pray: May all sentient beings be able to cast aside greed and anger, and abandon unwholesome mental states." This is one of the 141 verses on practicing mindfulness in daily activities, taken from the Purifying Practices Chapter of the *Avataṃsaka Sūtra*. I thank Ven. Zinai for this explanation.

26. Ding 1996: 431-42; Shi Zichun et al. 1992; Shi Jianhan et al. 1992. At some other temples, lay devotees, mostly women, do the cooking and daily chores, as a form of *dāna* and a source of merit. See Li Yuzhen's dissertation (2000), Chapter Six.

27. Shih Wu Yin, "Nisengjia jiaoyu de lixiang yu shixian" [The ideals and practice of nuns' education], *Xiang'guang zhuangyan*, no. 44, Dec. 20, 1995.

28. Shi Jianye 2001: 116, 148-49.

29. Shi Zichun 2002: 2. Up to now, the Taiwan government has not forbidden Ciji lay groups and teachers to teach *Still Thoughts* in public schools, or Luminary nuns to offer counseling in Kaohsiung-area public schools, activities which would have been impossible during the martial-law era.

30. These lectures were published in English as *Choosing Simplicity: A Commentary on the Bhikshuni Pratimoksha*. NY: Snow Lion Press, 2001.

31. The three-day Congress, called for and fully supported by the Dalai Lama, discussed how to establish full ordination for women in Tibetan Buddhism. See Conclusion.

32. Shi Jianxian, "Fojiao nuxing de tiaozhan yu weilai" [The challenge and future of Buddhist women]," *Xiang'guang zhuangyan*, no. 84, Dec. 20, 2006.

33. Shi Ziyao 2001: 56-59, 17-18, 25.

34. Ibid., 92-102.

35. Department of Statistics, Ministry of Interior, telephone call, August 14, 2006.

36. Shi Jianxian 2002: 17; Zeng Zhongming, General Editor. 2007. *Taiwan funu nianjian* [Taiwan Women's Almanac]: 39; 292-95; 444-54.

37. Bristow 2002. In southern Taiwan, I have seen billboards advertising "foreign brides from Southeast Asia: door-to-door service...a great package deal, no extra costs!"

38. http//www.taipeitimes.com/News/archives/2007/12/05/2003391173, accessed on Dec. 5, 2007.

39. Shi Jianxian 2002: 14; Zeng Zhongming, General Editor. 2007. *Taiwan funu nianjian* [Taiwan Women's Almanac].

40. Shi Zichun 2002: 3.

41. Shi Zichun 2002: 4–5.

42. Shi Jianxian 2002: 16–19.

43. Shi Jianxian, "Fojiao nuxing de tiaozhan yu weilai" [The challenge and future of Buddhist women], *Xiang'guang zhuangyan*, vol. 84, Dec. 20, 2006.

44. Shi Jianye 1999: 4–5, 136.

45. Shih Wu Yin, "Biqiuni jie gaishuo" [A general explanation of the *biqiuni* precepts], *Xiang'guang zhuangyan*, vol. 37, March 20, 1994.

46. *Xiang'guang zhuangyan*, 1990, 1994, 1997c.

47. Shi Zichun et al. 1992: 7.

48. Cheng 2003: 44–45.

49. Keown 2003: 138.

50. Ibid., 218.

51. Ding 1996: 427; Chern 2001; Jiang 1997: 49–60; Tsung 1978.

52. Chern 2001.

53. Chern 2001: 66–67 makes the point that Taiwan society values Buddhism primarily for its social utility.

54. Ding 1996; Jiang 1997: 49–60; *Xiang'guang zhuangyan* 1997b: 86–122.

55. As for women in China, Qin 2000 found that though today they are no longer necessarily confined to the domestic sphere, the wish to avoid the sufferings of marriage and motherhood was an important motivation for many women to join the nuns' order at Fuhu Temple in Sichuan, China. However, I never heard this wish directly stated by nuns in Taiwan as a possible reason for joining the *sangha*.

56. Li Lijun 2006. "Shi Jianduan fashi"[Master Jianduan], *Renlai lunbian yuekan* [Renlai Monthly: A Chinese monthly of cultural, spiritual, and social concerns], Oct., 44–45. See also Li Yuzhen's dissertation 2000, Chapter Six.

57. Qin 2000: 312–16; 434–41.

58. Cheng 2003: 44.

59. Ibid. Interview with Ven. Mingjia, Sept. 1999.

60. Interview with Ven. Wu Yin, Oct. 1999. To many women in Taiwan, the term "feminism" has very negative connotations, associated with the radical feminist social movement of the 1970s. Scott Simon (2003): 218 found that most Taipei women entrepreneurs whom he interviewed dismissed feminism as a Western discourse and did not credit feminism or the feminist movement as a reason for their success. Yet, in fact, thanks to the foundation built by social activists a generation ago, government and private groups in Taiwan (as in other countries) holding different political stances and ideological viewpoints are able to work on a diverse spectrum of issues related to women's rights and have brought about legal reforms which have greatly benefited women, whether or not women acknowledge this fact.

61. Shih Wu Yin 1999; Shi Zichun 2002: 5.

62. Luminary's Shi Jianxian has indeed posed the question, what links should Buddhist women have with women's groups in "Fojiao nuxing de tiaozhan yu weilai"

[The challenge and future of Buddhist women], *Xiang'guang zhuangyan*, vol. 84, Dec. 20, 2006. At present, there are hundreds of women's groups and committees in Taiwan. See Zeng Zhongming, General Editor. 2007. *Taiwan funu nianjian* [Taiwan Women's Almanac].

    63. Shi Zichun et al. 1992: 7, 132.

    64. The Taiwanese nun Tianyi worked closely with Baisheng, discussed in Chapter 1. Tianyi was considered to be his number one female disciple; he called her "king of the nuns." Shi Jianye 1999: 30–32, 78.

    65. Shi Jianhan et al. 1992: 8–9.

    66. Shi Zichun et al. 1992: 7.

    67. Ibid., 129.

    68. Shi Jianhan et al. 1992: 40.

Chapter 6

    1. Taixu and Yinshun did not provide English translations for the term *renjian fojiao*. There is no single satisfactory English translation, but scholars have variously rendered *renjian fojiao* as "humanistic Buddhism"; "worldly Buddhism"; "Buddhism 'of' or 'for' the human realm"; "Buddhism for this world"; and "Humanitarian Buddhism." This book employs "Buddhism for the human realm" as the translation best conveying the emphasis of modern Buddhists on action in the present, *human*, realm, rather than other Buddhist realms and lifetimes. As Chapter 3 discussed, the term "humanistic" is problematic, for it masks the vast differences between *renjian fojiao* (and Confucian humanism), and the "humanism" of Western religious and philosophical traditions.

    2. See also my "Mapping the Trajectories of Engaged Buddhism from China to Taiwan and Vietnam" in Karma Lekshe Tsomo, ed. *Out of the Shadows: Socially Engaged Buddhist Women*, edited by Karma Lekshe Tsomo, New Delhi: Sri Satguru Publications, India Books Centre, 2006: 261–81. Also see Chandler 2001, Chapters 3 and 4, for a lucid discussion of the differences between "Humanistic Buddhism" and Engaged Buddhism.

    3. See Thích Nhất Hạnh 1967, Queen and King 1996, Harris 1999; Đỗ 1999, Prebish and Baumann 2002, and Queen, Prebish, and Keown 2003.

    4. Bond in Queen and King 1996: 124.

    5. Ibid.

    6. Đỗ 1999: 260.

    7. Xiao Ping stresses the role of Japan as well in the Chinese Buddhist revival of the late Qing and early Republican periods. Interchange between the two countries included: reprinting of sūtras; Japanese Buddhist priests proselytizing in China; a revival of interest in Tibetan Buddhism; Chinese Buddhist monks and nuns in Japan for study and touring, and Japanese Buddhist monastics and laypeople in China for study and touring. Xiao Ping, "Zhong'guo jindai fojiao fuxing yu Riben" [China's Modern Buddhist Revival and Japan]. *Zhong'guo fojiao xueshu lundian*, no. 42, (Kaohsiung: Foguangshan wenjiao jijinhui, 2001): 1–4.

    8. Welch, 1968: 259. The discoveries at the Dunhuang caves (Gansu, China) in 1900 were a major stimulus to Buddhist studies in Europe and China.

9. Ibid., 260–62.

10. Ibid., 261.

11. Ma Tianxiang, "Wanqing foxue yu jindai shehui sichao," [Late Qing Buddhist Studies and Modern Social Thought]. *Zhongguo fojiao xueshu lundian*, no. 41, Kaohsiung: Foguangshan wenjiao jijinhui, 2001: 2–3.

12. Li Biwan, "Cibei xishe" [Being compassionate and happily letting go] in Lin Mingnan, ed. *Hongyi fashi hanmo yinyuan* [The Causes and Conditions of Master Hongyi's Art and Calligraphy], Taipei: Youshi meishu, 1996: 61.

13. On the basis of spiritual attainment, one may be reborn in the world of humans; in the heavenly realm; among those aspiring to be arhants; among the "solitary Buddhas," or among the buddhas and bodhisattvas. Pittman 2001: 171–74.

14. Bingenheimer 2007: 148; Pittman 2001: 203–4.

15. Pittman 2001: 89.

16. Welch 1968: 262–64. Chinese monasteries and laypeople throughout history, following the teachings and praxis of the Buddha and his followers, provided charity for the poor, ill, and homeless; Taixu knew this and urged Buddhists, as one way of practicing the Bodhisattva path, to place more emphasis on modern forms of social action, modeled on the work of modern Christians.

17. Pittman 2001: 182.

18. Ibid., 192–93.

19. Miaozheng, "Mantan jianshe renjian fojiao: wei jinian dashi zuo" [A casual discussion on establishing *renjian fojiao*, in the memory of the Master]. *Taixu dashi jinian ji*, Chongqing: Hanzang Jiaoliyuan, 1947: 90–91.

20. Pittman 2001: 182, 192.

21. The years 1925–1947 were a time of civil war, war against the Japanese, and a time of severe political oppression in China. Taixu's associates denied that he was a KMT member though Taixu received political and monetary support from the Nationalist government. Pittman 2001: 185.

22. Chen Yong'ge, *Ren jian chao yin: Taixu dashi zhuan* [Sound of the Tide of the Human Realm: Biography of Master Taixu]. Hangzhou: Zhejiang People's Press, 2003: 256, 259–60, 266–68, 271.

23. Ibid., 269–70.

24. Ibid., 272. Chen claims that Taixu was defeated by Chiang Kai-shek's Christian supporters, and by Chinese anti-Buddhist cultural conservatives. And, he should have added, due to the lack of support of senior monks.

25. Buddhists who remained in China formed a new Chinese Buddhist Association in 1953, firmly under the aegis of the Communist party-state; see below.

26. "Wode fojiao geming shibai shi" [History of my failed Buddhist revolution]. *Taixu dashi quanshu*, [Complete Works] 1956; 1970. 19.57.8:62–63.

27. Pittman 2001: 105–14; 118–30; 139–43. Pittman did not discuss Taixu's trip to Saigon in 1928, and Saigon and Hanoi, April 28–May 4, 1940.

28. Pittman 2001: 142–43. Holmes Welch notes that "Dharmapāla's ideal of a world Buddhist movement took root in China, first under the [efforts of layman] Yang Wenhui, 1837–1911, and later under Taixu." Welch 1968: 180.

29. This is a summary of points made by Taixu in a number of articles in his *Complete Works*.

30. See my chapter " 'Buddhism for this World': The Buddhist Revival in Vietnam, 1920–1951, and Its Legacy" in Philip Taylor, ed., *Modernity and Re-enchantment: Religion in Post-Revolutionary Vietnam*. Singapore: Institute of Southeast Asian Studies, 2007: 250–96, for more details about the links between China and Vietnam in the transnational Buddhist revival of the nineteenth and twentieth centuries.

31. Pittman 2001: 255–60.

32. See Zhe Ji's 2004 insightful article on the recent Buddhist revival in China in which he describes a three-sided relation of ongoing negotiations among the party-state, monastics, and lay supporters, each with varying economic, political, and symbolic interests. Needless to say, the growth of Buddhism in China today is inter-related with the tourist industry, the domestic and global economy, global politics, and the waning legitimacy of the official socialist meta-narrative. "Buddhism and the State, a new relationship: increasing numbers of believers bring great changes to the monastic economy in China." *Perspectives chinoises*, no. 55, Sept.–Oct. 2004: 2–3.

33. Until recently Taixu was seen as politically incorrect on *both* sides of the Taiwan Strait: too close to the Nationalist Party for (mainland) Chinese scholars, and too "radical" and controversial for scholars in Taiwan. See the excellent works by Chinese scholars recently published in a series called *Zhongguo fojiao xueshu lundian* (Academic Theses on Chinese Buddhism), such as vols. 41–43, by Foguangshan, Taiwan, and also Chen 2003.

34. Zheng Zimei, "Dangdai renjian fojiao de zouxiang: you zongjiao yu shehui hudong jiaodu shenshi," *Collected Papers from the 2004 Cross-Strait Conference on Yinshun and Humanistic Buddhism*, 38–39. Ven. Jinghui and his Bailing Temple were an integral part of Thích Nhất Hạnh's twenty-day trip to China, including *dharma* talks and retreats, in May–June 1999.

35. See Bingenheimer 2004.

36. Pittman 2001: 262.

37. Jones 1999: 110; 141–42.

38. Pittman 2001: 267–68.

39. Jones 1999: 131–33.

40. As mentioned in Chapter 1, after 1949, the various Buddhist factions from China not only competed with each other in Taiwan but also confronted a Buddhist landscape on the island that included lay vegetarian *zhaijiao* sects; temple lineages brought from Fujian and Guangdong before the twentieth century; and Japanese Buddhist schools. Jones 1999, Part III.

41. Jones 1999: 132.

42. In the 1950s, Yinshun founded the Huiri Lecture Hall in Taipei and the Fuyan Vihara and Fuyan Institute (1961) in Hsinchu. Yinshun and his students established the Zhengwen Publishers in 1980.

43. A search of Taixu's *Complete Works* found *renjian jingtu* mentioned 77 times; *rensheng fojiao* mentioned 66 times; and *renjian fojiao* 25 times. *Taixu dashi quanshu*, [Complete Works of Master Taixu-CD Rom] Hsinchu: Yinshun Culture and Education Foundation, 2005.

44. Taixu, *Taixu dashi quanshu*, [Complete Works] 1956; 1970, 47: 349–430.
45. Ibid., 47: 431–456.
46. Jiang Canteng, "Cong rensheng fojiao dao renjian fojiao," 1992: 180. In a special commemorative collection published by the Sino-Tibetan Buddhist Institute in Chongqing in 1947, Ven. Miaozheng wrote of his master Taixu that "... he worked hard for over forty years to reform the *sangha* system, attended to education, visited Europe, the USA, Burma, and India ... (in all this) his most important goal was purely to save the world's people ... his undertakings were all purely to realize *renjian fojiao* ... we can say that all of his life's writings were for the goal of establishing *renjian fojiao*." Hanzang Jiaoliyuan 1947: 89.
47. Chao Hwei 2003b: 8; 28.
48. Lu Shengqiang, "Yinshun daoshi 'Renjian fojiao' zhi pusaguan ji daocidi chutan," [Renjian fojiao: xinhuo xiangchuan: Di si jie Yinshun daoshi sixiangzhi lilun yu shixian xueshu yantaohui, *Humanistic Buddhism: Transmitting the Flame—The Fourth Conference on the Theory and Practice of the Venerable Yinshun's Teachings*, Page N-4, Lu is quoting from Yinshun's "Qili qiji de renjian fojiao," *Huayuji di sice*," pp. 48–50.
49. Ibid., N5. Lu is quoting from Yinshun's Ibid., pp. 57–63.
50. A number of Buddhist groups in Taiwan claim that they are the direct heirs and propagators of Taixu's and Yinshun's ideas and plans regarding *renjian fojiao*. To what degree these claims are accurate from a Buddhist studies' perspective is a topic beyond the scope of this book. See Marcus Bingenheimer, "Some Remarks on the Usage of Renjian Fojiao and the Contribution of Venerable Yinshun to Chinese Buddhist Modernism, in Hsu et al. 2007: 141–61, and Ting Jen-Chieh, "Renjian Buddhism and Its Successors: Toward a Sociological Analysis of Buddhist Awakening in Contemporary Taiwan," in Ibid., 229–67.
51. See Huang 2001; Pittman 2001; Queen, Prebish, and Keown 2003; Chandler 2004; and Hsu, Chen, and Meeks 2007. Socially engaged Buddhism is often translated into Chinese as *rushi*, "in the world," while a practice focused on study, meditation, seclusion, and so on, is termed *chushi*, detached, literally "exiting [the] world." "Engaged" [Buddhism] is also translated into Chinese as *canyu* (participatory) *fojiao* and *sheshi* (involved in the world) *fojiao*.
52. For example, see Chris Queen, "Introduction," p. 22, and Thomas F. Yarnall, "Engaged Buddhism: New and Improved?" p. 286, both in Queen, Prebish, and Keown, eds., *Action Dharma: New Studies in Engaged Buddhism*, London: Routledge/Curzon, 2003. Also Sallie B. King, "Thích Nhất Hạnh and the Unified Buddhist Church," in Queen and King, eds., *Engaged Buddhism: Buddhist Liberation Movements in Asia*, Albany: SUNY Press, 1986: 321–63. And see also, Nhất Hạnh 1967 and Chân Không 1993.
53. As far as I can tell, Jean-Paul Sartre developed his ideas on the politically engaged intellectual in *La nausée* 1938, and especially in his 1947 essay "Qu'est-ce que la littérature?" as well as the plays *Les Mains Sales* (1948) and *Saint Genet* (1952). More research is needed to know how Vietnamese intellectuals in France and Vietnam first interpreted and disseminated the works of Sartre and Camus; by the 1960s, existentialism was a frequently discussed topic in the Buddhist journals of South Vietnam. In the 1960s, two Vietnamese renderings of Sartre's term *engagé* were *nhập cuộc* and *dấn*

thân, but Thích Nhất Hạnh preferred his own term, *Tiếp Hiện*, Inter-being: *Tiếp* [to be in touch with, to continue], *Hiện* [to realize, to make here and now].

54. Buddhist journals in South Vietnam reported in depth on Bhave, who won the first Ramon Magsaysay award in 1958, and also on Sartre's opposition to the Vietnam War and his refusal of the Nobel Prize for Literature in 1964. For more discussion, see my chapter " 'Buddhism for this World': The Buddhist Revival in Vietnam, 1920–1951, and Its Legacy" in Philip Taylor, ed., *Modernity and Re-enchantment: Religion in Post-Revolutionary Vietnam*. Singapore: Institute of Southeast Asian Studies, 2007: 250–96.

55. See for example his *Vietnam: Lotus in a Sea of Fire*.

56. Jonathan Watts, International Network of Engaged Buddhists (INEB), Email, Feb. 4, 2004.

57. Laliberté in Clart and Jones 2003: 172–75. Fear of political retaliation, such as that which befell Yinshun, may have been a reason for Foguangshan and Ciji to eschew sociopolitical critiques during the martial law era. However, martial law ended in 1987; all civil and religious groups are free to engage in sociopolitical activism if they choose to do so.

58. Laliberté in Clart and Jones 2003: 178–79.

59. See www.ddm.org.tw for more details.

60. Laliberté in Clart and Jones 2003: 180.

61. Ibid., 179.

62. Jiang 1997: 104–11.

63. Ibid.

64. I borrow this phrase from Lan Jifu 2003. However he uses it in a different sense than I will here: He discusses what he thinks are the direct heirs to Yinshun and his thought, in the sense of written works, not in terms of praxis or actualization. Lan defines the "Yinshun Age" as comprising the years 1952–1994, from the year Yinshun came to Taiwan to the year when he ceased writing, due to ill health. Lan Jifu writes that since 1994, his students such as Chao Hwei and her colleagues such as Shing Kuang and Wu Yin at the Hongshi Buddhist Institute (all three are nuns); and the monk Chuandao of Miaoxin Temple in Tainan, have taken on the task of propagating, developing, actualizing, and answering criticism of Yinshun's work. Also included in this "generation" are monastic and lay scholars who have published criticism of Yinshun's work, either for textual/hermeneutical reasons, or in defense of the Tibetan, Pure Land, and Chan traditions critiqued by Yinshun.

65. Shing Kuang was born in Jiayi in 1962 and was ordained in 1982 at Haiming Temple. She, like Chao Hwei, is an activist-scholar, and has written works on Chan Buddhism; explications of Yinshun's writings, and Buddhist ethics, among other topics. She heads the Hongshi Institute; is chief publisher of Fajie Press, and teaches in the philosophy department at Dongwu University.

66. Chao Hwei was born in Myanmar and become ordained as a nun in 1978 while still an undergraduate in the Department of Chinese, National Taiwan Normal University. Unable to accept the conservative and authoritative atmosphere of her temple, she left on a study retreat and discovered the writings of Yinshun in 1982. She spent the years 1984–88 studying at Yinshun's Fuyan Buddhist Institute in Hsinchu. Li 2005: 104–6. There is no monograph about Ven. Chao Hwei in English

but there is a biography in Chinese, Tao 1995. Geoff Foy devotes a chapter to Chao Hwei in his PhD dissertation of 2002 and Li Lingyu's masters' thesis includes much valuable information about Chao Hwei. See also Shi Chao Hwei 2002 and Hongshi Buddhist Institute 2001.

67. Chao Hwei does not have her own tonsure disciples but the Hongshi Institute accepts students and nuns tonsured under other masters.

68. See Wen 2006: 221–48.

69. Gu Meifen, "Wurang zhichizhe duili huafen lun wei zhengdang de fuyung," *Taiwan ribao*, March 31, 2004: 3. The Humanistic Education Foundation in Taiwan lobbies the government and their efforts have, for example, led to a ban on corporal punishment in schools. This Foundation is also involved in conflict resolution and provides training in "alternative education" for Taiwan's teachers.

70. Chao Hwei 2003c.

71. Chao Hwei, "Shengren bu si, da dao bu zhi: Ping Ciji yiyuan heyueshu." *Hongshi tongxun*, no. 10, 1994.8: 3–8. Taipei: Fojiao Hongshi Xueyuan.

72. Geoff Foy, "Engaging Religion: An Ethnography of Three Religious Adherents in Taiwan's Academic Culture," PhD dissertation, Graduate Theological Union, 2002: 148–49.

73. Ibid.

74. Chao Hwei 2002: 3.

75. As for Foguangshan, Xingyun, like other Buddhist leaders in Taiwan, does not advocate feminism; he believes that essentialist differences between male and female determine their different social roles, and laywomen's primary roles are those of wife and mother. Shi Xingyun, "Fojiao de nuxing guan" [Buddhist View of Women] in Shi Xingyun, *Fojiao congshu* [Anthology of Buddhism] (Kaohsiung: Foguang) 10: 258–70. Yet, he has openly and consistently supported Buddhist women's education, and he has helped develop the nuns' order in Taiwan and worldwide. Chao Hwei, 2002: 35, Jiang Canteng in same, 253.

76. Tsomo 1999: 1; 30–31; Gross 1993: 291.

77. Tsomo 1999: 1, 31. For more details, see Karma Lekshe Tsomo, "Mahāprajāpatī's Legacy: The Buddhist Women's Movement, An Introduction." In Tsomo 1999: 1–44, and also *Sākyhadhitā Newsletter*, Twentieth-Anniversary Issue, vol. 16, no. 1, Summer 2007.

78. See Tsomo 2004c and Cheng 2007. Santikaro Bhikkhu,"Socially Engaged Buddhism and Modernity: What Sort of Animals are They?" http://www.bpf.org/tsangha/skbsebmod.html, accessed on August 15, 2007.

79. Taixu's Wuchang Buddhist Institute (1922–34) did have a section for female education, as did the branch in Beijing. Taixu sketched others plans to educate nuns and laywomen and he encouraged Buddhist nuns at extant temples to gain more training and education. Taixu, "Biqiuni de zeren" [The responsibilities of nuns], Speech at Dizang Nunnery Institute, Winter 1930. Shi Taixu 1970, "Speeches," Chapter 18: 323–24. Taixu's "Reorganization of the *Sangha* System" focuses on monks' education and monks' economic livelihood and spiritual cultivation; in one version of his plan, he suggests that nuns before the age of fifty labor part-time and "practice" the other half of their time, while after age fifty, devote their lives to full-time spiritual practice. "Fojiao sengsi caichanquan zhi queding" [The confirmation of Buddhist monastic temple property rights]. *Hai Chao Yin* [Sound of the Tide] (Summer 1928), vol. 9, no. 6.

80. Taixu said: "To become a monastic is hard enough for men, let alone women." "Funu xuefo zhi guifan" [The standards for women studying Buddhism] Sept. 1926, Speech at Min'nan Buddhist Youth Association, *Hai Chao Yin*, vol. 7, no. 10. "The nuns' order owes its existence to compliance with the Eight Special Rules . . . regarding nuns, quality is more important than quantity." *Letters to the Zhengxin Lay Association*, vol. 2, no. 2, Jan. 23, n.y.

81. "Youpoyi jiaoyu yu fohua jiating" [Laywomen's Education and the Making of Buddhist Families], Nov. 1935 speech at Donglian Institute, Hong Kong, *Hai Chao Yin*, vol. 17, no. 2.

82. Li Yuzhen, "Fojiao lianshe . . ." 2000: 270–78. In fact, Taixu was aware of the dearth of opportunities for women to study Buddhism, but this was not a priority in his reform program. Possibly due to the tradition of strict segregation between monks and nuns in Chinese Buddhism, he believed that nuns and laywomen should be trained to teach nuns and laywomen. "Questions and Answers," *Hai Chao Yin*, Jan. 29, 1935.

83. See Ester Bianchi 2001; quotation is from page 24. Ven. Longlian worked hard to re-establish dual ordination in China, absent from the Chinese Buddhist tradition for centuries, and in 1982 succeeded in ordaining twenty-one nuns. Bianchi 2001: 32. Dual ordination is becoming the norm for nuns in China, personal communication with monk instructor of Qixia Shan Buddhist Academy, Nanjing, China, Dec. 4, 2007.

84. Chao Hwei 2002: 18–19.

85. Mei 1998: 168.

86. Chao Hwei 2002: 3.

87. As part of this movement, Chao Hwei urged the fourteenth Dalai Lama on his two visits to Taiwan in 1997 and 2001 to restore full ordination for Tibetan nuns as soon as possible.

88. These "ugly gestures" refer to the eighty-four kinds of behaviors or attitudes, stereotypically attributed to women, which obstruct them from attaining nirvāna. Cheng 2007: 86–87, Note 36, 205–6; Li 2005: 102.

89. This "revolutionary" message was also addressed to the fourteenth Dalai Lama, who was in Taiwan at the same time. For more details, see Li 2005, Chapters Four and Five.

90. Cheng 2007: 86.

91. Xingyun diplomatically declared that Foguangshan long ago "froze" the Eight Special Rules and claims that this is not a problem at Foguangshan. Li 2005: 120–21.

92. Li 2005: 102. According to Wenjie Qin's observations, in China there is no open critique of the Eight Special Rules, but no consistent or systematic enforcement either. Qin 2000: 183–84.

93. Cheng 2007: 86; Bingenheimer 2004: 164.

94. Li 2005: 140–41. Wei-yi Cheng found that many nuns may agree with Chao Hwei's ideas, but not with her "extremist" (*jilie*) and media-savvy methods. Cheng 2007: 87–90.

95. Cheng 2004a: 184–85. "Nearly all of my nun informants, regardless of whether they accept the Eight Special Rules or not, expressed disapproval towards *bhikkhunī* Zhaohui's actions." Cheng 2007: 87.

96. Cheng 2007: 100.

97. Ibid., 98.

98. Li Lijun, "Shi Jianduan fashi [Master Jianduan]." *Renlai lunbian yuekan* [Renlai Monthly: A Chinese monthly of cultural, spiritual, and social concerns], October 2006, vol. 31: 44–45.

99. Li 2005: 102–3.

100. Chao Hwei 2002: 31, 34, 54–55.

101. Yikong 2004: 66. Cheng 2007: 99.

102. Jiang in Chao Hwei 2002: 253. Chao Hwei 2002: 158–62; 175–82.

103. Chao Hwei calls it "the pyramidal authority structure" in Taiwan's Buddhist organizations. Li 2005: 128. Monks have always held top leadership in Taiwan, despite the nuns' majority and nuns' active leadership roles in temple administration. Ibid., 64–65.

104. Li 2005: 139–41.

105. Chao Hwei 2002: 2. Li 2005: 140.

106. Li 2005: 134.

107. Shing Kuang, "Preface," in Chao Hwei, 1992: 1–6. *Wo yuan jiang shen hua mingyue* [I vow to become an illuminating light]. Taipei: Fajie. However, Chao Hwei told me that many Buddhists, lay and monastic, female and male, support her behind the scenes. Email, Nov. 23, 2002.

108. Marking a significant development for Taiwan's Buddhism, in September 2007, Chao Hwei and the Hongshi Buddhist Institute hosted the annual meeting for the International Network of Engaged Buddhists (INEB). The chief coordinator for this meeting was Dr. Yo Hsiang Chou of Foguang University, and the nun Lianchan of the Wuyan Association for the Protection of the Blind was a sponsor. The 2007 meeting's theme was "Engaged Buddhism: From Social Welfare to Social Change." During the course of the meeting, INEB members appointed Chao Hwei as the group's fourth (and sole female) spiritual advisor, joining the fourteenth Dalai Lama; Thích Nhất Hạnh; and the Thai monk Somchai Kusalacitto. For more details, see vols. 88 and 89 (August and October 2007) of the *Hongshi Bimonthly Journal*.

109. Don Swearer, "Centre and Periphery: Buddhism and Politics in Modern Thailand," in Harris 1999: 219.

110. Jon Watts, INEB, Email Feb. 4, 2004.

111. Ibid. A. T. Ariyaratne founded the Buddhist *Sarvodaya* rural development movement in 1958 (inspired by Gandhi's and Vinoba Bhave's movement; Gandhi first coined this term meaning "well-being of all"), in current parlance akin to "sustainable development." *Sarvodaya* has also put great efforts into building a pluralist alliance to end the civil war in Sri Lanka. George D. Bond, "A. T. Ariyaratne and the Sarvodaya Shramadana Movement in Sri Lanka," in Queen and King 1996: 121–46.

112. Queen 1996: 14–16.

113. Queen, Prebish, and Keown, eds., 2003: 21.

114. Chao Hwei, October 2, 2001, *Ziyou shibao* [Liberty Times], "Ziyou Guangchang [Freedom Square]" Section.

Conclusion

1. It is worth repeating that that was accomplished without strong sponsorship and money from the government, unlike the situation in other Buddhist countries.

2. Qin 2000. However, Yuan Yuan (PhD candidate, Duke University) reports from the field that the largest nunnery in China, the Pushou nunnery on Mt. Wutai, is a center for the growing female Buddhist movement in China.

3. See Kwangwoo Sunim, "Discipline and Practice of Buddhist Women in Korea," p. 175, and other chapters on Korean Buddhism in Tsomo 2006.

4. Thich Nu Dien Van Hue, "Buddhist Nuns of Vietnam," in Tsomo 2004a: 48-50.

5. Tsomo 1999: 13.

6. Two senior Taiwanese nuns, Vens. Heng Ching and Wu Yin, played important roles during the discussions at the First International Congress on Buddhist Women's Role in the *Sangha* held in Hamburg, Germany, July 2007. See Bhikkhu Sujato, "Dark Matter," [Summary of Congress Proceedings], Hamburg, Germany, July 27, 2007. The Congress voiced unanimous support for full ordination for women in Tibetan Buddhism but the exact details of how to proceed, most likely based on the Chinese *vinaya* of the *Dharmaguptaka* tradition, await future discussion and consensus.

7. Zhang Mantao in Nakamura Hajime, ed. *Zhong'guo fojiao fazhan shi* [History of the Development of Chinese Buddhism]. Taipei: Tianhua, 1984: 1092-93.

8. Taiwan also has followers of Tibetan Buddhism, new Japanese Buddhist sects, and Thai Buddhism.

9. Wang 1997: 3.

10. Su 1996: 23-37; 42-75.

11. Lu 2004: 223-43.

12. See DeVido 2004: 235-49.

13. Kaldor 2003: 9, 22.

14. Weller 1999: 100.

15. Ibid., 135.

16. Ibid., 140-42.

17. The groups studied are Ciji, Foguangshan, Fagushan, Zhongtai Chan Temple, Lingjiushan, and Fuzhi. Schak and Hsiao employ Robert Putnam's (2001) definition of social capital as the collective value of all social networks and the norms of reciprocity that arise from these networks. David Schak and Hsin-Huang Michael Hsiao, "Socio-Cultural Engagements of Taiwan's New Buddhist Groups." *Collected Papers of* the Taiwan-Japan Workshop on Civil Society Organizations in Contemporary Asia. Taipei: Center for Asia-Pacific Area Studies, Academia Sinica, 2004: 80–100. For a work in Chinese that takes a similar approach, see Zhang Peixin, "The Investigation in Social Capital Operated by the Religious and Non-Profit Organizations in Taiwan: Buddhist Tzu-Chi Merits Society As An Example," PhD dissertation, Department of Civic Education and Leadership, National Taiwan Normal University, 2004.

18. Kaldor 2003: 10.

19. Ibid., 12.

20. Lin 2003: 56-58. With all their experience in the areas of health-care, welfare, and relief, Ciji's experts could lobby or advise the government, but so far have declined this public role. Laliberté in Clart and Jones 2004: 175-76.

21. Gu 2002: 162, 165, 170, 188-89.

22. Ibid., 185.

23. Ting and Zhan in Lin, Ting, and Zhan, eds. 2004: xviii.

24. Ting Jen-Chieh, "Renjian Buddhism and Its Successors: Toward a Sociological Analysis of Buddhist Awakening in Contemporary Taiwan," in Hsu, et al., eds. 2007: 249–51. However, as Chapter 3 illustrated, Ciji is influencing education policies on the local level, with the teaching of Zhengyan's *Still Thoughts* in public schools.

25. Qin: 2000, Chapter 2, argues that the nuns of Fuhu Temple on Mt. Emei essentially recreated the patriarchal family structure, in all its glory, in their nunnery. Her chapter presents a grim picture of violent power struggles among the nuns. I do not have direct knowledge regarding monastic power struggles in Taiwan, but Li Xueping's informants told of nunneries in Taiwan that "reproduce the patriarchal hierarchy of the home," where abbesses, having sacrificed so much for their disciples, expect life-long obedience, loyalty, and personal service in return. Some abbesses aspire to absolute authority and nuns at their temples do not have the right of speech or discussion. Nuns' letters are opened, phone calls are restricted and/or monitored; reading of books, study at Buddhist institutes and unauthorized contact with others outside the monastery grounds are all forbidden. Li wonders to what degree abbesses make these demands for the good of their disciples' practice and training. Li Xueping 2000: Chapter Six.

26. Chen Ruoxi (b.1938 in Taipei) is the author of many works including *The Execution of Mayor Yin and Other Stories from the Great Proletarian Cultural Revolution* (1976).

27. See the discussion in Ding Min 2002.

28. Xinghe 2001: 78–79. Written before the appearance of Chen Ruoxi's novels, Mei 1998 critically explores the gender inequality in both Buddhist doctrine and within the institutions of contemporary Taiwanese Buddhism. See also Chao Hwei's essays in *Intonation for Thousands of Years: Buddhist Feminist Thought for a New Century* 2002 on gender inequality in Buddhism and on her movement to abolish the Eight Special Rules. Chao Hwei also publicly supported a nun who claimed to have been sexually harassed by her master. "Huan wo qingbai [Restore my innocence]" Press Conference, Oct. 1999, http://www.awker.com/hongshi/mag/41-7.htm, accessed on April 2, 2008.

29. A front-page story in Taiwan's *United News* reported that "society is opening up . . . lifestyles like women living with a partner, remaining single, or being an unmarried mother are no longer dishonorable . . . families and friends are gradually coming to accept the idea of 'not marrying.' " Li Chengyu, "Xingfugan: Yihunzhe jiang, weihunzhe sheng" [Happiness Drops Among Married, Rises Among Unmarried], *Lianhe bao* [United News], December 10, 2007: 1. Also see Gavin W. Jones, "The 'Flight from Marriage' in South-East and East Asia," in National University of Singapore, Asian Metacentre Research Paper Series, no. 11, 2002.

30. McNamara 1996: 629–32; 635; 639–43.

31. Interview with Ven. Mingjia, Sept 4, 1999, Jiayi.

32. In Taiwan though nuns outnumber monks and head two-thirds of Taiwan's Buddhist temples, top leaders in the Buddhist establishment such as the Buddhist Association of the Republic of China, the *Sangha* Protection Association, and the Chinese Buddhist Temple Association are monks. Lin Rongzhi 2004: 80. Furthermore, at Buddhist ceremonies and meetings, monks enjoy VIP treatment and generally speaking, still receive more lay donations than nuns. Cheng 2007: 130.

33. Ven. Chantal Tenzin Dekyi, "Visit at Luminary Temple in Taiwan." *Sangha: In the Footsteps of the Buddha*, Issue 7, November 1999: 4.

34. *Smyung gnas* practices focus on Avalokiteśvara and are undertaken periodically throughout the year. See the explication in Makley 1999: 184–89.

35. Cheng 2007: 149.

36. Li 2005: 27–30.

37. Traditional couplet, adapted by Mi Gao; thanks also to Marcus Bingenheimer.

Glossary of Selected Chinese Characters

Ba jingfa 八敬法
Baisheng 百聖
Baizhang 百丈
Baochang 寶唱
beiyuan, lixing, hehe 悲願, 力行, 和合
biedu 別渡
biguan 閉關
biqiuni 比丘尼
Biqiuni zhuan 比丘尼傳
canyu fojiao 參與佛教
chaogeng, yedu 朝耕, 夜讀
Chao Hwei 昭慧
Chen Ruoxi 陳若曦
chengdan rulai jiaye 承擔如來家業
Chongfan taohuayuan 重返桃花源
Chuandao 傳道
chujia 出家
chujia nai da zhangfu shi 出家乃大丈夫事
chushi 出世
cibei 慈悲
Cicheng dui 慈誠隊
da zhangfu 大丈夫
dazhuan xuefo yundong 大專學佛運動
dingning 叮嚀
dingtian lidi de da zhangfu 頂天立地的大丈夫
Dizang 地藏
Emeishan 峨嵋山
Erbu shoujie 二部受戒
Fagushan 法鼓山

Fangzhang 方丈
Faxiang zong 法相宗
Fayun 法雲
Foguangshan 佛光山
Fojiao ciji gongde hui 佛教慈濟功德會
Foying 佛瀅
Fujian 福建
fumu en nan bao 父母恩難報
fuquan 賦權
fuyan, muci 父嚴, 母慈
Gaoseng zhuan 高僧傳
gongmin shehui 公民社會
Guangqin 廣欽
Guanyin 觀音
Heng Ching 恆清
Hiuwan 曉雲
Hongshi 弘誓
houdun 後盾
Hs'ing Fu-Ch'üan 邢福泉
Huafan 華梵
Huijiao 慧皎
Huixinlian 慧心蓮
Huiyan 慧嚴
husheng, xifu 護生, 惜福
Jiji 集集
jijie 寄戒
Jiang Canteng 江燦騰
jiefang jiaoyu 解放教育
Jingsi jingshe 靜思精舍
Jingsi yu 靜思語
jiujing jietuo 究竟解脫
Jueli 覺力
jueshu renhua 覺樹人華
Kan Zhengzong 闞正宗
keji chongren 克己崇仁
keji fuli 克己復禮
Li Yuzhen 李玉珍
Lingjiushan 靈鷲山
li, yi, lian, chi 禮義廉恥
Linji 臨濟
Lin Mei-Rong 林美容
Longhu An 龍湖庵

Glossary of Selected Chinese Characters

Longlian 隆蓮
Lu Hwei-syin 盧蕙馨
Mazu 媽祖
Miaoshan 妙善
Miaoxin 妙心
Mingjia 明迦
mofa 末法
neng'gan 能幹
nuqiangren 女強人
Pilu Chansi 毗盧禪寺
pudu 普渡
pusa yuan xing 菩薩願行
Putuoshan 普陀山
qing'gui 清規
quanqiuhua 全球化
ren 仁
ren 忍
Renben jiaoyu jijinhui 人本教育基金會
renjian fojiao 人間佛教
renjian jingtu 人間淨土
rensheng 人生
rensheng 人乘
rushi 入世
sengni 僧尼
Shangren 上人
shangyou zhengce, xia you duice 上有政策, 下有對策
Shengyan 聖嚴
shijiehua 世界化
shijie zhuyi 世界主義
Shing Kuang 性廣
sheshi fojiao 涉世佛教
si weiyi 四威儀
Taixu 太虛
taoming, taoli 逃名, 逃利
tiankong 天空
"Tianxia mingshan shei shi zhu
Kongzhong wuwo xin ji fo"
天下名山誰是主,
空中無我心即佛.
Tianyi 天乙
tongyangxi 童養媳
Wangye 王爺

weishi 唯識
Wuliangyi jing 無量義經
wusheng laomu 無生老母
Wu Yin 悟因
Xiamen 廈門
Xiang'guang 香光
xianqi liangmu 賢妻良母
Xindao 心道
Xingyun 星雲
Xiudao 修道
Xiwang gongcheng 希望工程
Xu biqiuni zhuan 續比丘尼傳
yangnu 養女
yansi 巖寺
yibu, yijiaoyin 一步, 一腳印
yi ren wei ben 以人為本
yizheng bu ganzhi 議政不干治
Yinshun 印順
Yinxin Shuyuan 引心書院
Yongquansi, Gushan 湧泉寺, 鼓山
yuanfen 緣分
Yuanrong 圓融
Yuantong Chansi 圓通禪寺
yulu 語錄
yuhui 語彙
zhaigu 齋姑
zhaijiao 齋教
zhaodi 招弟
Zheng Cheng'gong 鄭成功
zhengquan 政權
Zhengyan 證嚴
Zhenhua 震華
Zhejiang 浙江
zhiquan 治權
zhizao suo 製造所
Zhongguo fojiao hui 中國佛教會
Zhongtai Chansi 中台禪寺
Zhou Xuande 周宣德
ziwo peili 自我培力
zhuangyan 莊嚴
zongwo zhiwu 縱我制物

Bibliography

Chinese Sources

Chen Huijian. 1983, 1984, 1989. *Zhengyan fashi de Ciji shijie* [Dharma Master Zhengyan's World of Ciji]. Taipei: Ciji Culture.

Chen Lingrong. 1992. "Riju shiqi shendao tongzhixia de Taiwan zongjiao zhengce" [Religious policies in Taiwan under the Shintō system during the Japanese occupation] Taipei: Zili wanbao chubanshe.

Chen Ruitang. 1974. *Taiwan simiao falu guanxi zhi yanjiu* [A Study of Laws Concerning Temples in Taiwan]. Taipei: Sifa xingzhengbu mishushi.

Chen Yong'ge. 2003. *Ren jian chao yin: Taixu dashi zhuan* [Sound of the Tide of the Human Realm: Biography of Master Taixu]. Hangzhou: Zhejiang People's Press.

Chern Meei-Hwa. " 'Linglei' nuxing: cong yige xinwen jianbao dang'an tan Taiwan biqiuni xingxiang de zaixian." ['An Alternative Woman': A Case Analysis of Newspaper Representations about Buddhist Nuns] *Taiwan Journal of Religious Studies*. Vol. 1, no. 2, October 2001. Taipei: Center for Buddhist Studies, National Taiwan University, 295–340.

———. 2002. " 'Linglei' dianfan: dangdai Taiwan biqiuni de shehui shijian" [An Alternative Paradigm: The Social Practices of Buddhist Nuns in Contemporary Taiwan] *Journal of the Center for Buddhist Studies*. no. 7, July 2002, 295–340.

Ciji Wenhua Zhiye Zhongxin [Ciji Cultural Mission Center]. 2000. "Xiwang gongcheng: kua shiji mengxiang tebie baodao." [Project Hope: Trans-Century Dream Special Report]. *Ciji yuekan* [Ciji Monthly], vol. 409. Taipei: Ciji Cultural Mission Center.

———. 2001a. http://news.tzuchi.net/HopeProject.nsf/HopeProject, accessed on August 25, 2007.

———. 2001b. *Ciji yuekan* [Ciji Monthly], 410: 92–101.Taipei: Ciji Cultural Mission Center.

———. 2001c. *Ciji yuekan* [Ciji Monthly], 412: 50–63. Taipei: Ciji Cultural Mission Center.

———. 2001d. "Xiwang gongcheng mao xinya." [Project Hope sprouts new buds] *Jingdian* [Rhythms Monthly], 39: 36–65. Taipei: Ciji Cultural Mission Center.

———. 2002. *921 gongcheng* [921 Building Projects]. Vols. 1–50. Taipei: Ciji Cultural Mission Center.

Ding Min. 1996. "Taiwan shehui bianqianzhong de xinxing nisengtuan—Xiang'guang nisengtuan de jueqi" [A new Buddhist nunnery in evolving Taiwan's society: The Luminary Buddhist Institute] in 1996: 415–469. *Diyijie zongjiao wenhua guoji xueshu huiyi lunwenji.* [Collected Essays from the First International Academic Conference on Religion and Culture] Taipei: Foguang daxue zongjiao wenhua yanjiu zhongxin.

———. 2002. "Chen Ruoxi fojiao xiaoshuozhong nuxing xingxiang yu zhutiyi—yi Huixinlian (2000), Chongfan taohuayuan (2001), wei tantao." [Images and themes of woman in Chen Ruoxi's Buddhist novels—The Story of Taiwan's Nuns (2000) and Return to Peach Blossom Spring (2001)]. *Collected Papers from the Third Conference on Humanistic Buddhism and Contemporary Dialogue.* VCD Set. Taoyuan: Hongshi Cultural and Educational Foundation.

Fan Rongda. 2001. "Zisha qici ta, cong Ciji zhaohui shengming" [She who attempted suicide seven times got her life back with Ciji]. *Lianhe wanbao* [United Evening News], April 23, 2001: 1.

Gu Meifen. 2004. "Wurang zhichizhe duili huafen lun wei zhengdang de fuyung"[Don't let supporters' oppositions and divisions get used by political parties]. *Taiwan ribao*, March 31, 2004: 3.

Gu Zhonghua. 2002. "Gongmin shehui zai Taiwan de chengxing jingyan" [The Making of Civil Society in Taiwan], in 2002: 161–196. *Fazhi, renquan, yu gongmin shehui* [The Rule of Law, Human Rights, and Civil Society]. Qu Haiyuan, Gu Zhonghua, Qian Yongxiang, eds. Taipei: Guiguan Books.

Hanzang Jiaoliyuan [Sino-Tibetan Buddhist Institute]. 1947. *Taixu dashi jinianji* [Collection to Commemorate Master Taixu]. Chongqing: Hanzang Jiaoliyuan.

———. 2001. "Zhenhua fashi yu Xu biqiuni zhuan" [Ven. Zhenhua and Lives of the Nuns, Continued]. *Juequn xueshu lunwenji* [The Juequn Collection of Academic Essays]. Beijing: Shangwu yinshu guan.

He Jianming. 1997. "Luelun qingmo minchu de zhongguo fojiao nuxing" [A brief discussion of Chinese Buddhist women in the late Qing-early Republic period]. *Foxue yanjiu* [Buddhist Studies] 6.

He Mianhan. 2006. "Shilun Taiwan dangdai fojiao chujia nuzhong de jueqi" [An exploratory discussion on the sudden rise of Taiwan's contemporary Buddhist nuns]. *Fayuan*, vol. 24 [Beijing: Chinese Academy of Buddhism]: 282–295.

Hongshi Jiaoyu Wenjiao Jijinhui. [Hongshi Education and Culture Foundation]. Feb. 2003. *Hongshi Buddhist Institute Bimonthly*, vol. 61, Special Issue: " 'Tanxue shijian': Shuiluo shichu" [The 'Pool of Blood Incident': The Truth Comes to Light Eventually].

Hongshi Xueyuan [Hongshi Institute]. 2001. *Linglei shisheng, linglei jingyan: xueyuan xiaoshe luocheng yizhounian jinian tekan* [Alternative teachers and students, an alternative experience: Special issue to commemorate the one year anniversary of the Institute's establishment]. Taipei: Fajie.

Huang Liling. 1999. "Cong wenhua rentong zhuanxiang quyu zhili—921 dizhen zaihou chongjian gongzuo dui 'shequ zongti yingzao' lunshu de tiaozhan" [From cultural identity to regional administration—post-921 earthquake reconstruction work regarding the challenge of 'total community construction']. *Chengshi yu sheji.* [City and Design] 9/10: 147–174.

Huang Xianian, ed. 1995. *Yinshun ji* [Collected Works of Yinshun]. Beijing: Chinese Academy of Social Sciences Press.

Huang Xiuhua. 1999. "Shouzhi budong: changzhu shifu pian" [Unwavering Will: The Nuns of the Still Thoughts Abode]. *Ciji yuekan*, no. 391. June 25, 1999: 52-75.

Huang Long-min and Chen Chien-zong. 2002. " 'Jingsi yu jiaoxue' zai guomin zhongxiaoxue shishi shiqiuxing zhi pingxi" [An analysis of the suitability of implementing the 'Still Thoughts Curriculum' in public primary and middle schools]. *Taichung shiyuan xuebao*, no. 16, July 2002, 159-76.

Jiang Canteng. 1992. "Cong rensheng fojiao dao renjian fojiao" [From 'Buddhism for human life' to 'Buddhism for the Human World'], in 1992: 169-188. *Taiwan fojiao yu xiandai shehui* [Taiwanese Buddhism and Modern Society]. Taipei: Dongda.

———. 1992. "Guangfuhou Taiwan fojiao nuxing jiaose de bianqian" [Evolution of the role of Buddhist women in post-1945 Taiwan], in Jiang Canteng 1992: 77-85; 82-3.

———. 1996. *Taiwan fojiao bainianshi zhi yanjiu* [Research on a Century of Buddhism in Taiwan, 1895-1995]. Taipei: Nantian.

———. 1997. *Taiwan dangdai fojiao: Foguangshan, Ciji, Fagushan, Zhongtaishan* [Taiwan Contemporary Buddhism: Foguangshan, Ciji, Fagushan, Zhongtaishan]. Taipei: Nantian.

———. 1997. "Cong zhaigu dao biqiuni: Taiwan fojiao nuxing chujia de bainian cangsang" [From "vegetarian auntie" to ordained nun: one hundred years of dramatic changes for Taiwan's Buddhist monastic women], in Jiang Canteng, 1997: 113-124.

———. 1997. "Huanjing baohu zhi 'fanxing zhuanyi:' yi Taiwan diqu fojiao sixiang he shijian moshi weili ['Paradigm shift' in the environmental protection: The case of Taiwan's Buddhist thought and praxis model], in Jiang Canteng 1997: 104-111.

———. 2001a. *Dangdai Taiwan renjian fojiao sixiangjia: yi Yinshun daoshi wei zhongxin de xinhuo xiangchuan lunwenji* [Modern Taiwan Renjian Fojiao Thinkers: "Transmitting the Flame" Collected Essays, centering on Master Yinshun]. Taipei: Xinwenfeng.

———. 2001b. *Riju shiqi Taiwan fojiao wenhua fazhan shi* [History of the development of Japanese era Taiwan Buddhist culture]. Taipei: Nantian.

———. 2003. "Cong 'Sihui ba jingfa' dao 'renjian fojiao sixiang' de chuanbo suyuan: you guan jinqi Taiwan renjian fojiao sixiang yu jielu bianfa de zhengbian wenti" [Tracing the roots of transmission, from "Tearing up the Eight Special Rules" to "Humanistic Buddhist Thought:" Recent debates about change in Taiwan Humanistic Buddhism Thought and Monastic Rules], in 2003: 259-267, *Taiwan jindai fojiao de bianqian yu fansi: qu zhiminhua yu Taiwan fojiao zhutixing queli de xin tansuo* [Change and reflection in Taiwan's modern Buddhism: New explorations in decolonization and the establishment of Taiwan's Buddhism subjectivity]. Taipei: Dongda Press.

———. 2005. "Taiwan jindai (1895-1945) fojiao shi yanjiu zhi zaijiantao" [Review of Studies on Buddhist History in Modern Taiwan, 1895-1945]. *Foxue yanjiu zhongxin xuebao*, vol. 10, (July): 287-326.

Jiang Canteng and Wang Jianchuan, eds. 1994. *Taiwan zhaijiao de lishi guancha yu zhanwang* [Taiwan's vegetarian religion: Historical observations and future prospects]. Taipei: Xinwenfeng.

Kan Zhengzong. 1999. *Taiwan fojiao yibainian* [One Hundred Years of Taiwan's Buddhism]. Taipei: Dongda Press.

———. 2004. *Chongdu Taiwanfojiao: zhanhou Taiwan fojiao* [Re-reading Taiwan's Buddhism: Post-war Taiwan's Buddhism]. Taipei County: Daqian Press.

Kan Zhengzong and Li Yuzhen. 2000. "921 zhenzai fojiao siyuan shoujuan yu zhenzai chubu diaocha" [A preliminary investigation of Buddhist temples' donations and disaster relief after 921]. *Taiwan zongjiao xiehui tongxun* [Taiwan Association for Religious Studies Newsletter]. Special Issue on the 921 Earthquake Disaster, 4: 38–61.

Lai Lijun. 2001. "Zouchu fengbao" [Emerging from the storm]. *Ciji daolu* [Ciji companion] 364.2, 2001. March, 16.

Lan Jifu, 1997. *Fojiao shiliaoxue* [Study of Buddhist Historical Materials]. Taipei: Dongda Press.

———. 2003. "Taiwan fojiao sixiangshishang de hou Yinshunxue shidai," in 2003: 265-285. *Tingyu senglu foxue zaji* ['Tingyu senglu' Buddhist Studies Miscellany]. Taipei: Modern Chan Press.

Li Lingyu. 2005. "You Taiwan fojiao biqiuni nuquan fazhan lai kan 'feichu ba jingfa yundong' [A study of 'The movement to abolish the Eight Special Rules' in light of the development of Taiwan's Buddhist Nuns' Feminism]. Master's thesis, Graduate Institute of Religious Studies, National Chengchi University.

Li Xueping. 2000. "Taiwan de biqiuni sengtuan ji qi butong de shengming jingyan: yige shehuixue de ge'an yanjiu [Taiwan Buddhist nunneries and their different life experiences: a sociological case study]. Master's thesis, Graduate Institute of Sociology, Tunghai University.

Li Yuzhen. 1989. *Tangdai de biqiuni* [Nuns of the Tang Dynasty]. Taipei: Xuesheng Shuju.

———. 2000. "Chujia rushi: Zhanhou Taiwan fojiao nuxing senglu shengya zhi bianqian"[Become a monastic and enter the world: The Evolution of Postwar Taiwan Buddhist female monastics' careers], in 2000: 409-4412. *Huigu lao Taiwan, zhanwang xin guxiang: Taiwan shehui wenhua bianqian xueshu yantaohui lunwenji* [Looking back at old Taiwan, looking ahead to a new native place: Proceedings of the Conference on Taiwan Social and Cultural Change]. Taipei: National Taiwan Normal University and Taiwan Provincial Documents Committee, 2000.

———. 2000. "Fojiao lianshe yu nuxing zhi shehui canyu: 1930 niandai Shanghai lianshe yu 1960 niandai Taiwan lianshe zhi bijiao" [The Buddhist Lotus Society and women's social engagement: A comparison of the 1930s Shanghai Lotus Society with the 1960s Taiwan Lotus Society], in Huang Kewu, Zhang Zhejia, eds., 2000: 255–312. *Gong yu si: jindai Zhong'guo geti yu qunti zhi chongjian* [Public and private: the remaking of the individual and the group in modern China]. Taipei: Institute of Modern History, Academia Sinica.

———. 2002. "Fojiao de nuxing, nuxing de fojiao: bijiao jin ershinian lai Zhong-Yingwen de fojiao funu yanjiu" [Buddhism's Women, Women's Buddhism: Comparing the past twenty years of Chinese and English scholarship on Buddhism and Women]. Paper presented at the "Third Conference on Humanistic Buddhism and Contemporary Dialogue," April 20, 2002, Academia Sinica.

———. 2003. "Munu qingjie: Taiwan nuxing chujia yu jicheng jiating jiaose de liangnan" [Emotional ties of mother and daughter: Taiwanese women's dilemma between becoming a nun and inheriting the family role], in Hu Taili, Xu Muzhu, Ye Guanghui, eds., *Qing'gan, qingxu, yu wenhua: Taiwan shehui de wenhua xinli yanjiu* [Affections, emotions, and culture: Research on Taiwan's society cultural psychology]. Taipei: Academia Sinica Ethnology Institute, 2003: 363–404.

Lin Huiwen. 2000. "Taiwan de Ciji, shijie de Ciji" [Taiwan's Ciji, the World's Ciji]. *Jianzhushi* [The Architect], 26(4): 106–109.

Lin Mei-Rong, Ting Jen-Chieh, and Chan Su-Chuan. eds. 2004. *Zainan yu chongjian: jiu er yi zhenzai yu shehui wenhua chongjian lunwenji* [Disaster and Recovery: the Social and Cultural Reconstruction after the 921 Earthquake]. Taipei: Institute of Taiwan History Preparatory Office, Academia Sinica.

Lin Minchao. 2000. "Wutu youqing, chang huai enxin" [My plans have sentiments, always having a grateful heart.] *Jianzhushi* [The Architect], 26(4): 106–109.

Lin Rongzhi. 2002. "Cong yige zishen jiaotuan gongzuozhe kan Taiwan fojiao nuxing de wenti" [A Senior Female Volunteer looks at the Question of Taiwan's Buddhist Women]. Abstract, Seventh Sākyadhitā International Conference on Buddhist Women, Taipei County: Huafan University, July 12, 2002.

Lin Su-wen. 2001. "Renjian fojiao de nuxing'guan: Yi Xingyun dashi wei zhu de kaocha" [Humanistic Buddhism's ideas on women: a study focusing on Master Xingyun]. *Pumen xuebao* [Universal Gate Journal], vol. 3 28–271.

Lin Yusheng. 2003. " 'Chuangzaoxing zhuanhua' de zaisi yu zairen"[Rethinking 'Creative Transformation'], in *Cong gongmin shehui tanqi* [On the topic of civil society], 31–61. Taipei: Lianjing Press.

Lu Hwei-Syin. 2000b. "Xiandai fojiao nuxing de shenti yuyan yu xingbie chongjian: yi ciji gongde hui weili" [The Body Language of Contemporary Buddhist Women and Gender Reconstruction: The Example of the Ciji Compassion-Relief Foundation]. *Collected Papers of the Institute of Ethnology*, Academia Sinica, 88: 275–311.

Lu Shengqiang. 2003. "Yinshun daoshi 'Renjian fojiao' zhi pusaguan ji daocidi chutan" [Preliminary exploration of Master Yinshun's Bodhisattva concept]. *Humanistic Buddhism: Transmitting the Flame-The Fourth Conference on the Theory and Practice of the Venerable Yinshun's Teachings, Collected Essays*, N1–30. Taoyuan: Hongshi Culture and Education Foundation.

Luo Rong, 2004. *Taiwan de 921 chongjian xiaoyuan* [Taiwan's 921 Reconstructed Schools]. Taipei County: Yuanzu Wenhua.

Mei Diwen. 1998. "Cong nuxing zhuyi jiaodu kan renjian jingtu," [Looking at the 'Humanistic Pure Land' from a feminist perspective], in 1998: 151–179. *Renjian jingtu yu xiandai shehui—di sanjie zhonghua guoji foxue huiyi lunwenji* ['Humanistic Pure Land' and Contemporary Society: Collected Papers from the Third Chinese International Buddhist Studies Conference]. Taipei: Dharma Drum Culture.

Pan Xuan. 2004. *Zhengyan fashi: liuli tongxinyuan* [Master Zhengyan: Crystal Concentric Circles]. Taipei, Taiwan: Tianxia.

Shanhui Shuyuan, ed. 1999. *Zhengyan fashi nalu zuji* [Ven. Zhengyan's Footprints]. Taipei: Ciji Culture Press.

Shi Chuanfa. 2002. "Dangdai Taiwan fojiao de shehui yundong: [Social movements in modern Taiwanese Buddhism]. Master's thesis, Graduate Institute of Religious Studies, Hsuan Chuang University.

Shi Jianchun. 2002. "Taiwan fojiao de shehui shixian: yi Xiang'guang nisengtuan weili" [Buddhist Social Practice in Taiwan: The case of the Luminary Buddhist Nunnery]. Paper presented at the Seventh Sākyadhitā International Conference on Buddhist Women, Huafan University, Taiwan, July 15, 2002.

Shi Jianhan, Shi Jianche, and Shi Zimao. eds. 1992. *Jueshu renhua—Xiang'guang niseng foxueyuan chengli shi'er zhounian zhuankan* [Jueshu renhua—Luminary Buddhist Institute's Twelfth Anniversary Special Issue]. Jiayi: Xiang'guang shuxiang.

Shi Jianxian. 2002. "Cong shequ fazhan tan waiji xin'niang jiaoyu" [Discussing foreign brides' education from the perspective of community development]. *Xiang'guang zhuangyan*, vol. 72, Dec. 2002: 1–20.

Shi Jianye. 1999. *Zouguo Taiwan fojiao zhuanxingqi de biqiuni: Shi Tianyi* [Shi Tianyi: A nun who went through the transitional period in Taiwanese Buddhism]. Taipei: Zhongtian Press.

———. 2001. "Fojiao linian yu shixian de ling yizhong duihua xingtai: yi Xiang'guang nisengtuan Gaoxiong zizhulin jingshe foxue yanduban weili" ['Another' Type of Dialogue Pattern Concerning Buddhist Ideas and Practices: A Case Study of the Bambusa Nana Luminary Study Group in Gaoxiong]. *Bulletin of the Institute of Ethnology* (Academia Sinica, Taiwan), no. 90:111–153.

———. 2003. "Yi nuxing xiuxingzhe kan zhanhou Taiwan fojiao zhi fazhan" [A study of the development of post-war Taiwan's Buddhism with a focus on its female Buddhist practitioners] in *Zai Yunhua xiansheng bazhi huadan shouqing lunwenji* [Collected essays to commemorate the 80th Birthday of Mr. Zai Yunhua], March, 449–487. Taipei: Faguang Press.

———. 2004. "Yi Xiang'guang nisengtuan qieyeshan jijinhui weili kan 9.21 zhenzai fojiao zhi jiuyuan" [Buddhist Rescue Acts of the 9.21 Earthquake Damage: A Case Study of the Gaya Foundation at the Luminary Buddhist Institute] in Lin, Ting, and Chan, 289–314.

Shi Huiyan. 1996. "Mingmo qingchu Min-Tai fojiao de hudong" [The Interactions of Fujian and Taiwanese Buddhism in the Late Ming-Early Qing]. *Chung-Hwa Buddhist Journal*, no. 9: 209–242.

———. 1999. "Cong Tai-Min-Ri fojiao de hudong kan niseng zai Taiwan de fazhan" [The Development of the Nuns' Order in Taiwan: An overview from the perspective of Taiwan-Fujian-Japanese Buddhist Interactions]. *Chung-Hwa Buddhist Journal*, no. 12: 249–274.

Shi Xinghe. 2001. "Foguo jingtu de zhenshi yu xuhuan—du Huixinlian yougan" [The real and the illusory in the Buddhist Pure Land: Comments on Reading Huixinlian]. *Guanghua zazhi* [Sinorama], Sept., 78–79.

Shi Taixu. 1956; 1970. *Taixu dashi quanshu* [Complete Works of Taixu]. Taipei: Taixu dashi quanshu yingyin weiyuanhui.

Shi Yikong. 2002. "Taiwan fojiao funu zhi gaishu" [A Perspective on Buddhist Women in Taiwan]. Abstract, Seventh Sākyadhitā International Conference on Buddhist Women, Taipei County: Huafan University, July 12, 2002.

Shi Yinshun. 1989. *Qiliqiji de renjian fojiao* [A truthful and timely Buddhism of the Human World]. Taipei: Zhengwen Press.

———. 1992. *Fo zai renjian* [Buddha in the human world]. Taipei: Zhengwen Press.

———. 2001. *Renjian fojiao lunji* [Collected Essays on Buddhism of the Human World] Xinzhu: Zhengwen Press.

Shi Zhengyan. 1989. *Jingsi yu* [Still Thoughts], vol. I. Taipei: Ciji Compassion Relief Enterprise Foundation.

———. 1992. *Jingsi yu* [Still Thoughts], vol. II. Taipei: Ciji Cultural Foundation.

Shi Zhenhua. 2005. *Xu biqiuni zhuan* [Lives of the Nuns, Continued]. Beijing: Xianzhuang shuju.

Shi Zichun, Shi Jianhan, and Shi Jianhao. eds. 1992. *Xiang'guang—Xiang'guang nisengtuan shi'er zhounian tekan* [Luminary: Luminary Nunnery's Twelfth Anniversary Special Issue]. Jiayi: Luminary Publishing Association.

Shi Ziyao, ed. 2001. *Zai anyeli dian deng: Xiang'guang nisengtuan 921.zhenzai xiezhu chongjian jishi* [Lighting a lamp in the dark night: A Record of Luminary Buddhist Institute's '921 Earthquake' Assistance and Reconstruction]. Taipei: Qieyeshan Foundation.

Shih Chao Hwei. 1994. "Shengren bu si, da dao bu zhi: Ping Ciji yiyuan heyueshu" ['If saints don't die, thieves won't cease': Discussing Ciji Hospital's Contract], in *Hongshi tongxun*, no. 10, 1994.8, 3–8.

———. 2001a. "Yige xiandai biqiuni de chujia jingyan yu shehui guanhuai" [A modern nun's monastic experience and concern for society], in Jiang 2001a: 267–378.

———. 2002a. *'Qian zai chen yin:' xin shiji de fojiao nuxing siwei* [Intonation for Thousands of Years: Buddhist Feminist Thought for a New Century]. Taipei: Fajie.

———. 2002a. "Fojiao yu nuxing: jiegou fomen nanxing shawen zhuyi" [Buddhism and women: Deconstructing male chauvinism in Buddhism], in Shih Chao Hwei, 2002a: 3–137.

———. 2002b. *Shiji xinsheng: dangdai Taiwan fojiao de rushi yu chushi zhi zheng* [New declaration for the 21st century: the debate on world-engagement and world-renouncing in contemporary Taiwan's Buddhism]. Taipei: Fajie Press.

———. 2003a. *Ru shi wo si* [Thus Have I Thought]. Taipei: Fajie.

———. 2003b. "Jieshao Yinshun daoshi" [Introduction to Master Yinshun], in Shih Chao Hwei, 2003b: 3–24. *Huoshui yuantou* [Ever-flowing source of living water]. Taipei: Fajie Press.

———. 2003b. "Tan Taiwan fojiao yu renjian fojiao" [On Taiwanese Buddhism and Buddhism for the Human World], in Shih Chao Hwei 2003b: 25–62.

———. 2003c. "Dangdai fojiao de rongjing yu yinyou" [Glories and Dangers in Contemporary Buddhism], Parts I–III, http://www.hongshi.org.tw, under "Ven Chao Hwei, Preview, Buddhist articles, Feb. 2003c.

Shih Heng Ching. 1995. *Puti daoshang de shan nuren* [Daughters of the Buddha on the Way to Enlightenment]. Taipei: Dongda Press.

Shih Shing Kuang. 1992. "Preface," in Shih Chao Hwei, 1992: 1–6. *Wo yuan jiang shen hua mingyue* [I vow to become an illuminating light]. Taipei: Fajie.

Shih Wu Yin. 1999. "Waiji xin'niang: Taiwan de xifu" [Foreign brides: Taiwan's daughters-in-law], in *Fangangji*, vol. 90, Sept. 3–4.

Su Qianling. 1996. *Buzai mofan de muqin* [Never again a 'model mother']. Taipei: Nushu wenhua.

———. 2002. *Wode mushi shijian* [My motherhood praxis]. Taipei: Nushu wenhua.

Tao Wuliu. 1995. *Shi Zhaohui fashi* [Biography of Master Zhaohui]. Taipei: Dacun Press.

Ting Jen-Chieh. 1999. *Shehui mailuozhong de zhuren xingwei: Taiwan fojiao ciji gongde hui ge'an yanjiu* [Helping Behaviors in Social Context: A Case Study of the Taiwan Buddhist Tzu-Chi Association]. Taipei: Lianjing Press.

Tsai Wen-ting. 1997. "Puti daoshang nu'er duo" [There are many daughters of the Buddha on the path to Enlightenment]. *Guanghua zazhi* [Sinorama] Dec. 1997: 89–101.

Wang Xinyi. 1997. "Liangxing huati yinbao zongjiao xuezhe lunbian" [Gender topic ignites religious scholars' debates]. *Zhongyang ribao* [Central Daily News] July 21, 1997: 3.

Wen Jinke. 2006. *Fojiao fandui sixing: Jingzheng huibian* [Buddhism Opposes the Death Penalty: A Collection of Scriptural Evidence]. Hsinchuang: Fu Jen University Press.

Xiang'guang zhuangyan zazhi she [Luminary Publishing Association]. *Xiang'guang zhuangyan*. Vol. 22 (1990); Vol. 37 (1994); vols. 49–51 (1997a–c). Jiayi, Taiwan.

Xie Yingjun, et al. 2001. "Zaiqu chongjian" [Disaster Area Reconstruction]. *Jianzhu zazhi* [Dialogue: Architecture, Design, Culture], 47: 70–87.

Xu Shirong. 1999. "Xin shehui yundong, fei yingli zuzhi, yu shequ yishi de xingqi" [New social movements, non-profit organizations, and the rise of community consciousness]. *Zhongguo xingzheng* [China Administration], 66: 1–19.

Yang Huinan. 1990. "Dangdai fojiao 'chushi' xing'ge de fenxi" [Analysis of Contemporary Buddhism's 'World-Renouncing' Character] 1990: 317–343. *Dongfang zongjiao yanjiu* [Eastern Religions Research], vol. 1, Oct. 1990.

———. 1991. "Cong 'rensheng fojiao' dao 'renjian fojiao' " [From 'Buddhism for human life' to 'Buddhism for the Human World'] 1991: 75–125. *Dangdai fojiao sixiang zhanwang* [Prospects in Contemporary Buddhist Thought]. Dongda Press.

Yang Liling. 2002. "Weixiao pusa" [The Smiling Bodhisattva] in *Rensheng* [Humanity] no. 223, March 2002: 62.

Yao Lixiang. 1988. "Taiwan diqu guangfuhou fojiao bianqian chutan" [A Preliminary Exploration of the Evolution of Buddhism in Post-1945 Taiwan], in 1988: 229–249. *Fujen xuezhi*, vol. 20.

Yao Shu'e. 1995. *Ciji daolu* [Ciji companion] 237: 6, Dec. 1.

Yao Taishan. 2003. "Shehuihua zhilixia feiyingli zuzhi de xieli celue: yi Ciji jijinhui '921 xiwang gongcheng' wei jianzheng duixiang" [Socialization governance's non-profit organization partnership strategy: examining the case of Ciji's '921 Project Hope']. Master's thesis, National Donghua University.

Yü Chün-fang. 2003. "Taiwan de fojiao nishi: yi Xiang'guang biqiuni weili" [Taiwan's Buddhist Nuns: The Example of the Luminary Nuns," in Li Shiwei, ed., *Taiwan zongjiao yanjiu tongxun*, vol. 5. Taipei: March 2003: 265–287.

Zeng Zhongming, General Editor. 2007. *Taiwan funu nianjian* [Taiwan Women's Almanac]. Taipei: Caituan faren funu quanyi cujin fazhan jijinhui [Foundation of Women's Rights' Promotion and Development].

Zhang Kaiping. 2005. "921 zaihou 'Xin xiaoyuan Yundong' huigu yu chongjian xiaoxue xiaoyuan diaocha yanjiu" [A study of the 'New Campus Movement' and the Elementary School Campuses Reconstructed after the 921 Disaster]. Master's thesis, Department of Architecture, Tunghai University.

Zhang Kunzhen. 2003. *Taiwan de lao zhaitang* [Taiwan's Old "Vegetarian Halls"]. Taipei County: Yuanzu Wenhua.

Zhang Mantao, ed. 1987. *Zhong'guo fojiao shi lunji: Taiwan fojiao pian* [Essays on the history of Chinese Buddhism: Taiwanese Buddhism]. Taipei: Dacheng Press.

Zhang Wei'an. 2000. "Renjian fojiao yu Taiwan shehui—yi shequ wei daochang, yi fuwu wei xiuxing" [Humanistic Buddhism and Taiwan society: community as temple, social service as Buddhist practice]. Paper presented at the conference, "Society, Culture, and Education in the New Century," Institute of Sociology, Qinghua University, Xinzhu, Taiwan, April 29.

Zhang Wei'an and Lin Yixuan. 1997. "Xingbie yu zongjiao: Taiwan fojiao jiaotuanzhong de nuxing diwei" [Gender and Religion: The Status of Women in Taiwan's Buddhist Community]. Paper presented at the International Conference on the Cultural Construction of Gender, (Xinzhu: National Qinghua University, May 24–5).

Zheng Zhiming. 1995. "Cong Taiwan Wanfohui tan fojiao de shehui canyu" [The Case of Taiwan's 'Wanfo hui' and Buddhist social engagement]. Tamkang University Department of History, Proceedings from the International Conference on Buddhism and Chinese Culture, vol. 1.1995.07, 125–155.

Zheng Zimei. 2005. "Dangdai renjian fojiao de zouxiang: you zongjiao yu shehui hudong jiaodu shenshi" [The Direction of Contemporary Humanistic Buddhism: An examination from a religious and social interaction perspective]. *Collected Papers from the 5th Cross-Strait Conference on Yinshun and Humanistic Buddhism*. Nangang: Academia Sinica, April 24–5, 2005, L1–L62.

Zhong'guo fojiaohui wenxian weiyuanhui bianjibu [Editorial Department, Documents Committee, Buddhist Association of the Republic of China]. 1975. *Zhonghua minguo liushinian lai fojiao lunwen mulu* [Index to articles on Buddhism in the Republic of China, 1912–1971]. Taipei: Zhong'guo fojiaohui wenxian weiyuanhui.

Zhonghua Minguo Jianzhushi Gonghui Quanguo Lianhehui Zazhishe. 2000. [National Federation of Architects, Republic of China] *921 jiji zhenzai xilie baodao zhi xiaoyuan chongjian teji* [Special Issue on the School Reconstruction in the 921 Jiji Earthquake Disaster Relief Serial Reportage]. *Jianzhushi* [The Architect], 26(4): 96–153. Taipei: National Federation of Architects Press.

Zhonghua Minguo Jiaoyubu, ed. 2004. [Republic of China, Ministry of Education]. *9.21 zaihou xiaoyuan chongjian zhuan'an xiaozu yuanzuo jishi* [Recovery from the 9.21 Quake: The Achievements of the Campus Rebuilding]. Taipei: Ministry of Education.

Zhonghua Minguo Jiaoyubu Xiaoyuan Chongjian Zhuan'an Xiaozu, ed. [Republic of China, Ministry of Education, School Reconstruction Small Group]. 2001. *9.21 ji 10.22 xiaoyuan chongjian jindu kong'guan shuang zhoubao* [9.21 and 10.22 School Reconstruction Progress and Control Bi-weekly Reports], vols. 1–14, March 1–August 28.

Sources in Other Languages

Adams, Carol J., ed. 1993. *Ecofeminism and the Sacred*. London and New York: Continuum International Publishing Group.

Apter, David E., and Tony Saich. 1994. *Revolutionary Discourse in Mao's Republic*. Cambridge, MA: Harvard University Press.

Arai, Paula. 1999. *Women Living Zen: Japanese Sōtō Buddhist Nuns*. Oxford and NY: Oxford University Press.

Bartholomeusz, Tessa J. 1994. *Women Under the Bo Tree: Buddhist Nuns in Sri Lanka*. Cambridge and NY: Cambridge University Press.

Batchelor, Martine, and Son'gyong Sunim. 2006. *Women in Korean Zen*. Syracuse: Syracuse University Press.

Bianchi, Ester. 2001. *The Iron Statue Monastery, Tiexiangsi: A Buddhist Nunnery of Tibetan Tradition in Contemporary China*. Florence: Leo S. Olschki.

Bingenheimer, Marcus. 2004. *Der Monchsgelehrte Yinshun (*1906) und seine Bedeutung fur den Chinesisch-Taiwanischen Buddhismus im 20. Jahrhundert* [The Scholar-Monk Yinshun and His Position in 20th Century Chinese Buddhism]. Heidelberg: Edition Forum (Wurzburger Sinologische iften).

———. 2007. "Some Remarks on the Usage of Renjian Fojiao and the Contribution of Venerable Yinshun to Chinese Buddhist Modernism," in Hsu et al., 141–161.

Bisnath, Savitri. 2002. "Eradicating poverty, including the empowerment of women throughout their life cycle in a globalizing world." http://www.un.org/womenwatchcswpanel-Bisnath.pdf, accessed on April 19, 2008.

Bond, George D. 1996. "A. T. Ariyaratne and the Sarvodaya Shramadana Movement in Sri Lanka," in Queen and King, eds., 121–146.

Bristow, Michael. 2002, Dec 25. "Taiwan's Foreign Brides." http://news.bbc.co.ukworld/asia-pacific/2603991.stm, accessed on March 19, 2007.

Brook, Timothy. 1993. *Praying for Power: Buddhism and the Formation of Gentry Society in Late-Ming China*. Cambridge: Council on East Asian Studies, Harvard University.

Cabezón, José I., ed. 1992. *Buddhism, Sexuality, and Gender*. Albany, NY: State University of New York Press.

———. 1992. "Mother Wisdom, Father Love: Gender-Based Imagery in Mahayana Buddhist Thought," in Cabezón, ed., 181–199.

Capra, Fritjof. 1996. *The Web of Life: A New Scientific Understanding of Living Systems*. New York, NY: Anchor Books.

Chandler, Stuart. 2004. *Establishing a Pure Land on Earth: The Foguang Buddhist Perspective on Modernization and Globalization*. Honolulu, HI: University of Hawaii Press.

Chang, Jui-shan. 1999. "Scripting Extramarital Affairs: Marital Mores, Gender Politics, and Infidelity in Taiwan," in *Modern China* (January): 69–99.

Cheng, Wei-yi. 2004a. "The Application of Feminist Theory to the Spiritual Practice of Buddhist Nuns: The Case of the Eight Special Rules," in Tsomo, 184–187.

———. 2003. "Luminary Buddhist Nuns in Contemporary Taiwan: A Quiet Feminist Movement." *Journal of Buddhist Ethics* 10: 39–56. http://jbe.gold.ac.ukcurrent10.html, accessed on July 27, 2007.

———. 2007. *Buddhist Nuns in Taiwan and Sri Lanka: A Critique of the Feminist Perspective*. Oxford and New York: Routledge Critical Studies in Buddhism.
Chern, Meei-hwa. 2000. "Encountering Modernity: Buddhist Nuns in Postwar Taiwan," PhD dissertation, Temple University.
———. "New Images of Buddhist Nuns in Postwar Taiwan." Paper presented at the panel "Against the Grain: Buddhist Nuns in Contemporary Taiwan." Association for Asian Studies Annual Meeting. March 23, 2001. Chicago.
Chuang, Tzu-i. 2005. "The Power of Cuteness: Female Infantilization in Urban Taiwan," in *Stanford Journal of East Asian Affairs*. (Summer), vol. 5, no. 2, 21–28.
Clart, Philip, and Charles B. Jones, eds. 2003. *Religion in Modern Taiwan: Tradition and Innovation in a Changing Society*. Honolulu, HI: University of Hawaii Press.
Clémentin-Ojha, Catherine, ed. 1997. *Renouveaux religieux en Asie*. Paris: ÉFEO.
Cole, Alan. 1998. *Mothers and Sons in Chinese Buddhism*. Stanford: Stanford University Press.
Crane, Hillary. 2001. "Men in Spirit: The Masculinization of Taiwanese Buddhist Nuns." PhD dissertation, Brown University.
DeVido, Elise A. 2004. "The New Funeral Culture in Taiwan" in DeVido and Vermander, eds., *Creeds, Rites, and Videotapes: Narrating Religious Experience in Taiwan*, 235–249. Taipei: Taipei Ricci Institute.
Đỗ, Thiện. 1999. "The Quest for Enlightenment and Cultural Identity: Buddhism in Contemporary Vietnam," in Ian Harris, 254–283.
Diamond, Irene, and Gloria Orenstein, eds. 1990. *Reweaving the World: The Emergence of Ecofeminism*. San Francisco: Sierra Club Books.
Duby, Georges, and Michelle Perrot. 1992. "Writing the History of Women," in Pauline Schmitt Pantel, ed. *A History of Women: From Ancient Goddesses to Christian Saints* (History of Women in the West, vol. 1). Cambridge: Belknap Press, Introduction.
Farris, Catherine S. P. 1988. "Language and Sex Role Acquisition in a Taiwanese Kindergarten: A Semiotic Analysis." PhD dissertation, University of Washington.
———. 2004. "Women's Liberation under 'East Asian Modernity' in China and Taiwan: Historical, Cultural, and Comparative Perspectives," in Farris, Lee, and Rubinstein, 325–376.
Farris, Catherine, Anru Lee, and Murray Rubinstein. eds. 2004. *Women in the New Taiwan: Gender Roles and Gender Consciousness in a Changing Society* [Taiwan in the Modern World Series]. Armonk, NY and London, England: East Gate M. E. Sharpe.
Faure, Bernard. 2003. *The Power of Denial: Buddhism, Purity, and Gender*. Princeton: Princeton University Press.
Findly, Ellison Banks, ed. 2000. *Women's Buddhism, Buddhism's Women: Tradition, Revision, Renewal*. Boston: Wisdom Publications.
Foy, Geoffrey E. 2002. "Engaging Religion: An Ethnography of Three Religious Adherents in Taiwan's Academic Culture." PhD dissertation, Graduate Theological Union.
Gold, Thomas B. 1994. "Civil Society and Taiwan's Quest for Identity," in Stevan Harrell and Chun chieh Huang, eds., *Cultural Change in Postwar Taiwan*, 47–68. Boulder, CO: Westview.

Gates, Hill. 1996. *China's Motor: A Thousand Years of Petty Capitalism*. Ithaca, NY: Cornell University Press.

Goossaert, Vincent. 2000. "Counting the Monks: The 1736-1939 Census of the Chinese Clergy," in *Late Imperial China*, vol. 21, no. 2: 40-85.

———. 2002. "Les sciences sociales découvrent le bouddhisme chinois du Xxe siècle," in *Archives de sciences socials des religions*. 120 (Oct.-Dec.): 33-45.

———. 2006. "Resident Specialists and Temple Managers in Late Imperial China," in *Min-su ch'ü-i* [Journal of Chinese Ritual, Theatre, and Folklore], no. 153: 25-67.

Grant, Beata. 1996. "Female Holder of the Lineage: Linji Chan Master Zhiyuan Xinggang (1597-1654)." In *Late Imperial China*, vol. 17, no. 2, Dec., 51-76.

Gross, Rita M. 1993. *Buddhism After Patriarchy: A Feminist History, Analysis, and Reconstruction of Buddhism*. Albany, NY: State University of New York Press.

Gutschow, Kim. 2004. *Being a Buddhist Nun: The Struggle for Enlightenment in the Himalayas*. Cambridge, MA: Harvard University Press.

Harris, Ian., ed. 1999. *Buddhism and Politics in Twentieth Century Asia*. London: Pinter.

Heirman, Ann. 2001. "Chinese Nuns and their Ordination in Fifth Century China," in *Journal of the International Association of Buddhist Studies*, vol. 24, no. 2, 275-304.

Hinsch, Bret. 2006. "Confucian Filial Piety and the Construction of the Ideal Chinese Buddhist Woman," in *Journal of Chinese Religions* 30.01: 49-75.

Hsieh, Evelyn Ding-hwa. 1991. "Images of Women in Ch'an Buddhist Literature of the Sung Period," in Peter N. Gregory and Daniel A. Getz, eds., *Buddhism in the Sung*, 148-187. Honolulu, HI: University of Hawaii Press.

Hs'ing, Lawrence Fu-Ch'üan. 1983. *Taiwanese Buddhism and Buddhist Temples*. Taipei: Pacific-Cultural Foundation.

Hsu, Min-tao. 1988. "Fitting in to the 'No Return Trip': Women's Perception of Marriage and Family in Taiwan," in *Proceedings of the National Science Council, ROC (C)*, vol. 8, no. 4, 527-538.

Hsu Mutsu, Jinhua Chen, and Lori Meeks, eds. 2007. *Development and Practice of Humanitarian Buddhism: Interdisciplinary Perspectives*. Hualian: Tzu Chi University Press.

Huang, Chien-yu Julia. 2001. "Recapturing Charisma: Emotion and Rationalization in a Globalizing Buddhist Movement From Taiwan." PhD dissertation, Boston University.

———. 2003. "The Tzu-Chi Foundation of Taiwan," in Queen, Prebish, and Keown, eds.,136-153.

Huang, Chien-Yu Julia, and Weller, Robert P. 1998. "Merit and Mothering: Women and Social Welfare in Taiwanese Buddhism." *Journal of Asian Studies* 57(2), 379-396.

Hughes-Shaver, Sarah and Brady Hughes. 1997. *Women in World History, Volume 2—Readings from 1500 to the Present*. Armonk and London, M. E. Sharpe.

Jones, Charles B. 1999. *Buddhism in Taiwan: Religion and the State, 1660-1990*. Honolulu, HI: University of Hawaii Press.

Jones, Ken. 1989. *The Social Face of Buddhism: An Approach to Political and Social Activism*. London: Wisdom Publications.

Jordan, David K. 1994. "Changes in Postwar Taiwan and Their Impact on the Popular Practice of Religion," in Harrell, Stevan, and Huang Chun-chieh, eds., *Cultural Change in Postwar Taiwan*, 137–160. Boulder, CO: Westview.

Kaldor, Mary. 2003. *Global Civil Society: An Answer To War*. Cambridge, UK: Polity Press.

Kawanami, Hiroko. 1990. "The Religious Standing of Burmese Buddhist Nuns (thilá-shin): The Ten Precepts and Religious Respect Words," in *Journal of the International Association of Buddhist Studies*, vol. 13, no. 1, 17–39.

Keyes, Charles F. 1984. "Mother or mistress but never a monk: Buddhist notions of female gender in rural Thailand," *American Ethnologist*, 11.2, 223–241.

Keown, Damien. 2003. *Dictionary of Buddhism*. Comp. Stephen Hodge, Charles Jones, and Paola Tinti. New York, NY: Oxford University Press.

Laliberté, André. 1998. "Tzu Chi and the Buddhist Revival in Taiwan: Rise of a New Conservatism?" *China Perspectives* 19: 44–50.

———. 2001. "Religious Organizations and Welfare Policy in Taiwan and China." *Taipei Ricci Institute Bulletin*. 4: 68–76.

———. 2003. "Religious Change and Democratization in Postwar Taiwan: Mainstream Buddhist Organizations and the Kuomintang, 1947–1996," in Philip Clart, and Charles B. Jones, eds., 158–85.

———. 2004. *The Politics of Buddhist Organizations in Taiwan, 1989–2003: Safeguard the Faith, Build a Pure Land, Help the Poor*. London: Routledge/Curzon.

Levering, Miriam L. 1982. "The Dragon Girl and the Abbess of Mo-shan: Gender and Status in the Ch'an Buddhist Tradition," in *Journal of the International Association of Buddhist Studies* 5:1 (1982): 19–35.

———. 1989. "Scripture and its Reception: a Buddhist Case," in Levering, ed. *Rethinking Scripture: Essays from a Comparative Perspective*, 58–101. Albany, NY: SUNY Press.

———. 1991. "Miao-tao and Her Teacher Ta-hui," in Peter N. Gregory and Daniel A. Getz, eds., *Buddhism in the Sung*, 188–219. Honolulu, HI: University of Hawaii Press.

———. 1992. "Lin-chi (Rinzai) Ch'an and Gender: The Rhetoric of Equality and the Rhetoric of Heroism," in Cabezón, ed., 137–156.

———. 1997. "Stories of Enlightened Women in Ch'an and the Chinese Buddhist Female Bodhisattva/Goddess Tradition," in Karen L. King, ed., *Women and Goddess Traditions*, 137–76. Minneapolis, Minn.: Fortress Press.

———. 1998. "Dōgen's Raihaitokuzui and Women Teaching in Sung Ch'an," in *Journal of the International Association of Buddhist Studies*, vol. 21, no. 1, 77–110.

———. 2000. "Women Ch'an Masters: The Teacher Miao-tsung as Saint" in Arvind Sharma, ed., *Women Saints in World Religions*, 180–204. Albany, NY: SUNY Press.

Levine, Sarah. 2001. "The Finances of a Twentieth Century Buddhist Mission: Building Support for the Theravada Nuns' Order of Nepal," in *Journal of the International Association of Buddhist Studies*, vol. 24, no. 2, 217–239.

Li Yuzhen. 2000. "Crafting Women's Religious Experience in a Patrilineal Society: Taiwanese Buddhist Nuns in Action (1945-1999)." PhD dissertation, Cornell University.

———. 2004a. "The Religiosity and Leadership of Taiwanese Bhiksuni Leaders: Guanyin and Bhiksunis Fuhui and Zhengyan," in Tsomo, 97-104.

———. 2004b. "The Path to Enlightenment: The Autobiographies of Two Contemporary Taiwanese Bhikusnis," in Tsomo, 360-364.

Lin Rongzhi. 2004a. "The Future of Buddhism in Taiwan: The Perspective of a Senior Female Volunteer," in Tsomo, 80-82.

Liu King pong, ed. 1997. *Lotus Flower of the Heart: Thirty Years of Tzu Chi Photographs*. Taipei: Still Thoughts Cultural Mission.

Lovelock, James E. 2000. *Gaia: A New Look on Life on Earth*. New Edition ed. Oxford: Oxford University Press.

Lu Hwei-Syin. 1998. "Gender and Buddhism in Contemporary Taiwan: A Case Study of Tzu Chi Foundation." *Proceedings of the National Science Council, Part C: Humanities and Social Sciences* 8 (4): 539-550.

———. 2000a. "Emotional Discourses in the Study of Religion." Paper presented at the 18th Quinquennial Congress of the International Association for the History of Religions, August 6-13, Durban, South Africa.

———. 2004. "Transcribing Feminism: Taiwanese Women's Experiences," in Farris, Lee, and Rubinstein, eds., 223-243.

Makley, Charlene. 1999. "Embodying the Sacred: Gender and Monastic Revitalization in China's Tibet." PhD dissertation, University of Michigan.

McCarthy, Kathleen D., ed. 1990. *Lady Bountiful Revisited: Women, Philanthropy, and Power*. New Brunswick, NJ: Rutgers University Press.

———, ed. 2000. *Women, Philanthropy, and Civil Society*. Bloomington, IL: Indiana University Press.

McHale, Shawn F. 2003. *Print and Power: Confucianism, Communism, and Buddhism in the Making of Modern Vietnam*. Honolulu, HI: University of Hawaii Press.

McNamara, Jo Ann Kay. 1996. *Sisters in Arms: Catholic Nuns Through Two Millennia*. Cambridge: Harvard University Press.

Mintz, Steven. 1995. *Moralists and Modernizers: America's Pre Civil War Reformers*. Baltimore, MD: The Johns Hopkins University Press.

Moon, Seungsook, 2002. "Carving Out Space: Civil Society and the Women's Movement in South Korea," *Journal of Asian Studies*, 61.2, May 2002, 473-500.

Overmyer, Daniel L. 1991. "Women in Chinese Religions: Submission, Struggle, Transcendence," in Koichi Shinohara and Gregory Schopen, eds. *From Benares to Beijing: Essays on Buddhism and Chinese Religion in Honour of Prof. Jan Yün-hua*, 91-120. Oakville: Mosaic Press.

Pascoe, Peggy. 1990. *Relations of Rescue: The Search for Female Authority in the American West, 1874-1939*. New York, NY: Oxford University Press.

Pittman, Don A. 2001. *Toward a Modern Chinese Buddhism: Taixu's Reforms*. Honolulu, HI: University of Hawaii Press.

Plant, Judith.1989. *Healing the Wounds: The Promise of Ecofeminism*. British Columbia: New Society Publishers.

Prebish, Charles S. and Martin Baumann, eds. 2002. *Westward Dharma: Buddhism Beyond Asia*. Berkeley, CA: University of California Press.
Primavesi, Anna. 2000. *Sacred Gaia: Holistic Theology and Earth System Science*. London: Routledge Press.
Qin Wenjie. 2000. "The Buddhist Revival in Post-Mao China: Women Reconstruct Buddhism on Mt. Emei." PhD dissertation, Harvard University.
Queen, Christopher S. and Sallie B. King, eds. 1996. *Engaged Buddhism: Buddhist Liberation Movements in Asia*. Albany: SUNY Press.
Queen, Christopher. Charles Prebish, and Damien Keown, eds. 2003. *Action Dharma: New Studies in Engaged Buddhism*. London: Routledge/Curzon.
Reed, Barbara E. 1992. "The Gender Symbolism of Kuan-yin Bodhisattva," in Cabezón 159–180.
———. 2003 "Guanyin Narratives: Wartime and Postwar," in Clart and Jones 186–203.
Ruch, Barbara, General Ed. 2002. *Engendering Faith: Women and Buddhism in Premodern Japan*. Ann Arbor, MI: Center for Japanese Studies, University of Michigan.
Salgado, Nirmala S. 1996. "Ways of Knowing and Transmitting Religious Knowledge: Case Studies of Theravada Buddhist Nuns" in *Journal of the International Association of Buddhist Studies*, vol. 19, no. 1, 61–79.
Sangharakshita. 2000. *What is the Sangha? The Nature of Spiritual Community*. Birmingham, England: Windhorse.
Sangren, Steven. 1983. "Female Gender in Chinese Religious Symbols: Kuan Yin, Ma Tsu, and the Eternal Mother" in *Signs: Journal of Women in Culture and Society*. 9:1, 4–25.
Santikaro Bhikkhu. "Socially Engaged Buddhism and Modernity: What Sorts of Animals are They?" http://www.bpf.org/tsangha/skbsebmod.html, accessed on August 15, 2007.
Sered, Susan Starr. 1994. *Priestess, Mother, Sacred Sister: Religions Dominated by Women*. Oxford and New York: Oxford University Press.
Sergiovanni, Thomas J. 2000. *The Lifeworld of Leadership: Creating Culture, Community, and Personal Meaning in Our Schools*. San Francisco, CA: Jossey Bass Publishers.
Shi Chuandao. 2004a. "Buddhist Women in Taiwan," in Tsomo, 63–65.
Shi Hengqing. 1999. "Buddhist Spirituality in Modern Taiwan," in Yoshinori Takeuchi, ed., *Buddhist Spirituality-Later China, Korea, Japan, and the Modern World*, 427–431. New York: Crossroad Publishing Company.
Shi Yikong. 2004a. "A Perspective on Buddhist Women in Taiwan," in Tsomo, 66–7.
Shi Zhengyan. 1993. *Still Thoughts*. Ed. Hsin-chiang Kao. Taipei: Chung Pao Printing Company.
Shi Zhengyan. 1993. *Still Thoughts* [trans. Lin Chia-hui], vol. I. Taipei: Still Thoughts Cultural Mission.
———. 1996. *Still Thoughts* [trans. Liu King-pong], vol. II. Taipei: Tzu Chi Cultural Publishing.
Simon, Scott. 2003. *Sweet and Sour: Lifeworlds of Taipei Women Entrepreneurs*. Lanham, MD: Rowman and Littlefield.

Skilling, Peter. 2001. "Nuns, Laywomen, Donors, Goddesses: Female Roles in Early Indian Buddhism," in *Journal of the International Association of Buddhist Studies*, vol. 24, no. 2, 241–274.
Sponberg, Alan. 1992. "Attitudes towards Women and the Feminine in Early Buddhism," in Cabezón, 3–36. Albany: SUNY Press.
Thích Nhất Hạnh. 1965. *Đạo Phật hiện đại hóa* [Modernization of Buddhism]. Sàigòn: Lá Bối.
———. 1967. *Vietnam: Lotus in a Sea of Fire*. New York: Hill and Wang.
Topley, Margery. 1978. "Marriage Resistance in Rural Kwangtung," in Arthur P. Wolf, ed., *Studies in Chinese Society*, 67–88. Stanford: Stanford University Press.
Travagnin, Stefania. 2004a. "Ven. Miaoqing and Yuantong Chan Nunnery: A New Beginning for Monastic Women in Taiwan," in Tsomo, 83–96.
———. 2004b. "Master Yinshun and Buddhist Women in Taiwan-Fayuan and Yitong Nunneries, Disciples of Guanyin in Northwest Taiwan," in Tsomo, 186–198.
Tsai, Kathryn Ann. 1994. *Lives of the Nuns: Biographies of Chinese Buddhist Nuns from the Fourth to Sixth Centuries: A Translation of the Pi-ch'iu-ni chuan, compiled by Shih Bao-ch'ang*. Honolulu, HI: University of Hawaii Press.
Tsomo, Karma Lekshe, ed. 1999. *Buddhist Women Across Cultures: Realizations*. Albany: SUNY Press.
———. 1999. "Mahāprajāpatī's Legacy: The Buddhist Women's Movement, An Introduction," in Tsomo, 1–44.
———, ed. 2004a. *Bridging Worlds Buddhist Women's Voices Across Generations*. Taipei: Yuan Chuan Press.
———, ed. 2004b. *Proceedings of the 8th Sākyadhitā International Conference on Buddhist Women: Discipline and Practice of Buddhist Women, Past and Present*. Kailua, HI: Sākyadhitā International.
———, ed. 2004c. *Buddhist Women and Social Justice*. Albany: State University of New York Press.
———, ed, 2006. *Out of the Shadows: Socially-Engaged Buddhist Women*. Bibliotheca Indo-Buddhica Series, no. 240. Delhi: Sri Satguru Publications, Indian Books Centre.
Tsung Shiu-kuen Fan. 1978. "Moms, Nuns, and Hookers: Extrafamilial Alternatives for Village Women in Taiwan." PhD dissertation, University of California, San Diego.
Welch, Holmes. 1967. *The Practice of Chinese Buddhism, 1900–1950*. Cambridge, MA: Harvard University Press.
———. 1968. *The Buddhist Revival in China*. Cambridge, MA: Harvard University Press.
Weller, Robert P. 1999. *Alternate Civilities: Democracy and Culture in China and Taiwan*. Boulder, CO: Westview Press.
Yang Chang-huey and Changyi Zhang. 2004a. "From Home to Buddhist Monastery: Links Between Female Lay Buddhists and Buddhist Nuns," in Tsomo, 272–277.
Yeh Wen-ying. "Good Husbands and Fathers: The Tzu Cheng Faith Corps." http://taipei.tzuchi.org.tw/tzquart/99fall/99fall.htm, accessed on July 2, 2007.

Yeshe, Bhiksuni Tenzin. 2000. "Nuns in Contemporary Taiwanese and Tibetan Buddhism." M. Phil. China Centre, Australian National University.

Yü Chün-fang. 2001. *Kuan-yin: The Chinese Transformation of Avalokitesvara*. New York: Columbia University Press.

Zhang Wei'an. "Silent Social Reform: The Compassion-Relief Tzu-Chi Foundation as a Model for Social Change." Paper presented at the Annual Meeting of the American Sociological Association, San Francisco, Aug. 21–25, 1998.

Zhou Yiqun. "The Hearth and the Temple: Mapping Female Religiosity in Late Imperial China, 1550–1900." In *Late Imperial China*, vol. 24, no. 2 (December 2003): 109–155.

Index

Page numbers in **boldface** indicate illustrations.

activism, Buddhist, 87, 96, 102, 104–105, 110, 151n57. *See also* Ciji: avoidance of politics by; Engaged Buddhism
adopted daughters (*yangnu*), 17, 39–40, 126n72, 131n30
animal rights, 101, 103, 105
architecture of schools, 52–54, **53**, 59
Article Six, 59, 137n56
Avalokiteśvara, 72, 75, 157n34. *See also* Guanyin

Baisheng (monk), 16, 90, 147n64
Baochang (monk), 23
BAROC (Buddhist Association of ROC), 15, 55, 82, 99, 107, 109
Benyuan Temple, 21
betel-nut, 12, 55, 56, 71, 136n41
Bhave, Vinoba, 100
bhikkhu chauvinism, 107, 109
Bingenheimer, Marcus, 150n50
Biographies of Chinese Nuns (Lianchan, ed.), 21
Biqiuni zhuan (Baochang), 23
Bodhisattva of Compassion. *See* Guanyin
Buddha Light Mountain (Foguangshan), 59, 121n15, 133n46; nuns of, 9–20, 67, 112, 126n83, 128n113, 151n57, 153n91. *See also* Xingyun (monk)
Buddhism, Engaged: global, 100, 105–106, 110; in Taiwan, 100–101; in Vietnam, 97, 100

Buddhism, global, 26
Buddhism for the Human Realm. *See renjian fojiao*
Buddhism for this world. *See renjian fojiao*
Buddhism in PRC, 7, 97–98, 110, 121n3, 129n122
Buddhism in Taiwan: decentralized nature of, 7, 108, 128n111; leadership and gender within, 79, 107, 109, 117, 156n32; three mountaintops of, 93, 121n15; unique features of, 15–16, 27, 111; valued for contributions to social welfare, 13, 88, 116. *See also* Buddhists in Taiwan; Buddhism in Taiwan, history of
Buddhism in Taiwan, history of: Qing era, 8–13; Japanese colonial period, 13–14; after 1949, 14–19
Buddhist activism, 87, 96, 102, 104–105, 110, 151n57. *See also* Ciji: avoidance of politics by; Buddhism, Engaged
Buddhist Association of ROC (BAROC), 15, 55, 82, 99, 107, 109
Buddhist campus movement (*dazhuan xuefo yundong*), 18–19
Buddhist laywomen, 3, 70, 120n9. *See also* Buddhists in Taiwan: preponderance of women among; Ciji: lay members of; *zhaigu; zhaijiao*
Buddhist nuns. *See* headings beginning *nuns, Buddhist*

181

Buddhist revival: in China, 94–98; global, 94, 97; in Sri Lanka, 94; in Taiwan, 1–2, 9, 14–15, 18–19, 90, 112; in Taiwan, civil society and, 2, 81, 104, 114; in Vietnam, 97
Buddhist teachings on gender equality, 16, 17, 27, 87, 107
Buddhist temples in Taiwan, numbers of, 120n6
Buddhists in Taiwan: interactions with Buddhists in China, 8–9, 13, 14; numbers of, 120n6; preponderance of women among, 2, 14, 15–16

candle *samādhi*, 43–44
Center for Buddhist Studies (National Taiwan University), 19
Chao Hwei (nun), **102, 103**; activism, 102–105; feminism, 105–109, 125n69; views on feminine qualities, 26
charisma: defined, 39; of Zhengyan, 38–39
charity in Buddhist tradition, 13–14, 23, 24, 70, 71–72, 148n16
charity in Taiwan delegated to private sector, 50, 78, 143n6
Chen Chien-zong, 60
Chen Ruoxi, 116–117
Chen Xiazhu (later Wu Yin). See Wu Yin
Cheng, Wei-yi, 80, 107–108, 122n5
chengdan rulai jiaye, 69
Chiang Kai-shek, 56, 128n24, 138n60
China, nuns' order in, 23–24. See also Fuhu Temple (Sichuan, PRC), nuns of
Chongfan Taohuayuan (Chen Ruoxi), 116
Christian missionaries, 56–57, 94, 106, 148n16
Christianity: competition of, with Buddhism, 19, 94–95, 114, 125n62, 148n24; and curriculum in Taiwan, 59; as model for Buddhist revival 94, 106, 148n16; parallels with Ciji of, 37, 41

Chuandao (monk), 101–102
Chuanqing (monk), 22
Chun Lei (pseudonym), 17–18
cibei. See compassion, Buddhist
Cicheng dui (Ciji Compassion Faith Corps), 63, 71, 78
Ciji (Ciji Compassion-Relief Foundation; Fojiao ciji gongde hui), 29, **64, 71**, 121n15; avoidance of politics by, 55, 71, 78, 100; commissioners of, 31, 63; and Confucian values, 31, 50, 53; cultural reform goals of, 56–57, 101; education programs of, 52, 58–60, 67; egalitarianism and hierarchy in, 38; and environmentalism, 54–55, 101; and feminism, 76–78, 112; global activities of, 134n8, 138n60; group identity of, 32, 36, 37, 38, 45–46, 71; headquarters in Hualian, 29, **32, 35**, 45–46; lay members of, 70–72; men of, 63, 70–71; narratives of, 45–47; nuns of, 65–68, 69; and *renjian fojiao*, 46; and self-reliance, 45, 66; spirit of, 52. *See also* Zhengyan
Ciji Compassion Faith Corps (Cicheng dui), 63, 71, 78
Ciji Teachers' Association, 29, 31, 56, 70. *See also* Still Thoughts Camp
civil society, 2, 7, 81, 96, 104, 114–116
coeducation in Taiwan, effect on monastic recruitment, 19
compassion, Buddhist, 90, 95, 111, 141n48, 142n72; and Ciji, 43, 44, 72, 75, 76; and Luminary Buddhist Institute, 80, 87
compassion, female, 26, 71, 75, 76, 90, 141n48
Compassion Faith Corps, Ciji (Cicheng dui), 63, 71, 78
Confucian values: and Buddhism, 127n96; and Ciji, 31, 50, 53
Conghui (nun), 81
Crane, Hillary, 129n121, 140n29
Crosby, Kate, 142n76

Index

da zhangfu, 68–69, 87, 89, 139n21, 140n29
Dalai Lama, 84, 112, 145n31, 153n87, 153n89, 154n108
Daoist clergy, 122n20, 123n29
dazhuan xuefo yundong, 18–19
death penalty, 103
Defu (nun), 69
Deni (nun), 67, 69
Deqin (nun), 14
Dharma Drum Mountain (Fagushan), 100–101, 113, 114, 121n15
dharma lecturing: by Luminary nuns, 79, 81–82, 87–88; by nuns, 14, 15, 22, 23, 81, 132n42
Dharmapāla, 94
Dijiao (nun), 21
Dizang Boddhisatva, 21, 72
dual ordination system, 16–17, 124n61, 125n69, 127n93

earthquake of Dec. 26, 2003 in Bam, Iran, 134n8
earthquake of Sept. 21, 1999 in Taiwan, 49; responses to, 84–85 (*See also* New School Campus Movement; Project Hope)
economic production of nuns, 66, 127n102
Eight Special Rules in Taiwan, 17, 27, 107–109, 110, 125n71
eighty-four ugly gestures of women, 107, 124n61
Emei, Mount (Emei Shan). *See* Fuhu Temple (Sichuan, PRC), nuns of
empowerment, 77–78, 80, 86, 90, 138n3
Engaged Buddhism: global, 100, 105–106, 110; in Taiwan, 100–101; in Vietnam, 97, 100
eremitic monastics, 21
essentialist notions of gender, 26, 76, 89–90, 113, 138n5
Eternal Mother (*wusheng laomu*), 10, 24, 41, 42, 72

Fagushan (Dharma Drum Mountain), 100–101, 113, 114, 121n15
family, relation of nuns to, 25, 67, 81, 128n111, 133n46, 144n7
fangzhang, 82, 143n4
female disadvantages, in Buddhist teaching, 16, 75–76, 87, 109, 124n61, 142n74
feminine qualities: negative perceptions of, 69, 124n61, 76; positive perceptions of, 26, 64, 72, 74–75, 76, 89–90, 142n76
feminism, 2, 26–27, 77, 80, 90, 146n60. *See also* women's movement in Taiwan
Fenglin clinic incident, 43–44, 132n45
fengshui, 56, 137n43
filial piety, 31, 52, 75, 127n96, 128n111
Five Hindrances, 124n61
Foguangshan (Buddha Light Mountain), 59, 121n15, 133n46; nuns of, 9–20, 67, 112, 126n83, 128n113, 151n57, 153n91. *See also* Xingyun (monk)
Fojiao ciji gongde hui (Ciji Compassion-Relief Foundation). *See* Ciji
foreign brides in Taiwan, 85–86
Foying (nun), 16
Fuhu Temple (Sichuan, PRC), nuns of, 90, 121n3, 133n46, 140n27, 141n55, 142n71, 146n55, 156n25
Fuhui (nun), 21
Fujioshi Jikai, 17
fuquan (empower), 80, 86, 138n3. *See also* empowerment
fuyan, muci, 72, 131n19

gender construction in Taiwan, 129n121
gender equality: in Buddhist institutions, 26–27, 69, 80, 87, 107–109, 117, 125n69; Buddhist teachings on, 16, 17, 27, 87, 107
gender essentialism, 26, 76, 89–90, 113, 138n5

gender roles in Taiwan, 18, 75, 88–89; in Ciji, 64, 71
globalization, 97
Goossaert, Vincent, 9, 12, 123n29
Grant, Beata, 23, 69, 132n42, 139n24
Gu Zhonghua, 115–116
Guangqin (monk), 18, 124n61
Guanyin, **11**; and Ciji, 29, 40, 64, 72–76 passim, 113; and Luminary Buddhist Institute, 87; and traditions in China and Taiwan, 8, 24, 59, 72–73, 74, 141n50; in Vietnam, 111, 141n50; and *zhaijiao*, 10–11, 72
Gutschow, Kim, 126n77

Henan Temple, 22
Heng Ching (nun), 19, 26, 125n69, 155n6
Hiuwan (nun), 19, **20**, 31, 67
Hongshi Buddhist Institute, 21, 102, **104**, 109–110, 152n67. *See also* Chao Hwei
Hsieh, Evelyn Ding-Hwa, 23, 69
Hs'ing Fu-Ch'üan, 8, 9
Huafan University, 19, 21, 67
Hualian, 22, 42–43. *See also* Ciji: headquarters in Hualian
Huang, C. Julia, 38, 39, 60, 63, 66, 129n3, 130n5
Huang Long-min, 60
hui (insight), 87
Huixinlian (Chen Ruoxi), 116–117
Huiyan (nun), 9
humanism: Buddhist, 50 (*See also renjian fojiao*); Confucian, 50; Western, 50
Humanistic Education Foundation (Renben jiaoyu jijinhui), 49, 50, 51, 152n69

immigration to Taiwan: of Chinese monastics in 1949, 14–15; of foreign brides, 8
infinite worlds (*tiankong*), 7, 118
insight (*prajñā*; *hui*), 87, 142n72

International Network of Engaged Buddhists (INEB), 110, 154n108
Iran, Ciji in, 134n8

Japan, nuns' order in, 119n1
Japanese Buddhism in Taiwan: opportunities for women, 14; sects in colonial period, 13
Japanese colonial government in Taiwan, 9, 12, 13–14, 123n40
Japanese-trained nuns in Taiwan, 14, 15, 41, 81
Jianduan (nun), 88–89
Jiang Canteng, 12, 20, 101, 109
Jianxian (nun), 86–87, 89, 146n62
Jingding (nun), 21
jingsi yu (still thoughts). *See* Still Thoughts (*jingsi yu*)
Jingsi yu (Zhengyan). *See Still Thoughts* (Zhengyan)
Jingxin (nun), 26
Jones, Charles B., 9, 12, 66, 120n9, 123n31
Jones, Ken, 110
Jueli (monk), 14
jueshu renhua, 87–88
Juzan (monk), 98

Kan Zhengzong, 9, 120n9
Kang Liwen, 138n63
karuṇā (compassion), 87, 142n72. *See also* compassion, Buddhist
keji chongren, 96, 116, 136n42
keji fuli, 56
kitchen work, 79, 89, 124n61, 143n2, 145n26
Korea, nuns' order in, 111, 119n1, 125n62

laywomen, Buddhist, 3, 70, 120n9. *See also* Buddhists in Taiwan: preponderance of women among; Ciji: lay members of; *zhaigu*; *zhaijiao*
Levering, Miriam, 23, 68–69, 132n43, 142n72

Li Yuzhen: on BAROC 7; on Guanyin worship, 73; on laywomen, 126n78; on nuns' achievements, 21, 23, 126n81; on nuns' background, 24; on nuns' family relations, 133n46; on nuns' struggle, 16, 27, 79, 124n54; on nuns' views, 124n61; typology of Buddhist women, 10–11; on Zhengyan, 40
Lianchan (nun), 21, 154n108
Liaoyi (nun), 20
Lin Yusheng, 115
Lives of the Nuns (Baochang), 23
Longlian (nun), 106, 153n83
Lotus Sūtra, 43, 73, 124n61, 130n4, 132n43
Lu, Annette, 128n114, 136n41
Lu Hwei-syin, 63, 113, 131n19
Luminary Buddhist Institute, 79–91; compared with Ciji, 67, 82, 85, 87; cultural mission of, 84, 113; and education 79, 84; and self-reliance, 144n7; social service of, 84–87; training of nuns by, 82–83, 113

Malalasekera, G. P., 97
Malaysia, Ciji in, 138n60
Mao Zedong, 41, 56, 139n15
marriage resistance, 122n23, 139n25, 146n55
masculine qualities, 68, 69, 71
maternal traits, 63, 64–65, 72–73, 74–77, 113
Mazu, 8, 41
Mencius, 87, 139n21
Miaoqing (nun), 14
Miaoshan, 73, 141n55. *See also* Guanyin
Miaoxiu (nun), 14
Mingjia (nun), 89, 117
mixed-sex *sangha*, 7–8, 89, 121n5–122n5
mofa, 15, 55
monastics, numbers of, in Taiwan, 120n4. *See also* nuns, Buddhist, in Taiwan: numbers of

monks, Buddhist, from China: dependence on Taiwanese women after 1949, 15, 106–107; as leaders of post-1949 Buddhism in Taiwan, 15
monks, Buddhist, in Taiwan: impediments to recruiting, 18, 128n113; ordination of, 9, 13, 14, 18; ratio of, to nuns, 1, 16
Museum of World Religions, 20

Nationalist government in Taiwan, 7, 9, 14–15, 96, 99, 126n78, 140n42
Nenghai (monk), 106
New Culture Movements in China, 56, 106, 138n60
New School Campus Movement, 49, 51, 54. *See also* Project Hope (Xiwang gongcheng)
New Taiwan Civilization, 50, 58. *See also* Ciji: cultural reform goals of
National Taiwan University, 19
nuns, Buddhist, biographies of, 21, 23–24, 126n81
nuns, Buddhist, in China, 23–24, 128n103. *See also* Fuhu Temple (Sichuan, PRC), nuns of
nuns, Buddhist, in Japan, 119n1
nuns, Buddhist, in Korea, 111, 119n1, 125n62
nuns, Buddhist, in Sri Lanka, 23, 112, 119n1, 142n74
nuns, Buddhist, in Theravādin countries, 84, 119n1
nuns, Buddhist, in Taiwan: diversity of, 7, 19–22, 108; during Japanese colonial period, 13–14; during Qing era, 12–13; education missions of, 19–20; family relations of, 25, 67, 81, 128n111, 133n46, 144n7; and feminism, 2, 26–27, 108; and gender identity, 69, 89, 144n11; high level of education of, 19–20, 88; improved social status of, 88, 90, 112; Japanese-trained, 14, 15, 41, 81; negative perceptions of, 13, 17–18, 24, 88, 120n9;

nuns, Buddhist, in Taiwan *(continued)*
  numbers of, 1, 119n1, 120n4;
  ordination of, 13, 14, 17–18, 127n93;
  ratio of, to monks, 1, 16; reasons
  for flourishing after 1949, 14–17, 19;
  social service missions of, 21–22;
  socioeconomic backgrounds of, 9–10,
  23, 24; technology use by, 19, 22,
  130n14, 144n16; training of, 16–17,
  67, 79–80, 82–83. *See also under* Ciji;
  Luminary Buddhist Institute
nuns, Buddhist, reasons for becoming,
  22–26; economic issues, 18, 24,
  122n23; family relations, 10, 17,
  24, 146n55; for independence and
  opportunity, 25, 88–89; spiritual and
  intellectual interests, 25
nuns, Buddhist, segregation from
  monks, 7–8, 12–13, 121n5, 153n82
  (*See also* mixed-sex *sangha*)
nuns, Buddhist, in Tibetan tradition, 84,
  117, 119n1, 126n77
nuns, Buddhist, in Vietnam, 111–112,
  119n1
nuns, Catholic, 44, 81, 117
nuns, Daoist, 122n20, 123n29
nuqiangren (superwoman), 57–58,
  137n49

ordination of Taiwanese monks: first in
  Taiwan (1917), 14; in China, 9, 13;
  standards, 18
ordination of Taiwanese nuns: first
  in Taiwan (1919), 14; mail-in, 13;
  standards, 17–18, 127n93
ordination status of nuns: global
  comparison of, 119n1; in Qing-era
  Taiwan, 12–13

phoenix halls, 10
pluralism in Taiwan, 86, 110
popular religion, Chinese, 1, 9, 64, 81,
  82, 84, 114; and Zhengyan, 41, 64,
  72, 73–74. See also *zhaijiao*
prajñā (insight), 87

PRC (People's Republic of China),
  Buddhism in, 7, 97–98, 110, 121n3,
  129n122
prison education programs, 22, 84
private charity in Taiwan, 50, 78, 143n6
Project Hope (Xiwang gongcheng):
  architectural critiques of, 53–54;
  architectural vocabulary of, 52–53,
  54; compared to Shigang project, 85;
  goals of, 50–51; green philosophy of,
  54–55; locations of schools for, 49

Qin Wenjie, 69, 121n3, 127n101,
  129n122, 153n92. *See also* Fuhu
  Temple (Sichuan, PRC), nuns of
Qing religious laws barring nuns, 12
Qing-era Buddhism in Taiwan:
  institutional history, 8–10; negative
  assessments, 9; nuns' order, 12–13;
  positive assessments, 9; roles of
  women, 10–11
quanqiuhua (globalization), 97

religion, Chinese popular, 1, 9, 64, 81,
  82, 84, 114; and Zhengyan, 41, 64,
  72, 73–74. See also *zhaijiao*
religion in public schools in Taiwan, 52,
  58–60, 126n78
religious revival in Taiwan. See *under*
  Buddhist revival
Renben jiaoyu jijinhui. *See* Humanistic
  Education Foundation (Renben jiaoyu
  jijinhui)
renjian fojiao: and Ciji, 46; formulation
  of, 99; and Luminary Buddhist
  Institute, 91; prevalence in Taiwan,
  93; and women, 106–109
rensheng, 95
Rongzhen (nun), 21

Sākyadhitā, 106, 129n115
sangha, mixed-sex, 7–8, 89, 121n5
Santikaro, 106
Sartre, Jean-Paul, 100
school architecture, 52–54, **53**, 59

schools, religion in, 52, 58–60, 126n78
segregation of monks and nuns, 7–8, 12–13, 121n5, 153n82. *See also* mixed-sex *sangha*
Shangren, 130n11. *See also* Zhengyan
Shanhui (monk), 13–14
Shanhui (nun), 22, 26
Shengyan (monk), 16, 17, 113, 125n71. *See also* Dharma Drum Mountain (Fagushan)
Shi or Shih (Master). *See names of individual masters*
Shigang Township, 84–85
shijie zhuyi (world-ism), 97
shijiehua (globalization), 97
Shing Kuang, 93, 102, 103, 151n65
si weiyi (four postures), 68
sign language and Ciji, 32, 131n17
silk industry, 122n23, 127n102
skillful means, 16, 26, 76, 110
smyung gnas, 117
social reform: Ciji agenda for, 56, 58; Luminary Buddhist Institute views on, 86–87; nineteenth-century Christian, 57
social transformation, 64–65, 80–81, 114
Sōka Gakkai, 37, 130n4, 131n21
Sri Lanka, nuns' order in, 23, 112, 119n1, 142n74
Still Thoughts (*jingsi yu*): origin and meaning of term, 30; pedagogy, 29, 31, 58–60, 138n60. *See also* Still Thoughts (Zhengyan)
Still Thoughts (Zhengyan), 30–31, 73–75. *See also* Still Thoughts (*jingsi yu*)
Still Thoughts Abode, **32**; as model and symbol, 52, 66; nuns of, 65–68, 69
Still Thoughts Camp, 31–38; audio-video documentation of, 35–36, 130n14; expectations for dress and behavior at, 32, 36, 130n12; schedule for, 33–34; small group system at, 31–32, 36; Zhengyan's role in, 36–38

Still Thoughts Hall, **35**; as model for Project Hope, 52
Su Qianling, 113
superwoman (*nuqiangren*), Taiwan, 57–58, 137n49
Sūtra on Immeasurable Meanings (*Wuliangyi jing*), 30

Taiwan aborigines, 85, 103, 136n41
Taiwan Economic Miracle, 39, 46, 101
Taiwan superwoman (*nuqiangren*), 57–58, 137n49
Taixu (monk), 14, 50, 91, 93, 95–97, 98, 106
technology use by nuns, 19, 22, 130n14, 144n16
temples, Buddhist, numbers of, in Taiwan, 120n6
Thailand, Ciji in, 138n60
Theravādin Buddhism and women, 75–76, 84
Theravādin nuns' order, 84, 119n1
Thích Nhất Hạnh, 100
three mountaintops of Buddhism in Taiwan, 93, 121n15
tiankong (infinite worlds), 7, 118
Tianyi (nun), 16, 81, 147n64
Tibetan Buddhism: nuns' order in, 84, 117, 119n1, 126n77; and Western women, 84
Ting Jen-Chieh, 116, 150n50
Topley, Marjorie, 10, 122n23
Tsomo, Karma Lekshe, 105–106, 125n71, 129n115
Tzu Chi. *See* Ciji

University of the West, 20

Vegetarian Halls. *See zhaitang*
vegetarian religions. *See zhaijiao*
Vietnam, nuns' order in, 111–112, 119n1
vinaya: and administration, 82, 83, 125n71, 128n112; and ordination, 16, 119n1, 125n66, 127n93, 155n6; and training, 16, 84, 121n5, 128n112

vinaya studies, 2, 20, 102

Wang Jinyun (later Zhengyan), 39–42. *See also* Zhengyan
Welch, Holmes, 94, 95, 128n104
Weller, Robert, 57, 63, 66, 114–115
Westernization, 19
White Lotus, 13
women and socioeconomic change in Taiwan, 2, 19, 88, 90, 112
women's movement in Taiwan, 113, 128n114
world-ism (*shijie zhuyi*), 97
Wu Yin, **80**; advocacy for women, 84, 86; biography, 81–82; views, 89–90, 117. *See also* Luminary Buddhist Institute
Wuliangyi jing (*Sūtra on Immeasurable Meanings*), 30
wusheng laomu (Eternal Mother), 10, 24, 41, 42, 72
Wuyan Association for the Protection of the Blind, 21

Xilai An Incident (1915), 123n40
Xinghe (nun), 116–117
Xingyun (monk), 31, 100, 131n19, 131n32. *See also* Foguangshan
Xinzhi (nun), 82
Xiudao (nun), 41–42, 132n38, 132n41
Xiwang gongcheng. *See* Project Hope
Xu Zongming, 42
Xiang'guang. *See* Luminary Buddhist Institute
Xiang'guang Temple, 82

Yang Chang-huey, 63
yangnu (adopted daughters), 17, 39–40, 126n72, 131n30
Yao Taishan, 58

yi ren wei ben, 50
yibu, yijiaoyin, 46
Yifa (nun), 20
Yikong (nun), 3, 17, 26, 109
Yinshun (monk), 16, 17, 91, 98–99, 106–108; and Zhengyan and Ciji, 42, 46
yizheng bu ganzhi, 96
Yü Chün-fang, 143n4, 144n7
Yuanrong (nun), 16, 124n54

zhaigu, 11, 15
zhaijiao, 10–11, 13, 123n40
zhaitang, 10–11, 13
Zhan Sujuan, 116
Zhang, Changyi, 63
Zheng Cheng'gong, 8
zhengquan, 96
Zhengyan, **30, 44, 64**; biographical narratives of, 39–44; charisma of, 38–39, 45; and Guanyin, 40; as Guanyin incarnate, 29; and her family, 39–41, 133n46; as mother or patriarch, 36–37; and nuns of Ciji, 65–66, 67; and popular religion, 41, 64, 72, 73–74; as rebel or traditionalist, 63; spiritual development of, 40–43; *Still Thoughts*, 30–31, 73–75; at Still Thoughts Camp, 36–38; teachings of, 30, 32, 53, 55–56, 73–75, 100; use of Southern Min dialect by, 36, 43, 45; vision and mission of, 43–44. *See also* Ciji
Zhenhua (monk), 23–24
zhiquan, 96
Zhiyuan Xing'gang, 132n42
Zhongtai Chan Temple Incident (1996), 128n111
Zhou Xuande, 18–19
Zichun (nun), 86, 87, 90

www.ingramcontent.com/pod-product-compliance
Lightning Source LLC
Chambersburg PA
CBHW030138240426
43672CB00005B/175